# Practical SharePoint 2010 Branding and Customization

**Erik Swenson**

**Apress®**

## Practical SharePoint 2010 Branding and Customization

ISBN-13 (pbk): 978-1-4302-4026-6

ISBN-13 (electronic): 978-1-4302-4027-3

President and Publisher: Paul Manning
Lead Editor: Joanthan Hassell
Technical Reviewers: Chris Arella, Robert Dornbush, and Matt Lally
Editorial Board: Steve Anglin, Mark Beckner, Ewan Buckingham, Gary Cornell, Morgan Ertel, Jonathan Gennick, Jonathan Hassell, Robert Hutchinson, Michelle Lowman, James Markham, Matthew Moodie, Jeff Olson, Jeffrey Pepper, Douglas Pundick, Ben Renow-Clarke, Dominic Shakeshaft, Gwenan Spearing, Matt Wade, Tom Welsh
Coordinating Editor: Annie Beck
Copy Editor: Jill Steinberg
Production Support: Patrick Cunningham
Indexer: BIM Indexing & Proofreading Services
Artist: SPi Global
Cover Designer: Anna Ishchenko

Distributed to the book trade worldwide by Springer Science+Business Media New York, 233 Spring Street, 6th Floor, New York, NY 10013. Phone 1-800-SPRINGER, fax (201) 348-4505, e-mail orders-ny@springer-sbm.com, or visit www.springeronline.com.

For information on translations, please e-mail rights@apress.com, or visit www.apress.com.

Apress and friends of ED books may be purchased in bulk for academic, corporate, or promotional use. eBook versions and licenses are also available for most titles. For more information, reference our Special Bulk Sales–eBook Licensing web page at `www.apress.com/bulk-sales`.

Any source code or other supplementary materials referenced by the author in this text is available to readers at `www.apress.com`. For detailed information about how to locate your book's source code, go to `http://www.apress.com/source-code/`.

*I dedicate this book to my wife, Karissa, for supporting me through this long process and to my boys, Gavin and Bryce, for encouraging me to always do my best.*

*—Erik Swenson*

# Contents at a Glance

# Contents

# About the Authors

**Erik Swenson** is a Solutions Architect for EMC Consulting. He received his bachelor degree in graphic design from Plymouth State University. His portfolio includes more than one hundred SharePoint based projects over the last seven years and has been a speaker at various SharePoint conferences. His expertise is focused on SharePoint Information Architecture, Wireframes, Visual Branding, and CSS/Master Page Front End Development. He currently resides in Jaffrey, NH with his wife, Karissa, and two sons, Gavin and Bryce. His blog can be found at `http://erikswenson.blogspot.com`.

# About the Technical Reviewers

**Chris Arella** is a Senior Solutions Architect and SharePoint Consultant focused on User Experience and Information Architecture. With a background in Graphic Design and Usability, he blends his award-winning creativity and technical savvy to deliver well-adopted, leading-edge solutions to his customers. When he's not travelling, working on projects, helping friends, or speaking at conferences, Chris can be found having fun with his loving and beautiful family in East Lake, Florida. To learn more, check out his website at www.chrisarella.com.

**Robert Dornbush** is an Information Architect specializing in Navigation Systems, Interaction Design, SharePoint Site Structure, Site Templates, and Wireframes documentation describing page layout and page flow that are provided as web site planning and design deliverables to ensure his consulting clients' work environments with an improved User Experience. Robert specializes in IA and UX analysis with extensive experience in eXperience Design and discovery, definition & planning aspects of UI related software design. He has fourteen years of experience as a Web Designer and twelve years as a Business Analyst capturing Software Design Specifications in a visual format utilizing MS Visio illustrations. Robert is a proven solutions architect and brings added value to software development projects by exercising his technical writing abilities with an emphasis on UX, Wireframes, UI REQs documentation, and Interaction Design. Check out his User Experience Design Blog At: http://consultingblogs.emc.com/robertdornbush/default.aspx.

**Matt Lally** is a Senior SharePoint Architect with extensive application development and infrastructure design and implementation experience. As a Senior Solution Architect for EMC consulting, Matt has been engaged with numerous Fortune 500 Clients leading on-shore and off-shore development teams to implement SharePoint .NET solutions, preparing SharePoint Server 2010 hosting infrastructures, providing technical guidance for SharePoint governance, and conducting client environment assessments. Prior to joining EMC Consulting, Matt was a Technology Manager at Johnson and Johnson where he led the design and implementation of what Microsoft reported as one of the largest SharePoint infrastructures in the world and participated in the Microsoft Customer Advisory Board for SharePoint 2010.

# Acknowledgments

As a first-time author, there were many unknowns when it came to writing a technical book. Writing a book as a single author takes a lot of time and research. I would like to especially thank my family, friends, and colleagues for giving me the encouragement to do my best. There were a lot of late nights and short deadlines, and my family was always there for support.

The technical review team did a great job with providing feedback during the review of my book. Chris Arella led this team and spent a lot of his personal time away from his family and busy schedule to provide detailed comments and suggestions within the book. Chris also helped with the chapter topics and the overall flow of the book. Matt Lally is an amazing developer and became the go-to guy for all of the technical support within the book. Matt also spent a significant amount of his free time to create the Visual Studio solution that is included in the SharePoint Branding Kit. Robert Dornbush was also a great resource who helped with the content review and organization, and also spearheaded the content around Information Architecture and Design. His knowledge of IA theory and process was invaluable.

The technical review team at Apress was very helpful and quick to respond to my endless questions. Thank you for keeping me to a schedule and pushing me to write the best book possible. I never would have written this book if it were not for Jonathan Hassell who found my blog in a sea of many talented SharePoint branding professionals and suggested that I write this book. With all of the questions that I had he was right there to provide me support. He also allowed me to be flexible with my book content and structure. Annie Beck and Jim Markham became my lifeline when it came to deadlines and chapter content reviews. I think Jim now knows more about SharePoint branding than he would like.

I would finally like to thank all of my co-workers within EMC for supporting me in my career path. Patrick Steger specifically pushed me to be a great designer and consultant. He taught me the values and benefits of being a good consultant and how each and every project will help me grow and learn new concepts and ideas.

Lastly I want to thank all of my clients for allowing me to spread the word of User Experience and design. For everyone else who has helped me through my career and given me the knowledge and support to do my best. I want to thank you for all of your support and contributions.

# Introduction

*Practical SharePoint 2010 Branding and Customization* cuts through the fluff and discusses accessible, easy-to-understand consulting and processes to create aesthetically pleasing, highly usable branded and customized SharePoint web sites. Designed to be a quick-reference how-to guide that lets you dive straight into the task at hand, you'll find this book's attention to detail and pragmatism make it an attractive companion during your branding experience.

SharePoint 2010 deployments are more common than ever, as is the desire to make the environment branded and attractive to your needs. However, since SharePoint is more than just a collection of web pages, customizing the look and feel and completing the process of branding the platform itself is complex and requires a knowledge of web development, web design techniques, and a familiarity with SharePoint administration—a curious niche, to be sure. Sometimes, you just need to make quick fixes, while at other times, building an entirely customized and branded environment is a multistep process with lots of stakeholder buy-in and development time required.

Whether you're interested in applying just a touch of style to a team site, or you're branding a public-facing Fortune 500 web site based on SharePoint, *Practical SharePoint 2010 Branding and Customization* is the only book you'll need to quickly, easily, and efficiently brand and customize your environment.

## Who This Book Is For

This book is for anyone who works within SharePoint sites and wants to make changes to how those sites look, whether they're minor changes or wholesale branding and customization efforts. As an Information Architect you learn how your role fits into the process and how your will support the organization, structure, and requirements for the site. As a designer you learn the tricks of the trade on how to create visually appealing designs that your developers can easily build. As a front-end developer you learn tips on how to build simple to advanced visual designs using CSS, master pages, and page layouts. As a Project Manager you learn the process of how all of these roles and tasks are achieved in a well-organized manner. As an Executive, Stakeholder, Information Worker, or other role within a project with branding you will get a better understanding of the benefits that come with branding a SharePoint 2010 site and its return on investment.

## How This Book Is Structured

This book is structured based on the process by which the visual branding is created. It starts with an introduction and then walks you through the UX process from gathering requirements, to creating the visual design, to building and testing the design. Many step-by-step instructions are included that guide you through the branding and designing tasks.

## Prerequisites

It is recommended that you have some basic knowledge of SharePoint 2010, HTML, and CSS.

## Downloading the code

The source code and SharePoint Branding Kit is available from the Apress web site `http://www.apress.com/9781430240266`. Click on the Source Code/Downloads tab from the book details page. The SharePoint Branding Kit .zip file is password protected: Use the password "SBK" without quotes to unlock the file. These files should not be distributed or sold, but used as a starting point for your projects.

# CHAPTER 1

# Intro to SharePoint 2010 Branding

**What's In This Chapter?**

- Why Brand SharePoint?
- Key Topics and Guiding Principles
- What to Expect and Things to Know
- Basic HTML
- Cascading Style Sheets
- SharePoint Master Pages

Whether you are starting your first SharePoint branding project or you have done it all before, this book helps guide you down the right path towards success. There are many things to consider and prepare for before you jump in. One is that SharePoint is a pre-built system composed of sites, lists, libraries, and web parts. It is critical to understand the basics of how SharePoint works before you begin the design. In this introductory chapter you learn about the benefits to branding a SharePoint site, some key things to expect, and some basic HTML, CSS, and master page definitions. This chapter is designed to serve as a refresher to these topics. The other chapters guide you through the design process and dive deep into preparing, designing, building, testing, and supporting the design. If you are new to SharePoint branding, you might find all this information intimidating at first. However, after you have gone through the branding process a couple of times, you will enjoy contributing to a great experience for your users.

## Why Brand SharePoint?

The user interface accounts for 99.9 percent of the visible end product of your SharePoint site. Creating a custom brand for your SharePoint site will help increase user adoption and provide a better experience to the end users. One of the most common challenges you will encounter is initially creating executive and stakeholder buy-in to invest into transformation from the standard SharePoint experience to a custom and tailored design. Author Douglas Martin puts it succinctly in his famous quote:

*Questions about whether design is necessary or affordable are quite beside the point: design is inevitable. The alternative to good design is bad design, not no design at all.*

# Key Topics and Guiding Principles

As you explore the branding process, keep the following key topics and guiding principles in mind; this will help make the experience fun and memorable. Before you jump into the design, you need to understand the portal that you are designing for. Is it a public Internet site that is heavy on news and information, and requires a high level of control over the content? Is it an intranet portal that will be used for collaboration, social networking, and document management? Will it include an extranet to allow information sharing with external partners? Other types of SharePoint sites are records management-, project management-, business intelligence-, and reporting-type portals. Knowing how the site will be used affects how you approach your design and your information architecture.

# What to Expect and Things to Know

The first thing to expect when branding SharePoint is that anything is possible. Some people will say, "I want SharePoint to not look like SharePoint." There are many ways to configure and brand SharePoint so that it does not retain the default look and feel.

You should also expect that you won't get it right on the first try. Everyone will have an opinion, and it's ok to have opposing opinions when it comes to design. Some people might like the color orange; some might not. This doesn't mean that you should scrap all orange from your design if that color is a valid choice in your palette.

As you move through the branding-definition process you will need to conduct peer reviews. Don't take anyone's criticism personally. When it comes to design, people have strong personal preferences. Take in the feedback, but stay true to your direction. Don't allow a committee to define your designs.

## Identify the Support Team

For small projects you might be the only person carrying the design from concept to production. But on larger projects make sure you identify and communicate regularly with your team members, business users, and stakeholders. Your team might consist of approvers, testers, developers, project managers, and program managers. Get involved and participate in weekly or daily calls to discuss blocking issues, risks, and other problems as they come up.

## Seek a SharePoint Community

You are not alone; there is a large community of people just like you that can help with any issues that come up. Explore blogs and forums, and attend a conference if you can. Start networking.

## Understand That All Projects Are Different

No two projects are the same. They might have similar features and functionality but differ entirely in brand approach. The scope and length of the project also determine how much customization you can apply to your site. Some projects might just need a simple facelift with the use of themes, while others require a complete overhaul. It's best to fully understand the scope of the work and set expectations early.

## Rely On Multiple Roles for Support

The success of the project depends on having good teamwork and synchronization among team members. On most projects you will be working with a variety of people with different skills sets. Make sure that you utilize those resources and capitalize on their strengths. If you're the sole person tasked with branding SharePoint, do not work in a bubble. Have others review your work, and conduct peer reviews often.

## Understand the Project Scope

With SharePoint you can turn a number of features on or off depending on users' needs. These features include Document Management, Business Intelligence, Reporting, Multimedia, News, Ratings, Commenting, Blogging, Social Features, My Sites, and Profiles. Including these features means additional time and effort for building out the information architecture and taxonomy. Make sure you understand the defined scope of the project so that you don't exceed the original scope with your wireframes and potentially add unplanned development work. Stay in communication with your project managers through regular status reports, and do your best to keep to a schedule.

## Take It One Step at a Time

If you haven't branded SharePoint before, it is advisable to take baby steps at first. Start small and work your way up to more advanced designs and configurations. First select a design on the web that you like—one that has similar characteristics to your basic SharePoint design. Then get access to a virtual development environment, and don't worry about making mistakes. If you happen to mess up, you can always revert back to a safe state and try again. Take that preexisting design and make small changes to the background colors, images, and fonts. You will be surprised by how quickly things start to come together.

## Don't Skip Ahead

Put down those crayons. Don't be tempted to skip ahead in the process and go straight for the fun stuff. There will always be the temptation to get your hands dirty at the beginning of a project with visual design. You need to understand who your users are and what they want out of the site. If you jump ahead, you run the risk of lots of rework and lost time.

## Don't Be Intimidated by SharePoint

As you begin to build out your newly defined visual design do not get intimidated by vast amount of styles that come with SharePoint. If you find yourself scrolling though the basic CSS style sheets wondering how you are ever going to make heads or tails of it, don't worry. This book covers the main CSS classes and the techniques for defining them. However, at times you might be at a complete loss on how to do something and will spend a ridiculous amount of time trying to figure it out. At this point you will need to dive deeper into the book and explore other options to get the look and feel that you are after. For example, if you are having issues with incorporating your own custom logo or header into SharePoint, the section on building the design steps you through the process.

## Learn the Basic Features of SharePoint

Before you start defining your portal it is critical that you understand the basic features of SharePoint and how it works. Get access to a development environment or online lab and explore ways in which you can edit and customize sites. In SharePoint 2010 the inclusion of the ribbon takes some time to get used to. The ribbon is used for list and library management—for example, uploading and managing documents. It is also a key component in the rich text editing of content on your page. Almost everything in SharePoint is a list, library, or configurable web part. Any list or library can have custom columns. Think of columns as containers for metadata. The main difference between a list and a library is that a library item needs to have a file attached to it, while a list is simply a collection of metadata. For example, an announcement list is just three simple columns of data: a title, body text, and an expiration date. If you wanted to have additional metadata for that announcement you would simply add an existing site column or create a new column. Within each list and library you can create custom views that allow you to sort and filter the data, display different columns, and group the content by a specific column's metadata. Some SharePoint web parts are configured on the page and allow you to consume or display data in different ways. The Summary links web part for example is a publishing web part that allows you to manage links directly on the page with different groupings and display styles.

## Remember the 80/20 Rule

When it comes time to build out the SharePoint visual design, you will find that you can quickly change the visual appearance. But implementing the final, small changes to get SharePoint to look exactly like your visual design composition takes up most of your time. Things like fonts, spacing, colors, and positioning are time-intensive. In most cases, if something is one or two pixels off position from your specifications, that is not such a big deal. But if objects are overlapping and the actual functionality of the site is degraded, then you need to spend time fixing the issue.

## Have Fun

Branding SharePoint should not be something that you despise. Make it a pleasurable experience, and have fun with it. Keeping a positive attitude helps boost the quality of work. There will be times when you are up late burning the midnight oil to meet a very tight deadline, but the reward of finishing a project and having it be a success makes it all worth it. Be proud of your work and enjoy the experience.

## Try New Things

Don't be afraid to venture outside the box every once in a while. You just might surprise yourself with a new idea. Sometimes people get tunnel vision and forget to explore new options. Look on the web to see how other people have done it. Ride the wave of the most current design trends and try new things. SharePoint has its limitations, and it's good to keep yourself in check with your development team so that you are not designing high in the sky without any boundaries. There always needs to be a balance between staying with what works and being completely out in left field.

## Identify the Design Types

There are a variety of different types of design projects. The first type is just using simple colors and fonts that relate to a theme. The second type is to take an existing design like a public web site and adapt it to SharePoint for an intranet or extranet. The last and most complex type of design is creating a custom design. These custom designs are defined by requirements, design inspirations, and moods. They are considered custom since they will require a large amount of development effort to transform them from the standard SharePoint look and feel to something completely different.

## Look Out for Pitfalls

Since SharePoint is a prebuilt system there are known pitfalls that you need to look out for. Some of these deal with vague requirements and definitions around approach. Others are more technical and pertain to the build and implementation of the design. The book covers some of these pitfalls and how to avoid them.

## Know Your Branding Limitations

With all systems come limitations. These limitations can be rectified with custom code and development, but that takes time and money. It is best to understand these limitations and clearly communicate them to set clear expectations. The last thing that you want is to ignore the problem and expect it to just go away. People in general will understand and accept the limitation or, if it is a must-have feature, they might be ok with the additional cost to fix it.

## Work With SharePoint, Not Against It

There may be times when you find yourself banging your head against the wall, with no clear understanding of why things are not working or why they aren't looking the way that you want them to. Don't give up, and don't be afraid to ask for help. Who knows? You might just need to make a simple configuration change, and then everything will go back to normal. If you find yourself stuck in a hole, try alternative methods. If all else fails, clearly communicate that there is a known limitation and that you might need some additional resources to help out.

## Make a Great First Impression

A first 5.250impression goes a long way. As new users navigate to your site you want them to feel excited to learn, explore, and spend more time on your site. You want them to leave having had a good experience and wanting to come back. You can accomplish this in a couple of different ways. The first is through the user experience. By having good information architecture, navigation, taxonomy, and up-to-date, relevant content, your users will get what they need. The second is by adding personalization and targeted content to allow users to feel like this is their portal. The third is through a memorable and exciting visual experience. If the images and colors are dull, drab, and inconsistent, users will immediately conclude that the entire site and its content are weak. You have a very small window of opportunity to capture a user's attention before they click away or navigate to another site. Make the most of it and provide the best experience possible. This will increase user adoption and give you the best return on investment (ROI).

## Be Prepared

A successful SharePoint branding project depends on the time and detail put into it. Take the time to do your homework. Listen to your users and discuss with them the primary objective for coming to your site. Develop use cases and test them. Organize your requirements and make sure to validate them. Create wireframes and detailed specifications to help your development team so that they don't have to guess or make things up as they go. Read through and use the design specifications that are given to you such as style guides, fonts, colors, and logos. The more prepared you are the easier the project will be.

## Maintain Brand Consistency

Throughout the design and development phases, be sure to stay consistent with your design styles. Don't make the user guess whether an element is a link or just text. If you add a design treatment to an image, such as a shadow or a border, keep that consistent across all pages. Reuse classes for consistency to ensure that when updates are made, changes are updated globally. Headers and web-part spacing should also be consistent.

## Allocate Time for Testing

There are different types of testing, and all of them will help make the user experience the best that it can be. Testing can be easy and does not require a team of skilled testers. For some tests you simply show the concept to a group of people and record their reaction. Throughout the process of building the visual design you will be testing your own code. It is important to test early so that you have time to make adjustments. Pay attention to how users react. Look for things like hesitation, facial expressions, and frustration. Ask participants to think out loud, and try not to lead testers in a particular direction that might skew the results.

Card sorting is a very effective exercise for testing out site maps and taxonomies. To prepare for a card sort write one word or phrase on each card. There are two types of card-sort tests. The first is called an *open card sort*. Participants are asked to create their own group labels. The second type is called a *closed card sort*. Testers have created a predetermined grouping for the participants to sort the cards under. To start the card sorting the participant is asked to sort the cards into logical groupings that make sense to them. Make sure to have a few blank cards in case a participant wants to put in additional items. Once you have completed the tests, record the organization and relationship of the cards into a spreadsheet. After repeating this with other participants review the results and look for clusters of similar groupings by the participants. You can also conduct card sorting online; a number of free web sites allow you to set up your own open or closed card sort. Most free sites allow for up to 30 participants and provide a graphical output of the results. The online card sorts often are a cheaper way to test, but you lose the live interaction between the tester and the participant.

## Don't Expect to Get It Right on the First Shot

Branding SharePoint takes patience. When working with CSS you often make multiple passes at creating the design. Refer to your style guide and plan ahead. Be organized and take it slow. If you rush you might end up missing key style attributes and end up having to do a lot of rework. When planning your schedule add in time for multiple phase releases.

## Know That There Is Never One Way to Do Something

When building out the design, you will discover multiple ways to get the same results. For example, to represent background color you can either create an image or use CSS. Also when placing something on the page, you can use padding, margins, or positioning to get the same effect. It is a good idea to know the pros and cons of each approach and test the results in different browsers. You can follow best practices to get the best performance out of your site. It is recommended not to use overly large images that will make the page load longer.

## Try Not to Take Shortcuts

If you're on a tight deadline, it might be tempting to take shortcuts when designing or building your design. In most cases, if a shortcut does not affect the overall user experience, then it should be ok. However, if you decide to simplify or alter the design just to make it easier to build, then you might run the risk that users notice the change, and the original experience becomes degraded. Some shortcuts, like creating inline styles, affect the manageability of the site going forward. Placing inline styles directly on an element—for example, `<div style="font-weight:bold; color:#000;">Text</div>` —means that if a change needs to be made to that element style, you have to modify it directly and it will not be global. It is best to use CSS classes like this: `<div class="bold-text">text<div>`. With this approach you can update all references to this class with one quick change.

## Understand the Purpose of the Site

Each site has different requirements and goals. Some sites are geared specifically toward the generation and publishing of news. In this situation you need to allow for content to be aggregated and rolled up to a higher level. There might also be different news styles such as featured news, company news, and reminders. The more advanced news sites might include rotating carousels, featured news, related news, ratings, and discussions. Other sites might be more collaborative and focus on knowledge management and content sharing. Sites may include social features that allow users to see what their colleagues are doing on the site. Given all of these scenarios you need to fully understand the purpose of the site and what your users want to get out of it. With this knowledge in hand, you can focus on those key features and provide the best user experience possible.

## Make SharePoint Not Look like SharePoint

As mentioned earlier, when you start gathering the requirements for the visual design, a common request is for the site not to look like SharePoint. This statement can be interpreted in many different ways. Some people will ask for this when they want the visual design to take on a completely different look and feel. Others make this request to indicate that some of the controls on the page should be moved around to allow for a new and different experience. It's best to ask what they mean by this and not assume anything.

## Keep Up With Design Trends

Stay up to date with new design trends. Start introducing these types of treatments and features to your designs and wireframes. Some trends have a short shelf life while others have been around for years. If you are out of touch with these trends, simply check a few top sites on the web and check for similarities. Design trends come in a variety of formats. Some design trends focus on look and feel while others are strictly functional or conceptual. Just be mindful of budget and time constraints as some features are not standard SharePoint functionality and therefore require considerable custom development.

## Offer Mobile Support

More and more people are using their mobile phones to access the web, so it is only natural that users of your site will want to view SharePoint from their mobile phones or tablet computers. While SharePoint 2010 has a mobile view that can be configured, in most cases this will not give users the functionality that they need. There are some third-party software companies that can be purchased for a better experience. Another option is to create your own mobile views or applications for the site.

## Provide Accessibility

Identify any special considerations that you need to account for when building out your site. This goes back to knowing your users and making sure you provide them with all the tools they need. Some sites require that you provide full accessibility feature to be compliant with Section 508 government-regulated standards. Other sites require only basic accessibility features. SharePoint comes equipped with some basic accessibility features designed to help users who have poor visibility.

## Learn Application Shortcuts and Quick Keys

To be efficient and productive when designing your site, it's recommended that you spend some time learning and memorizing application shortcuts and quick keys. Show off your Photoshop skills by creating custom actions. By learning application quick keys, you save yourself from having to use scroll bars or choose a zoom percentage.

## Avoid CSS Overload

SharePoint includes a lot of CSS style sheets and classes. Don't get overwhelmed by them; just use the ones that you need. Make sure you add comments to your CSS to identify what classes go with what section of the design or functionality. This will help with future updates and changes.

## Save Often and Create Backups

The worst thing that can happen is that you spend all day working on your design and then find out that the file has become corrupt, overwritten, or lost. Save your work often and create backups. You can also leverage the built-in publishing in SharePoint and use version control to manage previous copies of your files inside of SharePoint's content database.

With the foundation knowledge of what to expect and key things to consider, this next section will provide you with some background concepts of HTML and CSS.

# Basic HTML

HTML (hypertext markup language) is the core markup language that is used to render SharePoint's information onto your browser. HTML defines the overall structure of the page and the controls, while CSS is used to style those elements. Figure 1-1 shows the basic required elements for any HTML page.

```
1  <!DOCTYPE html PUBLIC "-//W3C//DTD XHTML 1.0 Strict//EN" "http://www.w3.org/TR/xhtml1/DTD/xhtml1-strict.dtd">
2  <html xmlns="http://www.w3.org/1999/xhtml">
3
4  <head>
5  <meta http-equiv="Content-Type" content="text/html; charset=utf-8" />
6  <title>Basic HTML</title>
7  </head>
8
9  <body>
10
11 </body>
12
13 </html>
14
```

***Figure 1-1.*** *Basic HTML structure*

Each element has an open and a closed tag. The closed tags are indicated by the slash "/". The head tags hold valuable references like title, CSS, and JavaScript references. The body tag is where the structural tags get declared. Some examples of these tags are: `<TABLE>`, `<TR>`, `<TD>`, `<DIV>`, `<SPAN>`. Tables are used just like you would see in a Microsoft Excel workbook. The TR tag is used for rows and the TD tag is used for cell items in those rows. DIV tags are used as a replacement for tables, and spans are used within DIV tags for not much other than adding styles to an element.

# Cascading Style Sheets

CSS is the method used to centrally manage all of the style attributes in SharePoint. There are many benefits to using CSS. One of these benefits is that instead of adding inline style properties to elements within the HTML, you can link off to external CSS files. Another benefit is if you need to make global changes to all sites and pages, you can simply edit the styles of the CSS and it automatically updates all areas where that CSS file is referenced and the class or ID is used. For example, if you remove all CSS references in SharePoint, then the site branding is stripped down to just text and icons, as shown in Figure 1-2.

*Figure 1-2. SharePoint 2010 with no style sheets applied*

Within the HTML of your content or page you can add a class or an ID to any element:

- **Classes**: For a Class you would use the following on a table.
  `<TABLE Class="custom-class">`

- **IDs**: For an ID you would use specify it like this on a DIV tag.
  `<DIV id="custom-id">`

That class or ID can then be referenced in your CSS file:

- **Classes Reference**: To reference classes you use a period in front of the name.
  `.custom-class`

- **ID Reference**: for an ID you would use a pound symbol
  `#custom-id`

Once you have referenced the classes in your CSS, you can add properties like fonts, colors, or background treatment.

In the head of your HTML you specify and point to your custom CSS file. As the page loads it identifies that an element has a class or ID, checks for that in all of the CSS files referenced, and then styles the element according to the properties that you have included in the CSS file (Figure 1-3).

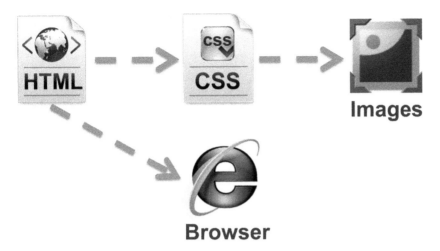

***Figure 1-3.*** *CSS connections*

There are three different ways to specify CSS within your master page, page layout, or content on your page:

1. **Internal.** When using internal styles, style attributes are added within the head of your page. This is commonly used in page layouts when you want a unique look and feel or padding for your page.

   ```
   <head><style type="text/css">CSS Content Goes Here</style></head>
   ```

2. **External.** This is the most common and best practice for specifying your CSS style sheets in your master page. The CSS class names and properties are stored in a separate file with a file extension of ".CSS". This file is located in the SharePoint Styles library within the SharePoint database or in a custom folder on the server.

   ```
   <link rel="stylesheet" type="text/css" href="stylesheet.css" />
   ```

3. **Inline.** When using inline styles you are adding unique attributes to a particular HTML element or control on the page.

   ```
   <p style="color: #ff0000;">Some red text</p>
   ```

The CSS syntax is the way that CSS rules are structured. The CSS class or ID is called a "selector," which can be an HTML element like a DIV. Each selector can have multiple properties. Each property has its own unique value. The structure is formed like this: `selector {property:value;}`. Using the following example, `.s4-search{color: red;}`, the selector would be "s4-search," the property would be "color," and the value would be "red." The curly brackets are used to contain all of the properties and values for each selector. Although the last property value can be left open, it is good practice to make sure that all property values end with a semicolon.

You can have multiple selectors for each set of properties as shown in Listing 1-1. The benefit to this approach is that you can share a set of CSS properties across all class names, and if a change is made, it is updated for all selectors specified.

11

***Listing 1-1.*** *Multiple CSS Selectors*

```
.s4-search, .ms-sbtable, .ms-sbscopes{
color: red;
}
```

■ **Note**  Each of the preceding selectors is separated by a comma. Make sure you do not have a comma between the last selector and the opening curly bracket or your style will not be rendered within the browser.

Within your custom CSS document it is recommended that you provide detailed comments to describe similar sets of selector class names. Comments can also be used to explain why you added certain selectors within your CSS file. This helps others who may see your file for the first time, or helps you remember an idea or updates to the file. For comments to be ignored by the browser they need to be structured such that they open with **/\*** and close with **\*/**, as shown in Listing 1-2.

***Listing 1-2.*** *CSS Comment Example*

```
/* This is the body class */
body {
  color: #000;
  background: #eee;
}
```

## Color Formats

There are multiple ways of specifying color values within your CSS. The most common way is to use hex colors. Hex colors use a combination of red, green, and blue. Hex codes use 16 digits for shades of those colors: 0 1 2 3 4 5 6 7 8 9 A B C D E F. "0" is full color and "F" is no color. Hex colors use 6 or 3 digits and start with a (#) symbol. Examples: #000000, #FFFFFF, #0DC5B2, #330099 (Figure 1-4).

■ **Note**  The first two digits are (Red), second (Green), last (Blue)

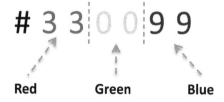

***Figure 1-4.*** *Hex color structure*

To simplify the preceding 6-digit hex color #330099, you can use shorthand to reduce the code to a three-digit number by simply removing the repeat value for each color. The three-digit code would be #309. It is important to note that three-digit hex codes only work where there are three pairs of repeating characters; these codes do not work with colors like #0DC5B2, where red is both 0 and D and not 00 or DD.

## CSS Property Tags

Following are just a few of the basic CSS properties that you should learn and understand. As you become more familiar with these classes you can start to include more advanced CSS techniques for your designs.

## Text Properties

The following are some example properties and styles that you can use to stylize the placement and form of the text on your page. Figure 1-5 shows a number of different text properties that can be used to stylize text on the page.

| | CSS | IE |
|---|---|---|
| Text Color | color: #FF0000; | Sample Text |
| Letter Spacing | letter-spacing: 5px; | S a m p l e   T e x t |
| Text Align | text-align: right; | Sample Text |
| Text Decoration | text-decoration: underline; | Sample Text |
| Text Transform | text-transform: uppercase; | SAMPLE TEXT |
| White Space | white-space: nowrap; | Sample Text Sample Text |
| Word Spacing | word-spacing: 10px; | Sample Text Sample Text |

**Figure 1-5.** *Text properties*

## Font Properties

Font properties are values that you set to make the font, size, style, and weight of text unique. As you can see in Figure 1-6 there are a variety of ways that you can enhance font styles just using CSS.

| | CSS | IE |
|---|---|---|
| Font Family | font-family: times; | Sample Text |
| Font Size | font-size: large; | Sample Text |
| Font Style | font-style: italic; | *Sample Text* |
| Font Variant | font-variant: small-caps; | SAMPLE TEXT |
| Font Weight | font-weight: bold; | **Sample Text** |

***Figure 1-6*** *Font properties*

## Background Properties

When using background properties you can specify HTML elements to have a specific background color or image, as shown in Figure 1-7.

| | CSS | IE |
|---|---|---|
| • Background | Background: #CCC url(images/bg.jpg) top left repeat-x; | 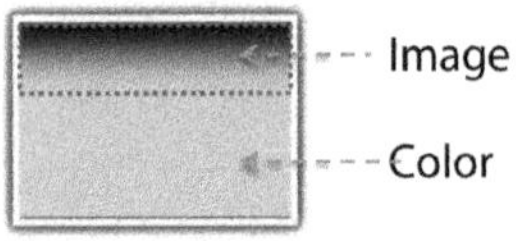 Image / Color |
| • Background Color | background-color: #CCC; | |
| • Background Image | background-image: url(images/bg.jpg); |  |
| • Background Position | background-position: top left; | 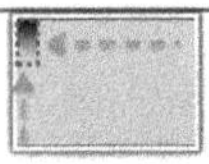 |
| • Background Repeat | background-repeat: repeat-x; | |

***Figure 1-7.*** *Background properties*

14

# Width/Height Properties

If you need to specify the height or width of an element or image, use the properties shown in Figure 1-8 to customize those values.

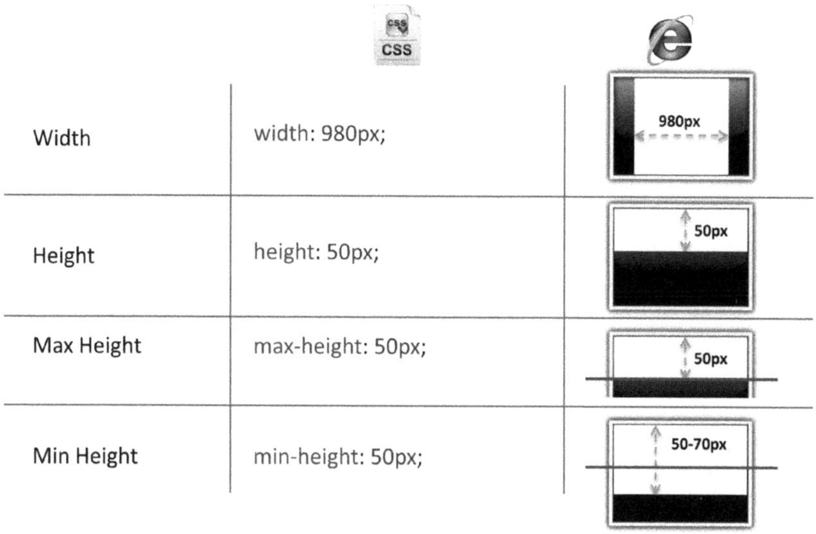

| | CSS | IE |
|---|---|---|
| Width | width: 980px; | 980px |
| Height | height: 50px; | 50px |
| Max Height | max-height: 50px; | 50px |
| Min Height | min-height: 50px; | 50-70px |

*Figure 1-8. Height/width properties*

# Boxed Model

The CSS boxed model is the basic way that you specify margins, borders, and padding. All content can use a combination of these properties to enhance the look and placement of your content elements. In Figure 1-9 the margin is used to space content away from something that has a specified border. Borders can range in style from a single solid-pixel black line to more complex borders that have multiple colors, widths, and styles. Padding is used to separate content from other elements. It is also used to add spacing from the content to its own border.

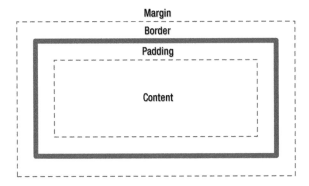

***Figure 1-9.*** *Boxed model*

For more information about the boxed model, check out the following link: `http://www.w3schools.com/css/css_boxmodel.asp`.

## Margins

The margin property declares the margin between an HTML element and the elements around it, as shown in Figure 1-10. The margin property can be set for the top, left, right, and bottom of an element. Margins can be individually specified or combined.

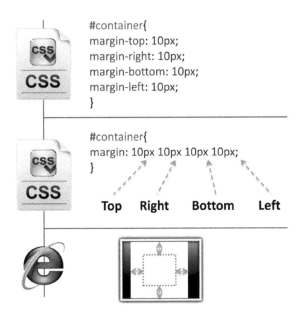

***Figure 1-10.*** *Margin structure*

## Border Properties

Borders are used to add colored lines around elements. Figure 1-11 shows that borders come with a variety of properties and values that you can specify.

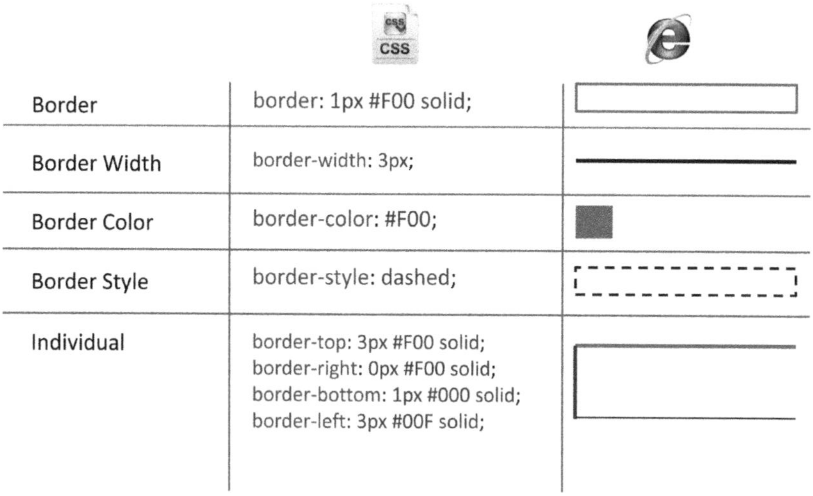

| | CSS | IE |
|---|---|---|
| Border | border: 1px #F00 solid; | |
| Border Width | border-width: 3px; | |
| Border Color | border-color: #F00; | |
| Border Style | border-style: dashed; | |
| Individual | border-top: 3px #F00 solid;<br>border-right: 0px #F00 solid;<br>border-bottom: 1px #000 solid;<br>border-left: 3px #00F solid; | |

**Figure 1-11.** *Border properties*

## Padding

The padding property is the distance between the border of an HTML element and the content within it. Most of the rules for margins also apply to padding, except there is no "auto" value, and negative values cannot be declared for padding. In Figure 1-12 the border property can be specified in multiple ways that allow you to get the exact border style that you need.

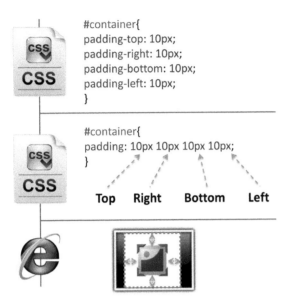

*Figure 1-12. Padding structure*

## Pseudo Properties

Pseudo codes are used to specify alternate attributes for a specific property. As shown in Figure 1-13 you can use pseudo codes to provide hover states on elements, images, text, and any other attribute that you want.

*Figure 1-13. Pseudo properties*

With the knowledge and understanding of the preceding CSS definitions and concepts you should have enough background information to get started on your design. You can find more information about CSS at http://www.w3.org/Style/CSS/. Tutorials can be found at http://www.w3schools.com/css/.

# SharePoint Master Pages

Master pages are the backbone for how SharePoint is built and rendered. Each site in SharePoint references two master pages. Master pages allow you to have a consistent experience across all of your sites within a single Site Collection. Together with page layouts, they produce output that combines the shell of the master page with content from the page layout. The master page creates the base HTML structure to your site. It also allows you to specify content placeholders such as the ribbon, site actions, navigation, and content.

One great thing about master pages is that if you make a change, it automatically updates all of the pages and sites that reference it. The master page also allows you to specify custom CSS files and JavaScript. Master pages are stored and managed within the master page gallery, which is accessible from the site settings page. You can view and modify the master pages with SharePoint Designer 2010.

---

■ **Note**   You do not need to have a custom master page to apply custom branding to SharePoint. Depending on what level of design complexity you want to achieve, there are different methods that you can use that do not require you to modify or create your own master pages. For example, you can use the OOTB SharePoint 2010 theme engine for simple text and color changes. Or you can use alternate CSS within publishing sites to link to your custom CSS file.

---

## SharePoint Page Layouts

Page layouts are used in publishing sites only and reference content placeholders on the master page to further define the structure and content of your publishing pages. Within the ContentPlaceholders you can control the order and placement of field controls, content, and web part zones. Page layouts can also override the default ContentPlaceholder settings and HTML within them. Web part zones allow content administrators to add, remove, or rearrange web parts within the page.

Page layouts relate back to unique page content types that allow you to add and display metadata associated with the page. Content authors create pages and then specify which layout that page is assigned to. These publishing pages are stored in a pages library that gets automatically created when the publishing feature is enabled on that site. Page layouts are also stored and managed within the master page gallery. Page layouts can be edited with SharePoint designer 2010.

In Figure 1-14 the master page is the outer shell that defines the overall structure of the site. The page layout is used to render the field controls and placement of the web part zones on the page.

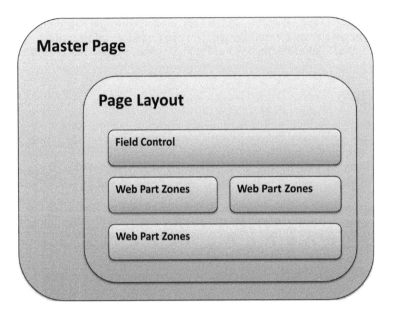

*Figure 1-14. Relationship between master page and page layouts*

# Summary

This introductory chapter provides an overview of the key components of how SharePoint is structured and built. After reading this chapter you should have a basic understanding of CSS, HTML, master pages, page layouts, and key topics to consider.

# CHAPTER 2

# Overview of UX/Branding Process

## What's In This Chapter?

- The 4 Ds
    - Discovery
    - Definition
    - Design
    - Development
- Roles and Responsibilities
    - Business Analyst
    - Information Architect
    - Visual Designer
    - Front End Developer

In this chapter you learn about the overall strategy for defining and building a SharePoint site from a user experience (UX) perspective. By its very nature, user experience is subjective since it refers to how a person feels about and reacts to an application or portal when they use it. User experience includes the user's perception of ease of use and efficiency, and captures users' overall thoughts about the site. This chapter covers four main phases—Discovery, Definition, Design, and Development—which include the process of gathering both system and business requirements, the benefits of creating and defining wireframes, the definition of visual design compositions, and the tools you use to build the design. Within this branding process you or others will be assigned to specific roles that help contribute to the ultimate user experience. Since many projects are scoped differently, you can use the following process as a guide. Some elements or definitions might be very valuable for one project but not as important for other projects. It is up to you and your team to decide which of these exercises add value to your project and whether or not you have the time or budget to include them.

# The 4 Ds

The four phases shown at the top of Figure 2-1, Discovery, Definition, Design, and Development, are the main user-centered design phases that are covered within this book. These four labels may differ based on the methodology that you use, but the tasks associated with each one are consistent across most projects.

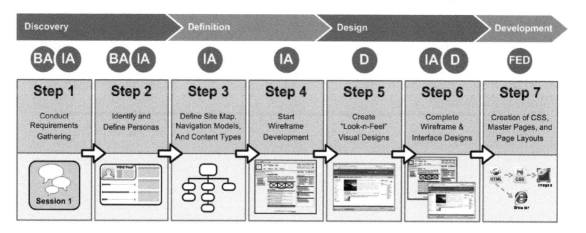

*Figure 2-1. UX process*

**Benefits** Having a process allows you to communicate with your stakeholders what types of things they will be reviewing and what stage you are currently in. It also gives the project manager an idea of when a specific role needs to be included and for what task.

## Discovery

Within the discovery phase the business analyst, information architect, and technical architect conduct sessions with business stakeholders to gather and define the business and system requirements. They also identify who the users of the system are and create personas as needed. The discovery phase has two steps, as shown in Figure 2-2. The first step is to gather business and system requirements. The second step is to identify user personas.

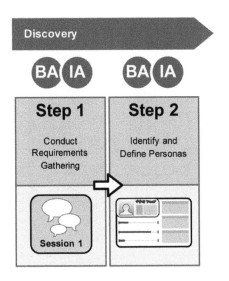

*Figure 2-2. Discovery phase*

## Discovery Documents

The documents that are created during the discovery phase set the foundation for how the portal will function. This phase is really the start of the project. There is a kickoff meeting to identify the purpose and scope of the site, introductions of team members, project schedule, critical success factors, deliverables/milestones, risks, and escalation paths.

The business analyst starts with interviews of the business users and key stakeholders to identify what the users need this site to provide and what features and functions it should have. All of the requirements that are gathered are compiled into the traceability matrix and organized into multiple columns, as shown in Figure 2-3. The traceability matrix can be created in Excel or managed directly in SharePoint as a custom list.

| | A | B | C | D | E |
|---|---|---|---|---|---|
| 1 | Req. Ref. ID# | Requirement Statement / Rule Description | RS# | Status | Benefi t |
| 28 | 200 | Home Page | | | |
| 29 | 201 | Ability to have a "base" home page (some areas of page cannot be changed by user) but has areas customizable by the user. | RS008 | | Must Have |
| 30 | 202 | Poll / Survey: ability to have polls / surveys within articles, on home page, etc. | RS018 | | Must Have |
| 31 | 203 | Have alerts from other systems/areas, such as eLearning, show up on the user's home page. | RS022 | | Must Have |
| 32 | 204 | Home page would show number of comments per article. | RS061 | | Must Have |
| 33 | 205 | Ability to display stock page as we do today – but could be open to discussion – users could subscribe. | RS062 | | Must Have |
| 34 | 206 | Third party content – open for discussions. (like CNN, financial news, weather, etc. | RS063 | | Not Needed – may be future |
| 35 | 207 | The system will provide an enterprise event calendar on the home page | | | Must Have |
| 36 | 208 | The system will display news on the home page, both corp. and dept. news if you belong to a dept. that puts out news | | | Must Have |
| 37 | 209 | The system will provide an easy way to add and display quick links on their home page, or favorite links | | | Must Have |
| 38 | | Ability to display BU news content on the home page for members of that BU, others can subscribe if they so wish | | | Must Have |
| 39 | 210 | The landing page will allow users to view a summary of their profile information, there will also be a link to update their profile. | | | Nice To Have |
| 40 | 211 | Ability to display the official news and postings that Company wishes to share with all users | | | Must Have |
| 41 | | | | | |
| 42 | 300 | Landing Pages | | | |
| 43 | 301 | Landing pages would show or represent high level content for each of the things in that section. | | | Must Have |
| 44 | 302 | All landing pages will have a contact box; can be email address or phone #, link to photos, etc. | | | Must Have |
| 45 | 303 | Communities landing page will show links to all community sites | | | Must Have |
| 46 | 304 | Communities landing page will show links to all community sites a user has joined | | | Must Have |
| 47 | 305 | Teams & Projects landing page that will show links to all sites a user has access to | | | Must Have |
| 48 | | | | | |
| 49 | 400 | My Site | | | |
| 50 | 401 | Ability for users to extend the functionality of their site by adding, configuring, moving, and removing web parts within their Private My Site Site Collection | | | Must Have |
| 51 | 402 | A user's My Site will provide a blog feature | | | Must Have |

**Figure 2-3.** *Traceability matrix*

■ **Benefits** The traceability matrix allows you to organize and capture all of the system and business requirements in a single document.

Another very helpful discovery document records the various personas and the defined users of the system. This document provides a detailed description of the "user by role." Personas can be as simple as the name of the roles to very detailed specifications, as shown in Figure 2-4. This type of diagram allows you to quickly identify what type of user they are. Here are some key questions that you will want to ask users when defining your personas:

- What are your current roles and responsibilities?

- How often do you use the current portal?

- What do you use it for?

- What do you like/dislike about it?

- Have you ever used SharePoint before? If so how often?

- Do you use any social websites like Facebook, Twitter, or Linked In?

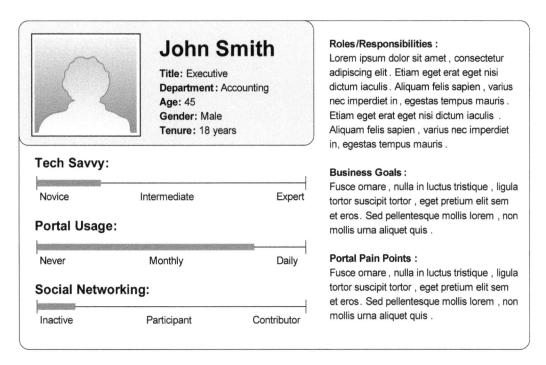

*Figure 2-4. Persona snapshot example*

# Definition

During the definition phase the information architect takes the business and system requirements from the traceability matrix and creates a variety of documents that help define the taxonomy, navigation, page layouts, and templates. The definition phase consists of two steps, as shown in Figure 2-5. The first is to define the site map, navigation models, and content types. This gives you a base set of information to then move to the second step, which is to start wireframe development.

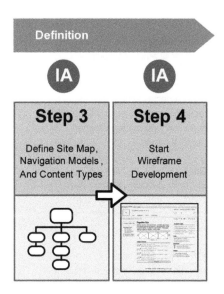

**Figure 2-5.** *Definition phase*

## Definition Documents

The types of documents that might be created in the definition phase are either visual representations of the requirements or groupings and labeling of information. To help define either a site map or a navigation model, conducting a card-sorting exercise, as shown in Figure 2-6, can identify how users group and label information.

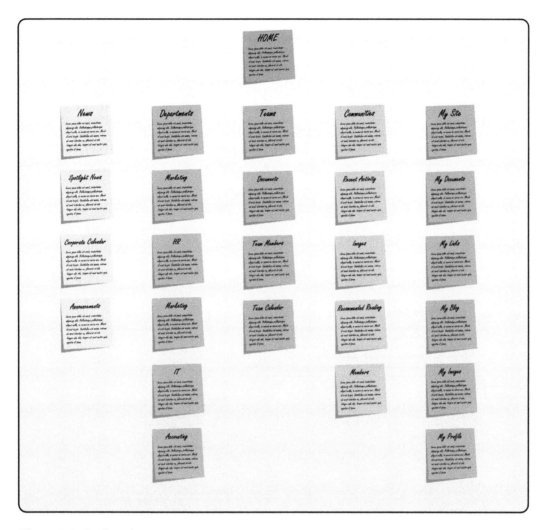

***Figure 2-6.*** *Card sorting*

■ **Benefits**  Conducting card-sorting exercises allows you to work with participants to quickly organize large amounts of information in a short period of time.

Creating wireframes is a very quick and effective way of displaying an idea or layout without having to be concerned with its visual appearance. Wireframes can start out as sketches and then mature into something much more polished. There are a few software applications that can help you create wireframe sets. Some people like to use OmniGraffle, iRise, or SketchFlow to create dynamic and interactive wireframes, but these types of programs can be expensive and hard to use. Visio is a simple yet effective tool that you can use to make and reuse wireframes, web parts, and UI controls for multiple projects. The information architect builds out wireframes to conduct usability testing and also shows them to the development team so that they have a better understanding of what the end result should look like. Wireframes can range from 5 to 10 pages for small projects and 50 to 60 pages for larger ones. This more involved type of wireframe, shown in Figure 2-7, contains a lot of detail and is easy for the development team to understand.

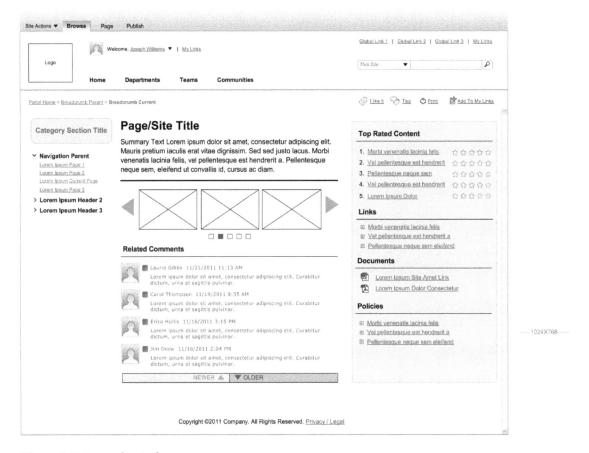

***Figure 2-7.*** *Example wireframe*

The site maps and navigation models that were generated by card-sorting exercises should go though some sort of usability testing. This testing can be as simple as showing the structured model to a variety of people and documenting any questions or concerns that they have. Another method is to provide the people you are testing with a task like, "Submit a time sheet," or, "Download PPT templates." Document how long it takes them to complete tasks and in what category they feel they would successfully accomplish their task.

Remember that site maps do not always have to be linear, parent-and-child categories in a traditional "boxes and arrows" tree hierarchy. In some cases you can afford to get very creative in mapping illustrations, and encourage your stakeholders to take part in creating a more innovative navigation model. For example, a non-linear site map can be very flexible. The goal is to provide system owners with an acceptable level of governance through controlled placement of content while giving end users the freedom to accomplish daily tasks and navigate the system unimpeded by labeling and navigation constructs. As demonstrated in Figure 2-8 not all sitemaps have to be boxes and squares. The size of the circles can represent importance and also the number of sites under them.

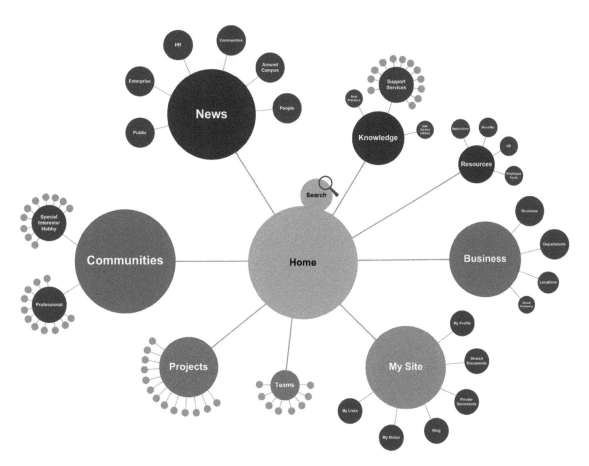

***Figure 2-8.*** *Graphical site map*

The last area of the discovery phase is site columns and content types. Site columns are just like any other list or library column in SharePoint but are managed at a higher level. When you combine multiple site columns together into a set you are basically creating a content type. Content types, a core component of the functionality and services within SharePoint 2010. Content types are designed to help users organize their SharePoint content in a more meaningful way. A content type is a reusable collection of site columns that you want to apply to a certain category of content. Content types enable you to manage the metadata and behaviors of a document or item type in a centralized, reusable way. They most often come from a business need to identify and group unique types of artifacts. SharePoint comes with some basic and very useful content types out of the box. Additional content types can be defined and then instantiated in SharePoint during implementation.

For example, consider the following two types of documents: software specifications and legal contracts. It is reasonable that you might want to store documents of those two types in the same document library. However, the metadata you would want to gather and store about each of these document types would be very different. In addition, you would most likely want to assign very different workflows to the two types of documents.

With content types you can store different types of content in the same document library or list. In the preceding example, you could define two content types, named Specification and Contract. Each content type would include different columns for gathering and storing item metadata, as well as different workflows assigned to them. Yet items of both content types could be stored in and effectively retrieved from the same document library.

# Design

Within the design phase the visual designer works with the information architect to transform the design requirements into visual design compositions and to create a style guide once the designs are approved. There are two steps to the design phase, as shown in Figure 2-9. The first is creating the visual design compositions. The second is taking the approved wireframes and adapting them to an approved design direction.

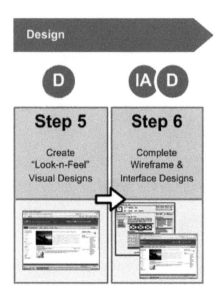

*Figure 2-9. Design phase*

The visual design composition shown in Figure 2-10 is usually created using photo-editing software like Photoshop. The designer manipulates colors, typography, background images, lines, and other design elements to create a visual interpretation of what the site will look like. This process can take time and is usually achieved in multiple review stages. For the first stage the designer would create a couple of design options for the stakeholders to choose from. These designs might come from a predetermined set of themes. After the first round of reviews, a decision on a particular design direction is typically made. The designer then goes back and makes any additional changes as requested by the review team. After the team is satisfied with the final design, the designer might be tasked with applying that design to some additional wireframe templates to give the front-end developer all of the design attributes and styles needed to build a complete system. Once all of the designs have been created and approved, the designer creates a style guide that defines the colors, fonts, heights, widths, margins, and any other specification that can help the front-end developer build the design.

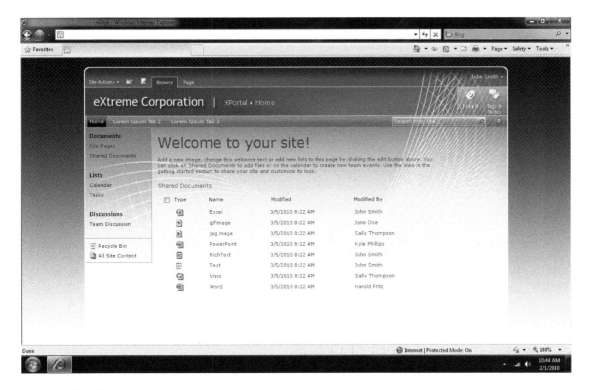

**Figure 2-10.** *Visual design composition*

# Development

The development phase, shown in Figure 2-11, is the last of the four phases that we will cover in this chapter. This phase includes the process of taking the final visual design comps and transforming them into a working prototype. During the development phase the front-end developer works with the visual designer to create cascading style sheets (CSS), images, master pages, and page layouts to transform

SharePoint based on the wireframes and visual compositions. This process requires a person on your team with a solid background in CSS, HTML, SharePoint master pages, and SharePoint page layouts. It is good if the front-end developer has at least some level of design background; there are likely to be UI detail elements present that require a designer's eye or a judgment call will need to be made on a design that wasn't fully predefined by the designer's comps or the design documentation.

**Figure 2-11.** *Development phase*

If custom master pages and page layouts are necessary, the front-end developer also needs to have some experience with SharePoint Designer 2010. The developer can use either SharePoint Designer (SPD) or Notepad to modify the CSS. SPD provides the benefits of color-coding and multiple undo options.

During this phase the requirements, information architecture, wireframes, and visual design compositions have all been approved. Now it is the front-end developer's turn to step in and start transforming those definitions into a working site. SharePoint Designer has multiple panels that the developer can use when creating the HTML and code, as shown in Figure 2-12. You can view the site in three different view modes:

- **Design:** In design mode you see the site in what is called the What You See Is What You Get (WYSIWYG) mode. The site should look exactly as you see it in the window.

- **Split:** In this mode the screen is split into two panels; one is the visual WYSIWYG form, and the other is code view.

- **Code:** This view allows you to see as much of the code as possible.

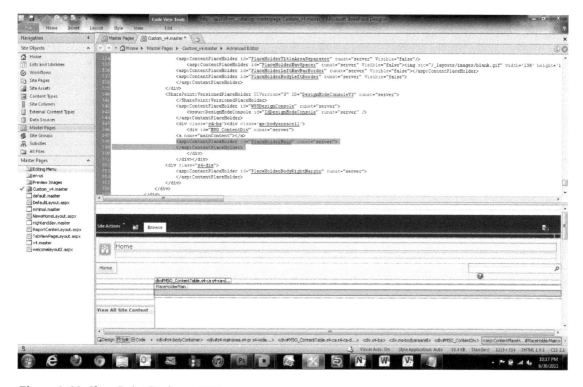

**Figure 2-12.** *SharePoint Designer 2010*

Throughout the four phases there are multiple roles that are needed to support the different tasks. Some of these roles will overlap within the project timeline. In some cases a single person can play multiple roles based on their skills and expertise.

# Roles and Responsibilities

Everyone on your software development team has a unique and important role. For example, the project manager keeps everyone on schedule and identifies or escalates any particular issues or obstacles that the team might have. In a "team design" scenario, there will be multiple roles that will collaborate and provide peer reviews and knowledge transfers throughout the project lifecycle.

The UX design roles that are defined in Table 2-1 are common across most project types. Each role is unique and in most cases has specialized skill sets. It is critical that team leads define the roles needed and team members understand their individual roles and how to map them to tasks, deliverables, and timelines early in your project.

Keep in mind that the roles that you need will vary on a project-specific basis. It might be necessary to have multiple business analysts on projects with many requirements that need to be identified and documented. Other projects might need more than one information architect to help define the taxonomies, wireframes, and navigation models. The project timeline also affects the number of resources needed. If your project has a very tight deadline, you might need more resources to cover the load in a short period of time. However, if the project duration is very long, you might have fewer resources (each responsible for multiple roles) for a more extended period of time.

The key to any project is clear and frequent communication. All resources on the project need to have good communication skills and be willing to participate as needed. Your project's success depends on the communication skills and group interaction dynamics (or "people skills") within your team. One example for clear communication is risk identification and issue resolution. If you or your team discovers an issue make sure to clearly identify and document it. This will prepare your team to accommodate for the changes needed and get the issue fixed or resolved in a timely manner.

It is important that everyone on the team understands the responsibilities and tasks for each role and member of the team. This promotes accountability, prevents duplication of efforts, and creates clear direction while empowering your team members to act independently.

In this chapter we focus on four main roles that help define the overall project experience within SharePoint. Each role provides details and definitions for the design. These roles and definitions span multiple phases of a project.

*Table 2-1. UX Roles Per Phase*

| Role | Discovery | Definition | Design | Development |
|------|-----------|------------|--------|-------------|
| Business Analyst | X | X | | |
| Information Architect | X | X | | |
| Visual Designer | | | X | |
| Front End Developer | | | | X |

## Business Analyst

 The business analyst (BA helps capture and define the business needs within the portal application. The BA acts as a middle tier between the development team and the business users and stakeholders. In most cases, the BA is responsible for analyzing business processes and capturing, documenting, and validating organizational requirements. The BA must be able to understand these needs and help organize and set priorities for each one. BAs often translate any "business goals" received from stakeholders into functional requirements that guide the development team. They work with the key stakeholders for approval of the requirements. For agile projects the BA also helps define the user stories and tasks assigned to each story.

## BA Responsibilities

The BA contributes to the following types of documents:

- **Business Requirements:** This document usually includes broad requirements that were identified by the business users. Examples:

  - Improved communication and collaboration between users

- Enhanced user experience for better user adoption

- Attractive and consistent branding across all sites

- Increased support and training materials

- **System/Functional Requirements:** This document includes specific requirements and features that help solve the business needs. Many of these types of requirements typically start with a directive statement or phrase such as, "The system must," or "The system shall provide the capability to." Examples:

  - The system will provide an enterprise event calendar on the home page.

  - The system will provide a mechanism to display news across all portal areas.

  - The system must provide the capability for a user to create a community-based site.

  - The system must provide a single federated search service with a results page that will include security-trimmed results.

  - The system shall provide global navigation, which is persistent and cannot be changed by an end user without going through appropriate governance processes.

  - The system shall enable the ability to navigate through and view content consistently within different browsers and operating systems.

- **Traceability Matrix:** This document (see Table 2-2), typically a Microsoft Excel spreadsheet, tracks all requirements through the different phases of the project. Each row in the document is a separate requirement, with some of the columns defined below:

  - Unique Reference ID

  - Title, Statement, and Summary

  - Status

  - I - in scope

  - O - Out of Scope

  - U - Under Consideration

  - D – Deferred

  - Benefit

  - Must Have

  - Desired

  - Nice To Have

  - Future

  - Need (need to consider for design purposes)

- Not Needed - may be future
- Level of Effort (LOE)
- High - 20 days +
- Medium - 1–20 days
- Low - Less than 1 day
- Target Release
- Phase 1
- Phase 2
- Future Phase
- Requirement Details
- Additional Comments

***Table 2-2.*** *Traceability Matrix Example*

| ID | Title | Status | Benefit | LOE | Release | Details | Comments |
|----|-------|--------|---------|-----|---------|---------|----------|
| RQ1 | Lorem | In Scope | Must Have | Low | Phase 1 | Lorem ipsum | Lorem ipsum |
| RQ2 | Lorem | In Scope | Must Have | Low | Phase 1 | Lorem ipsum | Lorem ipsum |
| RQ3 | Lorem | Out of Scope | Future | High | Phase 2 | Lorem ipsum | Lorem ipsum |

## BA Skills

A qualified business analyst has the following skill set:

- Is an outgoing public speaker and a good "people person"
- Is organized in terms of work output and time management
- Communicates effectively with stakeholders.
- Enjoys overcoming challenges and is an effective problem solver
- Facilitates diplomatic interview sessions and pays attention to what people are saying
- Is a "quick study" at learning and understanding how businesses are run
- Understands basic SharePoint features and functions and can communicate how to weigh and prioritize best practices to the client

## When to Include a BA

BAs should be included in the beginning or discovery phase of the project. They help with clearly and effectively gathering requirements from users and stakeholders. BAs work closely with information architects and developers.

# Information Architect

The information architect (IA) helps define the interface taxonomy, navigation, and page structure. The IA is a critical role in just about any SharePoint project. The origin of Information Architecture as a web design consulting practice comes partly from Library Sciences and partly from user interface design. This role has a deep understanding of how to categorize information in a coherent and logical structure. The IA will have multiple tasks throughout the project. Often the IA fills the role of BA if one is not identified.

The IA must have a basic understanding of how SharePoint works. It is recommended that your IA work directly with the development team, translating system requirements into the wireframes. Some system requirements might map directly to a feature that is out of the box (OOTB) within SharePoint, and should be represented as such within the wireframes. Whereas the BA captures "the what" in terms of documenting business goals and requirements, the IA's job is critical in defining "the how"—transforming the business vision from a list of requirements into usable illustrations. The IA's primary output in terms of deliverables is the wireframes document or grayscale blueprints providing developers with guidelines for how the system should operate from a user experience perspective. It is critical that the Information Architect work with the development team to review and verify the concepts and definitions that are being created within the wireframes.

---

■ **Benefits** The IA role is critical to have on any SharePoint Project. Nobody wants to use a site that has poor structure or is not user-friendly.

---

## IA Responsibilities

The IA contributes to the following tasks or documents:

- **Taxonomy:** Defining the navigation structure and organization of a web site is one of the most challenging tasks project teams face in the course of the project. It is also one of the most critical for ensuring project success because it helps users find what they need quickly and efficiently. Taxonomies are categories of information presented in a hierarchical format. Humans organize knowledge into systems. A good taxonomy is an intuitive system that helps users locate content. It's important to differentiate between the different taxonomies that appear in a web site. The global navigation is a site taxonomy that resides at the top of the collection or site. A page may have local navigation or information hierarchy unique to that page. Likewise, a document library may have a folder taxonomy that represents the folder structure of department information.

- **Card Sorting:** This is one of the most popular techniques used to define site taxonomy. It's very helpful in improving a system's "findability." Card sorting helps to reveal underlying structure in an unsorted list of information. It involves a facilitator, observer (helper), and one or more participants (card sorting can be done by individuals or in pairs). The facilitator writes each statement on a small index card and asks the participants to sort the cards into groups of related content, into categories that make sense to the participant. They also label the categories with titles that are familiar to them. The results of the individual sorts are then combined and analyzed to uncover common trends in categorization and labeling. As with other methods, the participants should be representative of the user population for whom the application is being designed. The benefits of a card sorting exercise is that it provides input into a final site hierarchy (taxonomy) that is representative of the user population, of how they expect ideas or functions to be presented.

- **Site Map:** Site maps show the overall structure and hierarchy of a web site. They can be used as the first step in laying out the web information architecture of a site, and provide the framework upon which to base site navigation.

- **Navigation Model:** SharePoint bases its navigation model on a hierarchical structure within a single site collection. Organizations need a consistent and global navigation across all site collections, so it is critical that a custom navigation model be defined and tested. Card sorting helps with the process of identifying the top level groupings and sub links within your navigation system.

- **Wireframes:** A wireframe is a schematic drawing that typically depicts a series of page layouts combined to form a site template such as the home page, team site, or project site. These flexible design artifacts allow you to explore patterns and ways of organizing sites to help finalize a design solution. In essence, wireframes are a tool for developing ideas about content, imagery, and functionality, and how they all come together to create an experience. Wireframes go through a series of reviews and revisions.

- **Content Types:** Content types are a reusable collection of settings you want to apply to a certain category of content. They enable you to manage the metadata and behaviors of a document or item type in a centralized, reusable way. A common custom content type would be a news article. Some articles will require specific metadata like start date, end date, byline, image, and body content. All of these metadata properties are combined into a single content type.

## IA Skills

An information architect should have the following skills:

- Is very organized
- Thinks structurally and reacts visually
- Has an understanding of labeling and language
- Works well as part of a team

- Can clearly explain how things work

- Shows attention to detail transcending a range of needs from requirements to design

- Recognizes design patterns and is skilled with problem solving

- Shows interest in labeling and indexing; having interaction design experience or a library science background is a plus

## When to Include an IA

IAs are used early on in a project, during the discovery and definition phases. They help organize and define the logical navigation within the system. The IA works closely with the development team to provide additional specifications and visual aids for how the system should be laid out and function.

# Visual Designer

The Visual Designer (VD) is the creative role that helps define the visual look and feel of the SharePoint site. It is recommended that the visual designer have some basic knowledge of how SharePoint works. Without that, you could end up with a captivating visual look and feel that doesn't conform to the SharePoint architectural framework and cannot be built within the scope of the work and schedule identified.

The designer works with the information architect and developers to create visual design compositions that will be reviewed and approved by the business stakeholders.

## Designer's Responsibilities

The IA helps contribute to the following tasks or documents:

- **Creative/UX Discovery Brief:** The UX brief summarizes the vision, strategy, requirements, and preliminary design work that were defined prior to starting the visual design. The creative brief is similar to a style guide in that it defines all of the identified visual requirements for the system. This type of document might include the following:

    - Referenced web sites

    - Colors

    - Fonts

    - Approved logo usage

    - Shapes, patterns, imagery

    - Browser requirements and resolution

- **Visual Design Compositions:** These flat visual designs are created based on the approved creative or UX brief documents. In most projects a designer is tasked with creating multiple design options, which could be based on the home, team, community, or departmental page. These options are reviewed by a set of approvers, who choose a particular design direction. Once the direction has been approved, the designer takes any changes or feedback and comes up with a second round of visual designs for another review. Normally there are no more than three rounds of revisions or changes. Once the design has been approved the designer could be tasked with adapting the design to additional templates defined in the approved wireframes.

- **Style Guide:** The style guide is a reference document that is used by both the front-end developer and the SharePoint development team. This guide consists of very specific heights, widths, spacing, colors, and fonts based on the approved visual design compositions.

## Visual Designer Skills

Designers should have the following skill set:

- Is highly creative/artistic

- Has the ability to think conceptually

- Shows great attention to detail

- Has experience with Photoshop or other photo-editing software

- Has strong communication and presentation skills

## When to Include a Designer

The designer can be included in the project once the majority of the wireframes have been approved. Bringing in the designer too early may force them to "fake" in navigation, content, and structure with the visual design compositions. The risk here is that the approvers of the visual design might pay more attention to those unfinished sections instead of concentrating on the actual visual look and feel of the site. It is best to start having branding requirement meetings after the wireframes have been approved or at least are mostly final.

# Front-End Developer

The front-end developer (FED) takes the look-and-feel designs defined by the visual designer and the wireframes defined by the IA and creates supporting files and images that are applied to SharePoint. The FED should have a solid background in HTML and CSS, and some experience modifying master pages, page layouts, and XSLT. Some designs require pixel-perfect precision and placement, so the FED must have an eye for detail. The FED also needs to be very organized in order to build cascading style sheets correctly. With some designs with hundreds of classes it is essential that they provide some type of hierarchy and commenting.

## FED Responsibilities

The FED contributes to the following tasks:

- **Supporting Build Files:** The FED works directly with the visual designer to translate the flat visual designs into optimized images, CSS, and HTML. The FED uses applications like SharePoint Designer 2010 to create custom style sheets, master pages, and page layouts.

- **Testing:** The FED will constantly be testing builds for consistency and accuracy according to the visual designer's approved design compositions and style guide. The FED works with the development team to identify and resolve any bugs and defects introduced by the new visual design.

## FED Skills

Front-end developers should have the following skills:

- Shows attention to detail

- Has experience with cascading style sheets (CSS) and HTML

- Has worked with SharePoint Designer

- Has experience with Photoshop or other photo-editing software

## When to Include a Front-end Developer?

The front-end developer should be included in the project any time after the visual designs have been fully completed and approved. The developer uses the style guide and works directly with the visual designer to ensure that all of the style elements have been defined and any image support files have been created.

# Summary

This chapter provides an overview of the UX process as it applies to SharePoint design. There are many moving parts within the software-design process, and it is easy for someone to get lost and confused. The intent of this chapter was to give you a better understanding of the different roles, the documentation, and the process involved, to help guide you through your project. The process described here is intended as an example model that you can follow. Other projects might follow a more iterative process, which would change how you define your activities and revise your deliverables and documentation.

CHAPTER 3

# Gathering Branding Requirements

**What's In This Chapter?**

- Key Questions to Ask
- The Value of Referencing Other Designs
- Things to Watch Out For
- Generating Creative/UX Discovery Briefs
- Estimating Effort Level and Time Required

In this chapter you learn what you need to do to prepare yourself for creating the visual design. Branding requirements are very different from standard business or system requirements. Design direction might come in the form of imagery, tone, and even fingernail polish colors. The process of gathering design requirements usually starts after the wireframes have been defined and approved. Figure 3-1, step 4b, shows the beginning of the Design phase. The designer (see the previous chapter for a definition of that role) is the primary person tasked with information gathering. The Discovery and Definition phases (steps 1–4) are important components of the user-experience process but since they are not focused around SharePoint branding they will not be covered in full detail within this book.

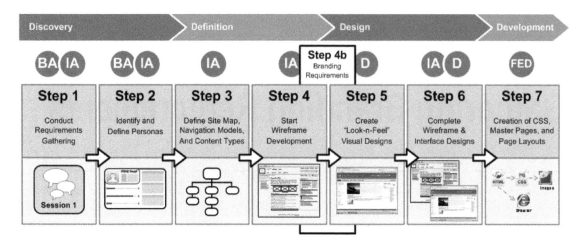

*Figure 3-1. Step 1: Gathering branding requirements*

As you learn the details involved in gathering branding requirements, it is important to understand all of the roles involved in the decision-making process. The visual designer holds the lead role in conducting the design sessions. The internal marketing or corporate communications team fills a key supporting role, as owners of the current visual branding. The team should be able to provide any existing style guides or documentation relating to the overall corporate brand, and, in most cases, will serve as the final approvers for the visual-design direction.

This chapter provides a variety of resources to help you with defining the visual design. These include a set of questions to ask your stakeholders and marketing teams. It also includes reference designs for inspiration, terms to watch out for, and definitions of a creative brief and why you need one. The last part of this chapter covers different levels of branding that can be applied and ways to estimate how long it might take to create.

# Key Questions to Ask

In preparing for your visual-design sessions you need to make sure you have everything required to get the ball rolling. These questions are intended to be used as topic starters, and to get people involved in the process. You can ask the questions before and during the design review meetings.

---

■ **Benefits** Getting answers to these questions helps you define your design, be better prepared, and allow your stakeholders to get involved. Responses also generate information for documentation that you can use for testing.

---

- **Q:** Has your company undergone any recent rebranding?
  - If yes, how long ago did it occur?

- **Q:** Do you have access to design support files?
  - Style guides
  - Layered design compositions
  - Font files for both Mac and PC
  - Images (approved and purchased photo libraries)
  - Screenshots of existing designs
- **Q:** Does the site have a name?
  - If yes, how is that name represented: text, logo, URL, other?
- **Q:** Do you need a custom logo?
- **Q:** What are the logo specifications?
  - Size
  - Treatment
  - Color
  - **Q:** Will there be multiple logos?
  - Corporate logo
  - Site logo
  - Divisional logos/images
  - Others?
- **Q:** Will there be any changes to the current design? If yes, what level?
  - **Level 1:** Theme (use current design for just colors and fonts)
  - **Level 2:** Brand adaptation (use current design as a guide)
  - **Level 3:** Custom brand adaptation (use some existing design parts)
  - **Level 4:** Custom design (create a completely new design)
- **Q:** How much customization is required?
  - Home page (customization of just the home page)
  - Site level (customization of only one site)
  - Portal level (customization of all front-facing pages (not admin or My Site))
  - Site collection (customization of all areas including admin and My Site)
  - Master page and page layout (customization of master pages and page layouts)

- **Q:** Do you need to change or include additional icons?
  - Drop-down arrows
  - Bullets
  - Chevrons
  - Input buttons
  - Document icons
  - Page-level icons
- **Q:** Who will be approving these designs?
  - Marketing (how many members of the team and who specifically?)
  - Board Executives (how many members of the team and who specifically?)
  - Project Managers (how many members of the team and who specifically?)
  - Others?
- **Q:** How many design reviews do you consider necessary?
  - 1st round (2–3 comps): 1 day for review; 1 day for revisions
  - 2nd round (2 comps): 1/2 day for review; 1/2 day for revisions
  - Final round (2 comps): 1 day for review; 1/2 day for revisions
  - 1 day for approvals and sign off
- **Q:** Is a different design required for each area?
  - Each department or office has its own design
  - Each site or functional area has its own color scheme
    - Portal
    - Team collaboration
    - Projects
    - Communities
    - My Sites
  - Each web part has its own header style
- **Q:** What type of treatments do you consider appropriate?
  - Gradations or flat colors
  - Rounded corners
  - Transparencies

- White text on dark background
- Tabbed navigation
- Pixel lines for separation
- Shadows
- **Q:** What branding style is appropriate?
  - Simple or complex
  - Bold or soft
  - Heavy imagery or soft color transitions
  - Heavy or light web-part title bars (Chrome)
  - Sharp square edges or soft rounded corners
- **Q:** What types of colors will be used from the approved color palette?
  - One color with tints for section definition
  - Many colors
  - Complementary colors
  - Soft, blended transitions
  - Hard edges between colors
  - Primary color with secondary color accents
- **Q:** What level of imagery is appropriate?
  - Large, bold marketing images
  - Soft watermark images to fill empty spaces
  - Enlarged, cropped images
- **Q:** What types of business rules will be applied?
  - All external links (open in new window or open with same page)
  - Fixed-width design versus liquid (resizes with browser)
- **Q:** Are there any accessibility requirements?
  - Need to accommodate for color blindness
    - Navigation cannot rely on just color alone
  - Need the ability to increase the font sizes in navigation components and content for users with poor visibility
  - Need the ability to navigate using only the keyboard

- **Q:** Does custom global navigation need to be created?

  - Do you want your site to have the same navigation on every page? If so, then you may need a custom global-navigation control

  - The top navigation control does not span multiple site collections

When it comes to visual design, in most cases people don't know what they want. The questions in this section get you most of the way there, but the best way to understand what people really want from a visual perspective is to ask them in a more graphical way using reference designs.

# The Value of Referencing Other Designs

People tend to find it hard to express, strictly in words, what they want their site to look like. They will probably say that if you show them something, they can let you if they like it or not. It's very useful to ask your participants to reference three to five web site designs that they really like. This will help inform your overall design-gathering experience.

---

░ **Benefits**   Getting answers to these questions helps jumpstart the process of defining what your stakeholders like and dislike. It also gets people involved and feeling like they have made a contribution to the design.

---

This should be considered a take-away action item or homework type of task. Give participants a day or so to compile and send you a list of web sites with bullets points highlighting the things that they like about each one. At the next meeting view the sites in front of the group, and ask participants to describe what they like about the designs. This interactive exercise lets you gather key data about preferred types of designs. After everyone has provided input, review the entire list, and ask the participants to come up with the top five sites that they all think are design worthy.

---

░ **Note**   These web sites should be used as a reference guide for tonal, emotional, and visual elements and should not be misconstrued as raw material to be copied as-is.

---

If the participants cannot come up with any web sites that they like, you might want to consider the following web sites, to give them a variety of design styles to look at. These sites serve as examples that you can review with your team. There are so many great designs out there coming out each day that it is hard to keep track of the best of class sites. Most public web sites update their designs about every one to three years. Some are major overhauls and others are just simple color or content changes.

- **Simple and Clean** (Figure 3-2): These web sites incorporate a lot of white space and use very simple color palettes.

  - http://www.apple.com

- http://www.whitehouse.gov

- http://www.facebook.com

- https://www.mint.com

- http://box.net

- http://www.wikipedia.org

- http://digg.com

- http://www.linkedin.com

- http://www.delicious.com

***Figure 3-2.*** *Example simple, clean web site design (http://www.wikipedia.org)*

- **Large Content Sliders** (Figure 3-3): These sites use graphical images within carousel-like sliders to help attract users and allow them to interact with the web site.

  - http://www.hulu.com

  - http://curiosity.discovery.com

  - http://www.nationalgeographic.com

- http://www.imdb.com

*Figure 3-3. Example large content slider web site design (http://www.hulu.com)*

- **Tiled Content** (Figure 3-4): In these examples the content is represented through small blocks of information that users can click on for more information.

    - http://www.ted.com

    - http://www.cnn.com

    - http://www.youtube.com

    - http://www.homedepot.com

    - http://www.etsy.com

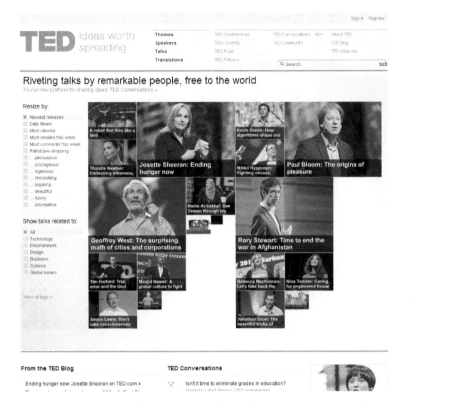

**Figure 3-4.** *Example tiled, content web site design (http://www.ted.com)*

- **Fun and Exciting** (Figure 3-5): Sometimes you just need to break the mold and start with something fresh and exciting that will draw your users into the site.

    - http://www.mtv.com

    - http://www.pottermore.com

    - http://www.lego.com

*Figure 3-5. Example fun and exciting web site design (http://www.pottermore.com)*

As you ask these questions and collect feedback on what people like and don't like, expect to be confronted with some vague responses. The next section addresses this situation.

# Things to Watch Out For

During the process of gathering design ideas you might hear some people use phrases or terms that are either vague or do not relate specifically to design or a particular direction. These terms are confusing in that they have multiple meanings.

---

■ **Benefits** When it comes to design, clearly understanding what your users want is important. There shouldn't be a disconnect between what you deliver and what people (in good faith) expected you to produce.

---

- **Flashy:** This term hints at animation, bright colors, and gradients, and could be interpreted in a few different ways.

- **Cool:** You really need to get further definition on what this term means. What might be cool to one person could have a different effect on someone else.

- **Clean:** Usually when applied to visual design, this term means making the site less cluttered and using more white space.

- **Wow factor:** There might be a hidden agenda with this phrase. Maybe the current site isn't attracting strong user adoption, and the stakeholders are looking for a new visual design that is inviting to new users.

- **Easy on the eyes:** This phrase is mostly used when you are designing for a site that users will stay on for an extended period of time or will go to multiple times a day—like an intranet or collaboration portal.

- **New aged:** This phrase is typically used when the current system is very outdated. You also might hear the phrases "Web 2.0" or "21st century."

- **Fresh:** Most people use this term when they are talking about relevancy or how updated the content will be. "Fresh" might not always relate back to the visual design.

- **Techy:** This one doesn't come up that often, but when it does more likely than not you are talking with an IT person who likes sites with hard lines and angles.

- **Lots of white space:** This is related to "clean" but is too vague to really know what is wanted.

- **Fun:** Watch out for this term. If people want their site to be "fun," they better be with a company that is targeting a younger audience or is trying to breathe new life into a dull, content-heavy site.

With all of these phrases and terms floating around, you'll need to ask for clarification and possibly request an example of what they mean. Respond to any vague requests by turning a statement into a question. For example, if people say that they want their site to be "cool," ask them what they consider that to be. Find out if there is a web site, design, brochure—basically anything design-oriented—that they think has a cool design. This gives you the best definition of what the business users or stakeholders want, so that you can consider incorporating that design treatment into your visual design compositions.

Now that you know what your stakeholders want, you need a way of documenting the requirements and design directions. In this next section you learn two different ways to capture this information.

# Generating Creative and UX Discovery Briefs

You can document all of the requirements and specifications that were provided during the visual-design requirements and design-direction sessions through the creative brief and the UX discovery brief.

---

▬ **Benefits** Documenting the visual requirements helps with the creation of the design. It also helps additional resources get up to speed on the overall approach.

---

# Creative Brief

The creative brief is used to outline general creative visual and tonal interface requirements. It describes visual/tonal design constraints and other factors necessary to provide a complete and comprehensive description of the graphic design/digital branding and user interface requirements for the system. It however should not be used as the basis for content needs, audience-specific functional requirements, and/or related business requirements. In most cases, an actual sign-off of this document is required before any design work is started. The creative brief will include the following sections.

- **Purpose:** This is a brief summary defining the reason for creating the document and its benefits to the project.

- **Scope:** This section is used to identify what portal this document applies to. The organization may have many SharePoint or portal sites, so it is important to define the precise target of the document.

- **Process:** This part describes the basic UX process to educate all team members assigned to the project. It can be as simple as bullet points, or you can provide more detailed descriptions if needed.

- **Definitions, Acronyms, and Abbreviations:** As with any documentation, you'll want to use abbreviations for items such as:

  - Creative brief (CRB)

  - User interface (UI)

  - User experience (UX)

  - Cascading Style Sheets (CSS)

  - Out of the box (OOTB)

- **Existing brand/creative:** Referencing existing brands helps the designer identify current designs that will coexist with or be replaced by the new design. It is important to identify the preferred design characteristics and the design elements that shouldn't be carried forward into the new design. Some existing sites might be very outdated and have no relevance to the new design direction. However, some recently designed sites might be used as the basis for the new design.

- **Vision and approach:** The vision is not intended as the overall vision of the system but is specific to the visual look and feel. It describes the impetus for the new design and where the design direction is coming from.

  - Example: The eXtreme Portal will have a custom design that uses some aspects of the referenced public-facing site's look and feel. The eXtreme portal site will include an updated design with custom elements to bring a more modern look and feel to the design.

- **Brand/identity:** Any corporate logos, portal names, and secondary logos are identified in this section, and specifications are provided for the approved usage of these logos. In most cases, the specifications that you will find are for print purposes and don't clearly indicate how the logos should be represented on the Web. Make sure to work with the marketing team to identify any gaps so that you are not just making stuff up as you go.

- **Colors:** The color palette should be included to show the colors that will be used throughout the site. Make sure the colors are converted to hex or RGB. Some style guides for print only include a PMS, Pantone, or CMYK color code, which might not translate well when converted to the Web. Communicate any color issues early on to avoid hurdles later in the process.

- **Fonts:** For basic designs, you don't typically change the fonts in SharePoint. But as the demand for more custom designs grows, fonts are starting to be changed more often. Some clients might want to change all content-based fonts and headers to a standard font, like Arial San-Serif. The issue with some predefined company fonts is that they are not system fonts and are used primarily in print media. It's a good idea to check to see if the specified font is a base PC/Mac system font; if it isn't, identify any close alternatives that can be used.

- **Structural elements:** This section of the document is really focused around any particular design element—like a fixed-width design or a unique left- or right-hand navigation. You can also use this section for specifying any hover states or visited styles.

- **Shapes/patterns/imagery:** It is recommended that you identify if there will be an image repository available with purchased media.

- **User personalization information:** Within this section you identify any part of the portal where users or site owners will be able to choose their own themes, banners, icons, and other elements.

- **Iconography:** SharePoint comes with well over 2,000 images and icons that support the default branding. You should state up front if there will be any updates to these icons. In most designs, icons such as the search button, list bullets, and drop-down arrows can be customized and changed quite easily using CSS.

- Browser requirements/resolution: This section defines how the design will interact with any specified browser and operating system.

    - Optimized for 1024 x 768 or higher resolutions

    - The site width will be 980px (centered within the browser)

    - Browsers supported: IE 7.x or higher, Firefox, Safari, Chrome

    - Minimal testing will be performed on any browsers not mentioned above

- **Accessibility features:** This section identifies any special features that you need to include when building out your site. This goes back to knowing your users and making sure you provide them with the right tools to meet their needs.

## UX Discovery Brief

The UX discovery brief is created to summarize all the vision, strategy, requirements, and preliminary design thinking that has been generated prior to starting the user-experience design work. Developing this document provides the following benefits:

- Ramps up new team members quickly

- Organizes learning already known about the users or business

- Uncovers new insights important to designing the user experience

- Raises key issues about the project

- Suggests areas for additional learning

- Contributes to the creative design

- Allows for all team members to have a clear understanding of the UX direction

In this brief you describe the project background, vision, goals, audience, and UX strategy. Within the strategy you describe success criteria for all of the roles and phases. It is important to also cover the top business and system requirements. This gives you a solid base on which to define the UX strategy. If any personas have been defined, make sure to identify those user types.

A big part of this document involves identifying either functional concepts or any unique interface-design considerations. For example, you might talk about user personalization and customization that allows users to add, remove, or change the web parts on the page. The last component to a UX discovery brief is to identify any existing branding guidelines that need to be met. This includes fonts, colors, logos, and design treatments.

# Estimating Effort Level and Time Required

This section is intended to teach you how to estimate the length of time it might take to define, create, and build a SharePoint visual design. It is really important to identify ahead of time what level is appropriate for your project. The different types of projects are organized into these four main levels.

## L1: Basic Theme

A basic theme takes a company's predefined color palette and applies the colors to background colors, icons, lines, and text. You can also specify what font types to be used in themes. An alternative way of creating SharePoint 2010 themes is to create a theme in PowerPoint, export it, and then import it into SharePoint 2010. If you modify the theme for a site, you can use the picker shown in Figure 3-6, selecting an OOTB or custom theme. You also have the option to choose your own color scheme using the following elements.

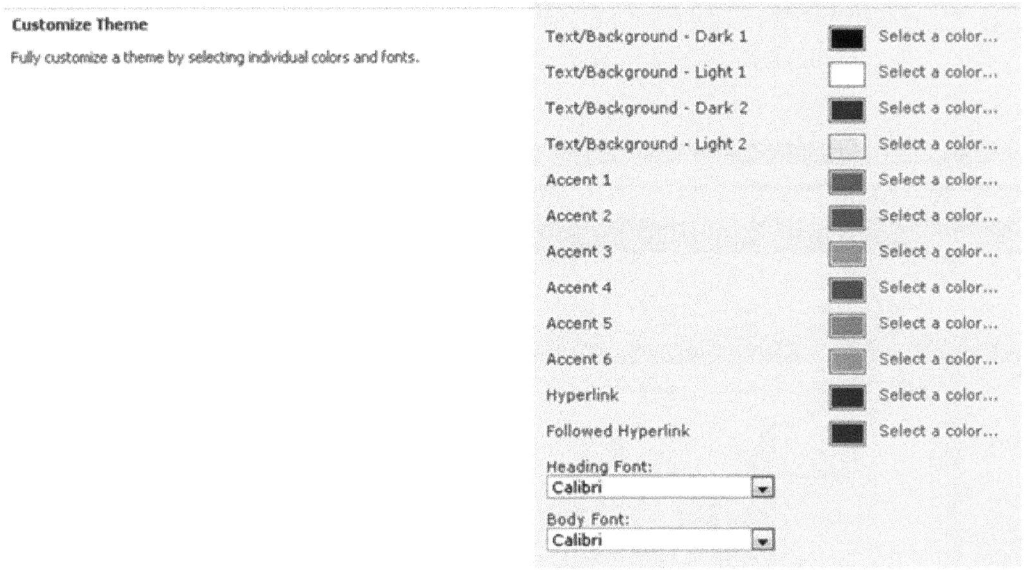

**Figure 3-6.** *SharePoint 2010 theme creator*

You can create themes quite quickly if you just want to change the colors and basic font types. Themes can also be small updates to a custom CSS file that you can centrally manage. This gives you the flexibility to enhance the design later and not be limited by the OOTB theme engine. An example of this type of design treatment is shown in Figure 3-7.

- **Details:** Looks like SharePoint but with different colors and images

    - Design from existing site/reference

    - Use existing logo

    - Update some colors within defined palette

    - Use existing SharePoint fonts

        - Verdana (body text)

        - Tahoma (navigation)

    - Basic CSS changes

    - No master page or page layout edits

- **Level of effort:** ~1–2 weeks

    - Gather branding requirements (4 hours)

    - Create design comp: (10–20 hours)

    - Create optimized images (4–8 hours)

- Create CSS (14–24 hours)

- Testing/bug fixes (8–16 hours)

**Figure 3-7.** *Example SharePoint theme*

# L2: Brand Adaptation

A brand adaption is a little bit more complex than a theme as you might make slight changes to a custom master page. This is more of an advanced theme where you might move an element like the search box or create a custom header. Overall, it might still look like SharePoint, but the inclusion of colors and design elements allows you to match an existing design like a company's public web site. This would be a great entry-level project for someone just starting out with creating and building a SharePoint design. An example of this type of design treatment is shown in Figure 3-8.

- **Details:** Incorporates corporate colors and fonts with slight modifications to the master page

  - Design from existing site/reference

  - Use existing logo

  - Update most colors within defined palette

  - Use existing SharePoint fonts

- - Verdana (body text)
  - Tahoma (navigation)
- Minimal customizations to master page
- No custom page layouts
- **Level of effort:** ~3–4 Weeks
  - Gather branding requirements (4–6 hours)
  - Create design comp: (24–40 hours)
  - Create optimized images (8–16 hours)
  - Create CSS (24–40 hours)
  - Create master page (8–16 hours)
  - Testing/bug fixes (24–40 hours)

***Figure 3-8.*** *Example SharePoint brand adaptation design*

## L3: Custom Brand Adaptation

For this level of branding you take an existing design and make SharePoint not look like SharePoint. The process involves creating custom CSS, master pages and page layouts. Since there is a current design direction, you can save time defining the design. But the time to actually build the site can take up more of your time since you have to do a lot more testing. This type of branding is handled by front-end developers, who have created multiple designs in the past and are experienced with SharePoint Designer and master pages. This type of design treatment is shown in Figure 3-9.

- **Details:** Uses an existing design as a model and requires custom modifications to master pages and page layouts.
  - Custom design from existing site/reference
  - Use existing logo
  - Update most colors within defined palette
  - Update base fonts to defined types
  - Minimal customizations to master page
  - 1 to 2 custom age layouts
- **Level of effort:** 3–4 weeks
  - Gather branding requirements (8–16 hours)
  - Create design comp: (32–48 hours)
  - Create optimized images (8–16 hours)
  - Create CSS (32–48 hours)
  - Create master page(s) (16–24 hours)
  - Create custom page layout(s) (16–24 hours)
  - Testing/bug fixes (32–48 hours)

*Figure 3-9.* *Example SharePoint custom brand adaptation design*

# L4: Custom Design

This level of customization does not come from any existing design but is created by translating tone, treatments, moods, and colors. This unique design requires more development time because you don't have anything to base the structure on. You'll probably go through more review cycles to further define the design. In most cases this custom design will use heavy gradients, iconography, and large and bold fonts. These types of designs are more suited for public-facing sites where the content is more controlled for heights and widths. This will allow for design treatments like a centered fixed width and rounded corners. Figure 3-10 shows an example of this type of design treatment.

- **Details:** Uses an existing design as a model and requires custom modifications to master pages and page layouts.

    - Creation of custom design

    - Create new or customization of logo

    - Custom color palette

- Custom fonts
- Multiple custom master pages
- Multiple custom page layouts
- Custom navigation and web-part styles
- Silverlight, jQuery, XSLT

- **Level of effort:** ~6–8 Weeks
  - Gather branding requirements (16–24 hours)
  - Create design comps: (40–80 hours)
  - Create optimized images (16–24 hours)
  - Create CSS (40–60 hours)
  - Create master pages (20–40 hours)
  - Create custom page layouts (20–40 hours)
  - Testing/bug fixes (40–80)

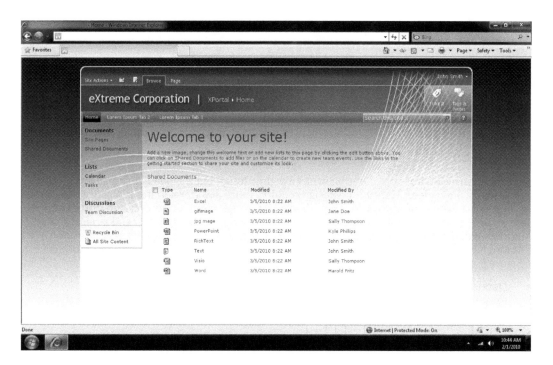

*Figure 3-10. Example SharePoint custom design*

# Summary

This chapter has guided you through the process of gathering design requirements that include fonts, colors, logo usage, and browser specifications. By asking the right questions, you'll now be prepared with a checklist of your stakeholders' web site design preferences. As you are aware, when it comes to defining the design, there are some known pitfalls. People have their own opinions, and you can't please everyone. You have also learned a few techniques on how to identify what your stakeholders like and what they do not like when it comes to web site design. This chapter identified a couple of ways to document your findings in either a creative brief or in a UX discovery brief. Each of these documents should provide you with enough details to proceed to the next stage of the UX process, which is the definition of the visual design.

CHAPTER 4

# Creating the Visual Design

## What's In This Chapter?

- Design Preparations
- Creating the Design
- Design Grids
- Conducting Design Reviews

This chapter takes you through the process of defining, creating, and presenting visual design compositions for SharePoint 2010. The visual designer takes on the role of defining and creating these documents. All of these tasks are part of step 5 within the design phase, as shown in Figure 4-1. The visual design compositions will be based on the branding requirements gathered from the previous chapter. The visual designer uses approved wireframes, the creative brief, and UX discovery briefs as a guide during the design process.

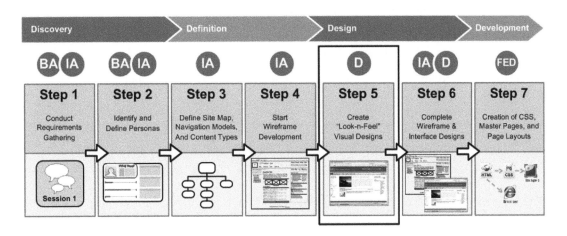

*Figure 4-1.* Step 5

Depending on the project scope, this process can be as simple as adding a logo to the site to as complex as creating a completely custom design with multiple iterations. Designers can choose from many different types of photo-editing software to create the visual design for SharePoint. Here I will be referencing Adobe Photoshop because it is one of the more popular software tools for creating designs for SharePoint. I'll spend a little time going over the tool before diving back into design grids.

This chapter will also cover the resourcing and review cycles needed to get the visual design approved. For larger projects, that could include multiple designers and information architects. It is critical that they are able to communicate and delegate tasks effectively.

# Design Preparations

Before launching into the creative process, the designer needs to gather and review information on what has already been defined. This includes reviewing the style guides, information architecture, creative and UX discovery briefs, taxonomy, and any additional business and system requirements that have been documented.

---

■ **Benefits** It is important for the visual designer to have all the material that has been approved to ensure that their visual designs are accurate and represent the overall structure and functionality specified. Having these files on hand speeds up the creative process and frees up the designer to be truly creative.

---

## Review Final Wireframes

The designer uses the wireframes as a basis for the placement and layout of the functional controls, navigation, and web parts needed on the page. Wireframes should reveal the positioning of the main portal features such as the header, navigation, content layouts, and footer links. The designer normally is tasked with creating multiple versions of designs using a single design template specified within the wireframes. In most cases this template is the homepage for the site. Depending on the time allocated, the designer might also be tasked with extending the design to other pages or templates such as community, department, team, and My Sites templates. The ultimate goal is to create a visual style for all of the unique design elements on the page. The designer will need to work with the IA to identify these elements and determine whether any special cases need to be designed. Special design elements might include custom filters, modal windows, and custom controls. The wireframes should not drive the design direction.

---

■ **Note** The designer uses the wireframes for overall layout and placement of controls and web parts.

---

The designer should also work with the development team to identify anything that would add technical complexity and expand the scope of the project. In most cases the designer should be flexible and find alternatives that still promote the best user experience possible—either with out-of-the-box solutions or using an easier way to implement the custom solution.

Specifications within the wireframes help the designer and the developer understand requirements that cannot be represented in a visual format, as shown in Figure 4-2. You'll want to capture a few key elements (purpose, audience, layout, and content inventory) for each wireframe that gets created.

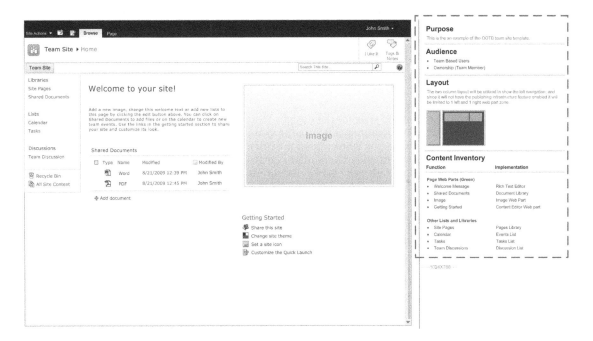

***Figure 4-2.*** *Example wireframe specifications*

The first task is to define the **purpose** of the wireframe, clearly identifying why the wireframe exists and how it should be used. The second element is to specify for each wireframe the **audience** that the wireframe is targeting. Some wireframes show administrative functions or display the page in edit mode. Clearly identifying who the audience is for each wireframe helps the designer and the development team know what should be visible to readers versus administrators or content authors. The third item is to clearly define what type of page **layout** is being used. Typically, any SharePoint projects that include publishing sites will have custom page layouts. Some are as simple as just one for the homepage and one for the top-level publishing content site. However, with more advanced portal sites you might have 10 to 15 custom page layouts that have their own unique web part zone layouts and configurations. The last specification that should be included in each wireframe is the **content inventory**. This inventory list clearly defines all of the web parts and custom controls that are visible on the page. For each component it then provides a best match for either an OOTB web part or specifies if something is custom. This makes it easier for the developer to scope out the level of effort necessary to create the defined wireframe.

It is always a best practice to ensure that a complete knowledge transfer occurs between the information architect and the visual designer. These two roles need to work very closely together to ensure that functionality is not lost while transforming the wireframes into final creative designs.

## Review Requirements

The visual designer must review and become familiar with all of the specified requirements for the specific pages that are to be created. It isn't enough to rely solely on the wireframes because some requirements might not have been addressed during wireframe development. Some of these requirements (or story tasks if you are using an agile methodology) further define the business or system rules for how the site should function.

## Review UX/Creative Brief

The visual designer looks to the UX discovery brief and creative brief as the primary documents for giving the direction on the tone and style for the design. The business stakeholders need to have reviewed and signed off on these documents before the visual designer starts creating the visual designs. Because the designer is usually the one who created the brief to begin with, there's already a familiarity with the specifications and requirements. There might be an extended period of time between the creation of a brief and when it actually gets used as a reference for the design. If this is the case, the designer should review the approved brief again with the business stakeholders to make sure nothing has changed since its approval.

## Establish Review Cycles and Schedules

The designer should work with the project manager to identify the number of review cycles needed and communicate to the stakeholders the amount of time they will need to set aside for review meetings. For smaller design projects there will be between two and three design-review meetings. The first review meeting usually takes around two hours. The second and third review meetings should not take more than an hour to review the changes and achieve sign-off of the designs. For larger projects, the designer will be creating a greater number of visual design compositions and extending them to multiple templates and pages. This will require multiple iterations and more time from the stakeholders. The first initial meeting should be no more than 2 hours. In these meetings it might cover the transition from wireframe to visual design. Before bringing any designs to the stakeholders for review, the designer should work with the project manager on scheduling weekly review meetings with both the development team and the information architects. This allows the internal team to make slight adjustments to the schedule to ensure that what they show to the review team represents the most accurate designs that can feasibly be built within the scope of the project.

# Creating the Design

With all of the basic reference material at your fingertips it's time to have fun! Here you'll learn about the different methods on how to start creating the visual designs. It is important that you take your time and do it right the first time. Some designers dive deep into designing and don't emerge for a breath of air. The trouble with tunnel vision is that you might have spent a lot of time on a particular design direction that ultimately gets scrapped for something more simple and elegant.

■ **Benefits** The value of visual design compositions is that they help define the overall look and feel of the portal. The designs give the front-end developer a guideline and specifications for what the overall site should look like before beginning the build process.

## Create Sketches

Wait, you mean actually draw something, on paper? Yes, for designs that aren't adaptations from an existing design, and before I actually jump into Photoshop, I like to go "old school" and make sketches showing different concepts. Creating sketches of the design concepts allows me to come up with patterns, forms, and quick representations of what the site might look like. These sketches shouldn't take longer than 10 to 15 minutes per design idea.

■ **Note** Not all projects require sketches, but stakeholders usually react really well to great creative talent.

At the beginning of my consulting career I was tasked with creating 100 sketches of different visual design options before the next day. I thought this was a crazy assignment, but I decided to take the challenge. I worked as hard as I could and ended up with 40 different design ideas. I felt bad that I couldn't even get close to 100 but felt the ones I made were solid enough that I wouldn't get in trouble. I came to find out that it was all just a test. If my manager had asked me to create 40 design options I more than likely would have created only 20 to 30. The moral of this story is that these sketches are meant to be quick design thoughts and shouldn't take up a lot of time. You can review these preliminary sketches with your team and get feedback on the top 5 options to pursue.

Once you have the general direction for your design you'll want to use a design program that allows you to create high-fidelity (to the pixel) visual designs. The next section presents a few software options that you can choose from for this task.

## Photo-Editing Tools

We're going to focus on Adobe Photoshop as the primary photo-editing tool. However, there are other alternative applications that have similar features. Here is a list of tools that could be used to create the visual design compositions.

- **Adobe Photoshop:** One of the most preferred software tools for photo editing and SharePoint design definition
  - http://www.adobe.com/products/photoshop.html
- **Xara:** Priced lower than Photoshop and similar features
  - http://www.xara.com

- **Corel PaintShop Pro:** A less expensive alternative for photo editing.
  - http://www.corel.com
- **Gimp:** A free client-side software alternative
  - http://www.gimp.org
- **Paint.net:** Another free photo-editing software tool
  - http://www.getpaint.net
- **Photoshop Express Editor:** An online photo-editing tool with basic editing features
  - http://www.photoshop.com/tools/expresseditor
- **Picnik:** An online photo-editing tool with very basic features
  - http://www.getpaint.net

If you are going to do any major design updates to SharePoint I would strongly encourage you to spend the extra money and purchase a license for the latest version of Adobe Photoshop. It has been a long-time, best-in-class application for creating high-fidelity visual design compositions and photo-image manipulation. It also offers a great way to optimize the size of your images and icons that you will be creating for your site.

## Base SharePoint Design

In any SharePoint design that I do I usually work from either a base Photoshop document that includes all of the OOTB SharePoint layered files or an existing design that I have created in the past. Each component is a different layer that allows me to easily swap out images, colors, fonts, and other elements, as shown in Figure 4-3.

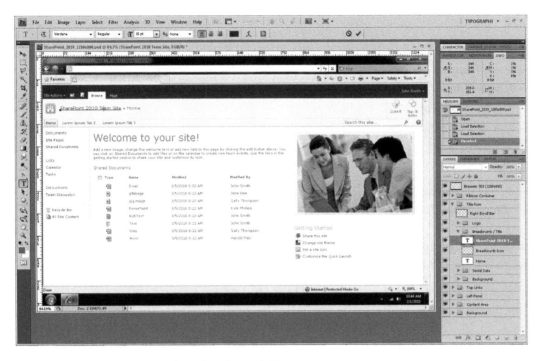

***Figure 4-3.*** *SharePoint 2010 Photoshop layered file*

This file can be downloaded from my blog post here: `http://erikswenson.blogspot.com/2010/02/sharepoint-2010-layered-photoshop-file.html`. You must have Adobe Photoshop installed. The file provides editable text for every element on the page. This allows you to customize the top navigation, left-side navigation, and the content within the page. You can quickly hide elements like the help icon, social tags and notes, and even the site actions and ribbon components if you need to target the design for what a reader would see versus what an administrator sees.

# Adobe Photoshop Basics

Photoshop is an advanced tool that you can use for multiple purposes. The topics below are included as a starter guide for beginner to novice users. You can find more advanced techniques on the web or in other technical books specializing in this software.

## Photoshop Tools

There are many different tools that you can use to create your designs. Figure 4-4 shows the top tools that you can rely on as you build the visual design. The letters in parentheses after the label are quick keys that you can press on your keyboard to quickly switch between the different tools.

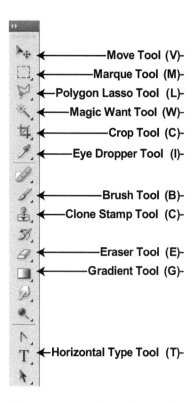

**Figure 4-4.** *Top Photoshop tools*

- **Move tool (V):** Move the current elements in the layers that are selected. You can use the Shift key while you drag elements to keep them inline vertically or horizontally. You can also use this tool to drag items at a fixed, 45-degree angle.

- **Marquee tool (M):** Select elements on the selected layer with either a square or an elliptical shape. Once you have selected the element, only the elements in that selection get affected by colors, sizing, deletions, or other actions.

- **Polygon Lasso tool (L):** Select complex paths to crop out an element that is not rectangular or circular, including things like people's faces,

- **Magic Want Tool (W):** Select similarly colored elements within your design. This is helpful if you need to select a background color behind an element, solid horizontal lines, or any other type of similar colors. There is a threshold that you can set so that either the exact colors or similar colors can be selected.

- **Crop Tool (C):** Mainly used for photo editing to minimize the dimensions of the currently opened file. This tool crops the size of the canvas or file and not just the layer selected.

- **Eye Dropper tool (I):** Identify and capture a single pixel of color or a combined sample of a radius of 3 to 5 pixels. This is useful if you need to sample a very specific color.

- **Brush tool (B):** Can be used for more creative tasks as it allows you to freely add color to a layer with either a sharp or a blended edge by default, or load artistic brushes for even more special effects.

- **Clone Stamp tool (C):** A unique tool that allows you to paint an exact representation of the selected area. This could be used for touching up elements or blemishes in images or faces.

- **Eraser tool (E):** Delete particular sections of the selected layer. It acts much like the paintbrush tool, but instead of adding color to the design it removes it.

- **Gradient tool (G):** Easily add a gradient of the specified foreground and background colors to the selected layer. You will mainly use the marquee tool to select a specific area where you want the gradient. This could be the background to a web part title area or the header of the site.

- **Horizontal Type tool (T):** Quickly add text to a new layer. Once you have typed in the text, you can easily change its font, color, and style.

Other useful Photoshop tools are the paint bucket, smudge, rectangle/ellipse, and the magnifying glass tool. As you become more familiar with these tools and shortcuts, you'll be able to create your designs faster and easier.

## Photoshop Windows

Within Photoshop there are windows that you can make visible to help define and provide details on the selected elements. There are over 20 different panels that you can show, minimize, or hide depending upon your preferences. The main windows that I constantly refer to and have available are the Character, Info, History, and Layers windows, as shown in Figure 4-5. These provide the best reference information for accurately creating my design.

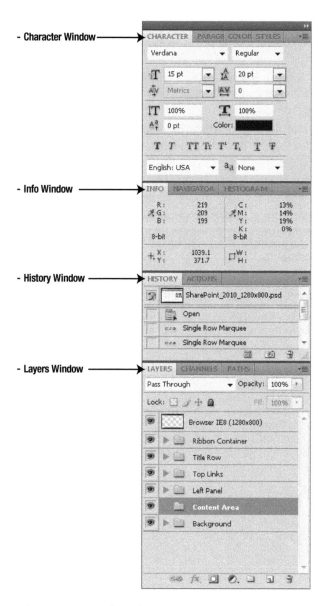

- Character Window
- Info Window
- History Window
- Layers Window

*Figure 4-5. Top Photoshop windows*

- **Character window:** Select elements on the selected layer with either a square or an elliptical shape. Once you have selected an element, only the elements in that selection get affected by colors, sizing, deletions, and other actions.

- **Info window:** Provides a variety of details like the location and color of the pixel that the cursor is on. This can be useful when you are looking at background colors for consistency. The width and height are some of the most used properties in this window. If you are using your marquee tool or cropping tool, you will get exact heights and widths for your selection.

- **History window:** Both informational and also functional. It is basically the list of actions that you have taken since you opened the document. Photoshop allows you to use *undo* (CTRL Z) only once, but if you click on any of the event items in the list, you can undo multiple changes. However, once you backtrack and make a change, there is no way of getting back to the previous state.

- **Layers window:** Probably the most important window that you will have open. It allows you to visually organize multiple layers of elements. If you are new to Photoshop it might take a little bit of experimentation to fully understand how to use and organize your layers. Each layer can have its own label and color. Layers can also be locked so that you do not accidently edit or delete them. You can organize layers in folders and also merge them with other layers. You can turn each layer off so that it is not visible on the screen. By simply turning on or off a content layer, you can create multiple pages within a single file.

Now that you are familiar with how to use Photoshop, you can focus on creating the base structure of your visual design.

# Design Grids

One of the first things that you will want to determine is the width of the design. Refer to the creative brief or UX discovery brief to identify if the site is going to be a fixed-width or fluid design. Out of the box, SharePoint is configured for fluid designs. The HTML and CSS are written such that as the browser size gets bigger the site expands with it. Fluid designs are traditionally used for internal collaboration sites where the content width is variable. Users might want to view lists with many columns that would expand beyond a fixed-width design. In a fixed-width design the whole site or the content area is set to an exact width and either rendered flush left or centered on the page. A fixed-width design frames the content better and provides a better visual experience for the user. It is common to use a fixed-width design on a publishing site where the content can be controlled more. However fixed width designs do take more time to build and test.

In either case you should consider using a grid-based system for your new design. The most common is the 960 grid system (`http://960.gs`), which was created by a front-end designer named Nathan Smith. This grid can be 12, 16, or 24 columns wide, and the columns have an equal amount of spacing between them. These columns provide a consistent way of placing and organizing content within your design. The reason for the number 960 is that it can be divided easily into multiple whole numbers. The fixed-width design also provides a nice visual experience in most standard browser windows. In the 12-column version, as shown in Figure 4-6, the smallest column is 60 pixels wide. Each column then increases in size by 80 pixels. The column sizes for this type of layout would be: 60, 140, 220, 300, 380, 460, 540, 620, 700, 780, 860, and 940 pixels.

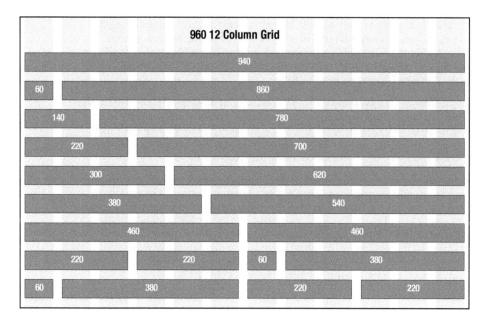

***Figure 4-6.*** *960 12-column grid system*

You can download the grid and place it into a locked layer. Locate the layer near the bottom of the list of layers so that all of the content will be visible on top of it. In a fixed-width design, position the outer border of your site to the very edges so that it equals 960 pixels. Each column has 20 pixels of separation between them. If you have a complex page layout, place your web part zone content into any one of these column sizes. There are many different types of layout configurations. See Figure 4-7 for some examples.

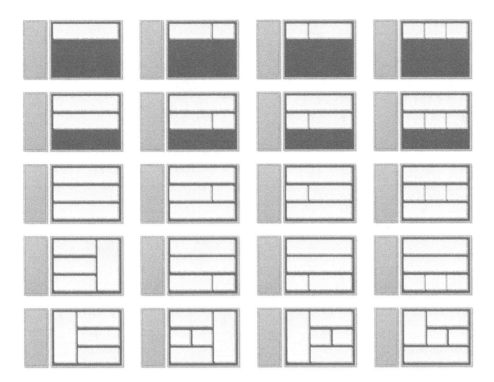

*Figure 4-7. Page-layout configuration examples*

The most common layout in SharePoint 2010 is the two-column, 70/30 split. It is used for all of the team collaboration sites. If publishing is enabled, you are allowed to create your own custom page layouts and add HTML and additional web part zones, to produce a more advanced page-layout configuration.

## Base Shell Styles

Now that you have your reference material, Photoshop skills, base file, and a grid, it is time to have some fun. In this section I walk you through the process of creating the basic design components. In these examples we adapt a brand from an existing design to SharePoint 2010. The base shell consists of the following elements, as shown in Figure 4-8.

*Figure 4-8. Basic design elements*

- **Body background:** Visible only on sites with fixed-width designs. This could be a simple, flat, solid color or could include gradients and repeating patterns.

- **Frame:** Used to provide a visible container for the header and content to fit within. The frame could include a border, background color, and, in the example above, a background image.

- **Header and logo:** Should be consistent across all sites. The logo is both visual and functional. Clicking on the logo brings users to the top-level landing page for the site collection that they are within.

- **Top navigation:** On smaller sites you can use the standard SharePoint navigation control that is limited to a single site collection. However, you can change this to a global navigation control that spans all site collections. These controls can have many different types of styles such as simple text, tabs, and buttons.

- **Left navigation:** The left-side navigation or Quick Launch has multiple elements that you can style, including headers, links, and administration links like recycle bin and view all site content links.

- **Content area:** A separate container that holds all of the web parts and content controls on the page. Some designers separate this section by adding borders, margins, and also background colors.

- **Footer:** Not included by default but this style can be added to the master page if needed.

# Web Part Styles

Most standard SharePoint 2010 web parts share the same basic CSS classes. A web part can have four main types applied: none, title and border, title only, border only. To apply these styles, click on the web part configuration arrow and choose to "Modify Shared Web Part." The Web Part Properties panel will appear (usually on the right side of the page). In the Web Part Properties panel expand the appearance section and click on the drop-down menu next to the label "Chrome Type." The drop-down provides the following options.

1. **None:** This chrome type shows only the content and does not show the web part title or a border. You would normally use this type of style for web parts like a content editor web part where you just want to display the rich text content or for image web parts.

2. **Title and Border:** The title and border chrome type shows both the web part title and a border around the web part. You might want to use this type of display for web parts that show a lot of content that need a visual separator from the other web parts on the page.

3. **Title Only:** This shows only the web part title with no border. This basic type works well for small pieces of content like lists of links.

4. **Border Only:** This type shows a border around the web part and does not display the title. It is best used when you want to highlight text or frame a list of links.

The web part title or *chrome* is a common element that you want to be sure to define a style for. The chrome is broken up into multiple classes, which allows you to style it in a number of ways. You can easily add gradients, background colors, and borders. For more advanced styles, you can create rounded corners and unique frames.

# Content Frame

In some designs you can style the container of the web part to make it appear separate from the background. This helps your users easily distinguish one web part from another. A common design theme is to set the content area to have a light gray or dark background, as shown in Figure 4-9. For each web part, you then make the background color white. This creates an effect of each web part floating at the top of the page.

***Figure 4-9.*** *Web parts with white backgrounds*

Be sure to give the content within the web parts enough padding on the outside so that the content has some space to breathe. Another way to give the content frame some visual interest is to add a border and light content color in all of the web parts on the page.

# Final Polish

To complete the design I recommend that you update the standard icons, bullets, and fonts. Making updates to these elements really helps give the design a final, polished look. Having standard icons and bullets that show through detracts from the overall user experience. Most of the bullets in SharePoint are specified through CSS and can be easily changed. For example, the standard link list icon is a small gray square, as seen in Figure 4-10.

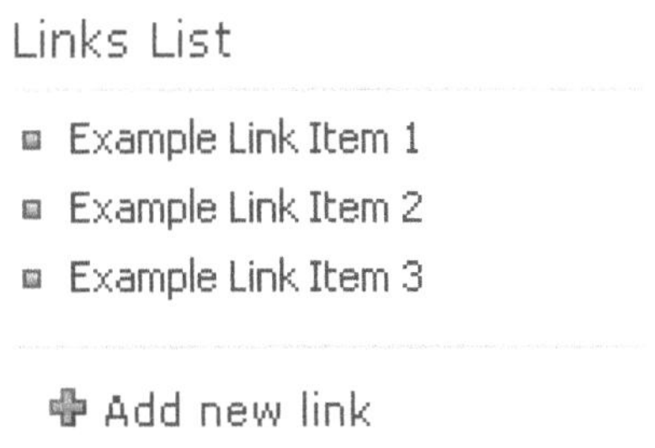

Links List

□ Example Link Item 1

□ Example Link Item 2

□ Example Link Item 3

✚ Add new link

**Figure 4-10.** *Links list web part icon*

The Summary Link web part link style is slightly different. This icon is a smaller orange square, as shown in Figure 4-11, and in most designs it sticks out like a sore thumb.

Summary Links

▪ Example Link Item 1

▪ Example Link Item 2

▪ Example Link Item 3

**Figure 4-11.** *Summary link web part icon*

Changing this icon is relatively easy. You just need to create a new icon and specify it as a background image using the **.bullet** class. That class is specified within the controls.css file located in the style library at the top-level site collection with publishing enabled.

# Conducting Design Reviews

The goal of design-review sessions is to gather feedback from the stakeholders and approvers on the visual designs. These sessions should be scheduled well in advance so that all participants have a chance to review the designs and provide full attention to the review process.

---

**Benefits** Design reviews allow you to gather feedback from stakeholders, to make your designs better.

---

There are three types of design meetings that you should schedule. The first meeting type is called a *peer review*. This is a review of the design with other designers that can provide constructive feedback that strengthens the design. The second type of review is the *technical review*. You need to make sure that the development or technical team is on board with the design direction and what is achievable within the scope of your project. The third meeting type is the *client review* or *stakeholder review*. Within these sessions you will gather feedback on what they like and what needs improvement. The ultimate goal is to get sign-off so that the design is ready to be built. It can be tricky to identify who should be in each one of these meetings and how long you should meet for.

## What to Include

With all design reviews it is important that you show only the designs that you feel are the strongest. There might be some cases that you have some back-pocket designs or concepts. Most peer reviews are ad-hoc and normally do not require much preparation. It could be as simple as asking your design colleagues to come look at your screen or print-outs and provide instant feedback. In the technical review sessions it is a good idea to have predefined elements that you want to cover. The developers aren't there to provide usability or design direction—only whether it's technically feasible—so you need to make sure you specify which elements the developer should be focusing on. For the design stakeholder meetings the presentation should be well organized and to the point, with a section for feedback and next steps. If you feel strongly about going in a particular design direction you might want to save that for the last slide that you review. This will keep the design fresh in their minds and, more often than not, people react to things that they have seen most recently. If you are showcasing multiple design options, include a summary slide that shows all of the design options in one screen, so that participants can clearly react to all options without having to scroll back through your deck.

## How to Organize

PowerPoint is one of the easiest applications to use to prepare your designs for review. The tool lets you easily swap out screens and build the context around the design concepts. The designs can be easily exported into a non-editable PDF for sharing before or after the meeting. I would advise against sharing the design deck with the stakeholders too far in advance of the meeting, as that would spoil the big "reveal." For users who are attending remotely, you might need to send the deck through email or upload it to a SharePoint site. Keep it simple and don't provide too many blocks of heavy text. If you spend over one minute per slide you will need to trim it down. The structure of the presentation should include the following:

- **Introduction/purpose:** This section of the presentation covers the necessary details about who you are, what this meeting is about, any ground rules (like cell-phone use and checking of emails during the meeting), and the overall goal of the meeting.

- **Agenda:** This is a standard slide that you will briefly cover that identifies what is going to be covered in the session.

- **Design comps:** This is the meat and potatoes of the presentation. It includes all of the design compositions that you have created and any variations on the design. You might want to provide a teaser slide for each design, and then talk about its characteristics.

- **Overview:** The overview showcases all of the design options in a single slide.

- **Q&A:** Make sure to save time at the end for any questions that may come up.

- **Next steps:** Clearly identify the next action steps—whether it's a sign off, request for feedback, or something else.

## Who Should Attend

You shouldn't have more than 10 people at a design-review session. The more people involved, the harder it is to get a consensus on a particular design direction. In larger groups some people might not speak up for fear of being criticized by their peers. In most cases there are no stupid questions, and all feedback is welcome. As the designer you just have to decide what feedback you will use to make the design better. The stakeholders in the room should be the ones signing off on the design. The internal marketing group is usually the most important set of attendees. The stakeholders will be looking to them for advice on what is within the corporate standards and how much flexibility you have with the design.

# Summary

This chapter provided helpful tips to give you all of the assets you need to create a beautiful design. You learned the basics of Adobe Photoshop, using the 960 grid system, and quick ways to get started with the design process. This chapter also included things to think about for preparing and presenting your visual designs to your stakeholders.

# CHAPTER 5

# Development Environment Setup

## What's In This Chapter?

- Virtual Environment or Physical Server
- Choosing Your SharePoint Edition
- Running SharePoint on Windows 7
- Virtualization
- Server Configurations
- Minimum Requirements for Branding
- Remote Desktop
- Required Access Levels
- Features That Affect Branding
- List of Required Applications
- Source Control
- The 14 Hive

Here you'll learn about the different options, configurations, and tools that you can use to build out your visual design. This chapter does not cover the step-by-step instructions on how to install SharePoint but it will point you in the right direction on what features to enable and what things you can do without. In most cases, you will just need a basic installation or SharePoint on a development box that you can customize as much as you want without any restrictions. You will also want to have the ability to save and retract any major changes that you have made to the server. This is where virtualization comes in handy. If you have ever used VMware workstation there is a concept of "Snapshots" that you can easily create of the virtual server. This allows you to go back to previous image snapshots and start fresh or go back to a previously saved safe state.

As you build out your site you might need to turn on features like publishing, which allows you to easily create pages and page layouts. With publishing you can easily work with master pages, page layouts, and XSLT list item styles all within a single site collection so access to the actual server is not really needed. For more global branding the files will more than likely be stored on the server in what is called the "14" hive. This location is where all of SharePoint 2010 configuration and system files are stored. By creating your own folders within this directory, you can easily manage your files in one location so that they don't have to be copied for every site collection that needs branding applied.

# Virtual Environment or Physical Server

One of the first decisions that you will have to make is if you are going to go with a physical development box or a virtual environment. A physical box will cost more money and has some limitations as it can only have one instance of SharePoint running on it. A virtual environment will probably be your best option for a simple development environment. A virtual machine can be stored on any internal or external hard drive. The setup that I use is actually pretty simple and inexpensive. I use VMware Workstation 7 installed on my local laptop and store all of my Virtual images on an inexpensive external hard drive. In most cases you will just be doing basic branding changes so you do not need anything crazy when it comes to the RAM or disk space availability. Virtualization also allows you the ability to make your image portable. Since the image is stored on your laptop or an external drive, you can easily access it from anywhere—even without an Internet connection. With a physical server you would be required to have direct access to the server, and connectivity and performance might be an issue depending on your connectivity.

---

▪ **Benefits**   One of the best things about having your own virtual environment is that you can experiment freely without affecting other development efforts.

---

Overall, I think your best option for a simple development environment is to go virtual. The speed, flexibility, quick backups, quick restoring, and overall portability makes a great case for going with a virtual environment. I discuss this in more detail later in this chapter. Once you have decided on the hardware, you need to choose the edition of SharePoint that you are going to install.

# Choosing Your SharePoint Edition

SharePoint comes in three versions or editions that you can install on your development environment. The basic install is SharePoint Foundation, which includes the majority of the basic functionality at no cost but does require the software to be registered. The second is the Standard SharePoint Server licensed edition that adds on my sites, web analytics, publishing, enterprise wikis, tags and notes, and many other features. The third type is the Enterprise edition that only requires a different license key for upgrade. This includes additional features like more enhanced search results, Microsoft Office Access, Visio, Excel, and InfoPath Forms services. The following site provides a helpful comparison of these editions: http://sharepoint.microsoft.com/en-us/buy/Pages/Editions-Comparison.aspx.

- **SharePoint Foundation (Free):** This free version of SharePoint gives you the basic features of SharePoint, including Basic Sites, Lists, Libraries, Top/Left local site navigation, and a variety of basic web parts.

- **SharePoint Server 2010 (Licensed):** This is the full version of SharePoint 2010 and comes with a couple levels of license types.

    - **Standard:** This version includes all foundational features with the addition of the following features:

        - Audience Targeting

        - Web Analytics

        - My Sites

    - **Enterprise:** This version includes all of the standard features with the following additions:

        - Enhanced Search Results (Thumbnails, Previews)

        - Business Intelligence (Dashboards, PerformancePoint)

        - Access Services

        - Visio Services

        - Excel Services

        - InfoPath Forms Services

Knowing which version to choose really depends on your current project. You would not want to install SharePoint foundation on your development server if the portal that you are designing for will have a fully licensed Enterprise version. There are enough differences between the two that Foundation would limit your development efforts. In most cases, the Standard license would be sufficient and you more than likely would not need to have Enterprise installed to build out your visual design.

## SharePoint Foundation (free)

Microsoft offers this version free of charge, to help people get their feet in the door and experiment with SharePoint 2010. It can be effectively used for very small companies with around 10–50 users. You can install it with an express version of SQL database to store up to 10 Gigabits (GB) of data per database with the limit of 1 CPU and 1GB of RAM. You can also download and install the free Search Server 2010 Express that allows you to search within all of your sites and provides a basic search center site template. (The Search capability you get from the SharePoint Foundation install will only allow you to search single sites, with no special search center site template.) For developers, SharePoint Designer 2010 is provided as a free tool that you can use to customize your SharePoint master pages and CSS.

If you don't have a Windows Server image to install SharePoint Foundation on, you can also install SharePoint Foundation 2010 directly on a Windows 7 machine.

---

■ **Note**    You will need to have x64-bit to run SharePoint foundation on Windows 7. You will not be able to install it on Windows 7 Home Premium 64-bit or any 32-bit versions.

---

# SharePoint Server 2010 (Standard)

The Standard edition of SharePoint gives you all of the features that you need to brand SharePoint. This version is not free and requires you to pay for a variety of different licenses to use the product. This version includes these major features:

- **Standard Lists and Libraries:** The core of SharePoint is its content management system that gives you the ability to create list items or upload documents. When you are applying your brand, verify that your SharePoint lists and library views stay consistent with your brand.

- **Standard Web Parts:** You will also want to make sure that the styling of common web parts such as content editors and image web parts is also consistently branded to match your design. You'll want to stylize the content area to include enough space around rich-text content to prevent it from blending into other web parts.

- **Publishing Web Parts:** Enhanced web parts such as content query, summary links, and media web parts rely on both CSS styles and XSLT templates for formatting and layout.

- **My Site and My Profile:** If you are rolling out SharePoint 2010 My Site features to your users, make sure that you have an idea of how you intend to brand these types of sites. For example, within the My Profile pages there are a few unique elements such as the profile tabs on the user profile pages that you will want to stylize to be consistent with your brand direction.

- **Meeting Workspaces:** The meeting workspace site templates are a bit different from most sites as they have their own master page. The reason for this is because of the custom page options that you see on the left side of these types of templates. If you are on a meeting workspace template and click on site actions, you will notice two options: one for adding a new page and one for managing the pages.

- **Search:** Standard SharePoint search comes with four primary pages: The first is the search center, which is a site with minimal branding applied to it and the search box centered on the page. The second is the advanced search site, which allows you to add additional search filters. The third is the search result page, which includes facets or refiners on the left and the results on the right. The last page is the people result page, which shows a more graphical result. You can customize and brand all of these pages and sites.

# SharePoint Server 2010 (Enterprise)

There is no harm in using the Enterprise edition for basic branding if you already have this type of license. The Enterprise server licensing fees are higher than Standard since they include additional features. You get the added option of turning on those services that do not come with the Standard licenses. Ultimately, choosing between Standard and Enterprise versions depends on what you will use for your production server. When it comes to Excel, InfoPath, Visio, Access, and other services, there are only a few web parts that you would want to stylize to match your overall branding design.

Another option that you have is to install SharePoint 2010 on a Windows 7 environment.

# Running SharePoint on Windows 7

There are some pros and some cons to running SharePoint on Windows 7. One of the benefits is that you do not need to have Windows Server in this installation type. This allows you to easily connect to your site quickly without waiting for a remote desktop session to connect or for a virtual image to load.

---

■ **Benefits**  Windows 7-based SharePoint installs give you the ability to quickly demo and showcase your sites.

---

However, there are some limitations, one being that your production server probably isn't based on a windows 7 machine. It is always recommended that you have the same configurations in your development environment (or as close as you can make it) and your production server. Another issue is that you will be adding a lot of server-based applications and configuration files to your local machine. The biggest issue with using your base machine for a development environment is that you can't make snapshots of your SharePoint environment. Unlike with a virtualized environment, you can't back up and restore all of the changes that you make.

# Virtualization

Virtualization is the process of using a physical machine and some software to create and host multiple operating systems. You have a few different options to choose from. Some are free options like VMware Player that you can try out, or you can download a trial version of VMware Workstation. A single license for VMware workstation won't break your bank at around $189.

---

■ **Benefits**  You can use VMware Workstation to create snapshots of a running virtual instance. It also allows you to clone, restore, and delete previously created snapshots.

---

Another option is to purchase and run your base desktop with Windows Server 2008 with Hyper-V attached. I have had great success with VMware Workstation. It is easy to use, and the snap shot option is fantastic, as shown in Figure 5-1. It allows you to create a snapshot of the operating system when it is both powered on and off. You can clone and delete each snapshot without affecting the other snapshots. You can go back to a previous snapshot and start a new branch of the tree. I find that I create snapshots for each major branding release that I create. This gives me the freedom to experiment and try new things without worrying that I am going to break the site. If I do break it, I can always revert back to my previous safe state.

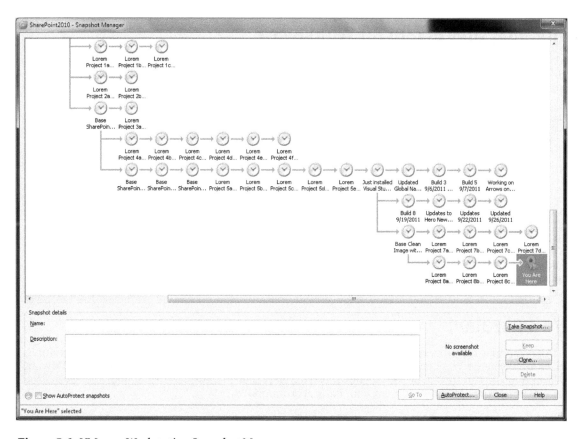

***Figure 5-1.*** *VMware Workstation Snapshot Manager*

# Server Configurations

The different configurations for your environment really depend on the type of hosting that you are using. If you have a virtual environment you need to dedicate almost half of the available resources to your base operating system and the other half to the virtual server. During the setup of the virtual image you can specify how much RAM, disk space, and processors you will dedicate to the server.

## Minimum Required Specifications (Development)

SharePoint is a bit of a resource hog, requiring quite a bit of horsepower to keep it going. The requirements for a development environment aren't as involved as those for a full production server.

To run a SharePoint 2010 development image, Microsoft recommends that you have at least the following specifications:

- **Operating Systems:** For SharePoint installation, you need a Windows 7 64-bit or Windows Server 2008 64-bit operating system.

- **RAM (Random-Access Memory):** You can run SharePoint Foundation on 2GB of RAM, but if you can allocate up to 4GB you will have better performance. For SharePoint Server 2010 it is recommended that you free up at least 3GB of RAM; anything over 4 is good if you can spare it.

- **Processor:** It is recommended that you have at least two processors.

- **Hard Disk Space:** According to Microsoft, you should dedicate about 80GB to your virtual environment, but for branding purposes, anything above 40 should be fine.

- **Applications:** You can install SharePoint Designer directly on the virtual operating system, but I prefer to run my virtual machine in the background and use my Windows 7 hosting laptop to view and edit the site in SharePoint Designer 2010.

## Standalone vs. Server Farm

By now, you are beginning to see that if you want to brand SharePoint you will not need more than one server to develop your customizations. To create a stand-alone server, you can install SharePoint either on a Windows 7 workstation or within a Windows Server 2008 operating system with a built-in database. This keeps the administration overhead to a minimum and allows you to start up a site and begin the branding.

---

■ **Benefits**   A stand-alone image allows you to have full SharePoint features and functions with just one virtual environment. This decreases the amount of administration overhead on managing multiple servers.

---

In my opinion, creating a full server farm for a branding development environment is a bit of overkill. A SharePoint farm is for use on production sites that require high availability and high performance. In a small farm, you could have one or two web front-end servers and one dedicated SQL server. But for development purposes, you should not need more than one server.

Now that you have your server and SharePoint software configured, it's time to start creating the base SharePoint sites for your branding.

# Minimum Requirements for Branding

If you're just looking to spin up a vanilla SharePoint 2010 site to get your branding groove on, then all you really need is a stand-alone server with a single web application. For more complex branding projects, you might want to create additional sites but a single server is all that you need. Installing

SharePoint should be as simple as installing the prerequisites, and then watching the configuration wizard as it goes through its installation steps. Once SharePoint is installed, you might want to configure search, user profile service, and my sites.

---

■ **Benefits**  You can easily be up and running with a base install of SharePoint by choosing the default configurations within the wizard.

---

After you have configured all of the services, it's time to create a basic top-level site collection. Knowing what site template you should use depends on the features that you want enabled by default. SharePoint 2007 included a site collection template called "Collaboration Portal" that automatically created a home Publishing site, News Site, Search Center, and a Site Directory site. This template was great because it combined both collaboration and publishing features in one. In the 2010 version of SharePoint, however, this type of template isn't available.

You could create a publishing site collection, switch back its base master page to v4.master, and turn on collaboration features. You'll also want to delete the approval workflow on some of the standard libraries like the master page gallery, Site Collection Images, and style library. More than likely, you are going to be doing quick changes to the files within these libraries, and this type of approval workflow is not needed within your development environment.

The other option is that you could create a blank site and then enable the publishing features. Once they are enabled, you can create a new page for use as your new homepage. In either option, you'll have to do some manual site configuration to get both the publishing and collaboration features within your site. The publishing features will provide more visibility into master page configurations and the use of page layouts. The base collaboration features provide the basics for document and list management.

Sometimes you may be doing branding development for a company that will require you to do all of your work on its development environment. This environment might require you to use Microsoft Terminal Services Remote Desktop client to access the site and branding support files.

# Remote Desktop

Remote desktop gives you access over a network connection to servers that are hosted externally to your base operating system. The network connectivity speed is what drives the performance and refresh rate of the server. One of the benefits of this option is that the server that you remote desktop into does the majority of the processing. The local machine that you are using to connect to the server can have a fraction of the resources since all it needs is the ability to refresh the data that is being sent from the server.

---

■ **Benefits**  Using remote desktop allows you to access the development servers from anywhere.

---

You can turn on options before you remote into the server to allow you to share the clipboard and drives from your local machine to the server. One drawback of remote desktop is that administrators sometimes set up security restrictions that block the ability to connect your local drives, and you can't easily copy and paste files from your local machine to the server. I would recommend using remote desktop if it is the only way that you can get access to a development environment.

Once you have established the method for gaining access to the site and server files, you will want to make sure that you have the correct level of permissions for creating and applying the branding.

# Required Access Levels

For your SharePoint design build-out, you need enhanced permissions on the server and on the site. You'll need to provide different levels of access depending on the type of branding that you'll be doing. These security permissions are broken down into the following roles:

- **Server Administrator** (AKA, member of the Local Administrators group on the server): You have full rights to configure, add, edit, and delete files on the server. This role is primarily granted when you have your own server and want to easily add and change files on the server. In most cases, this also gives you the highest level of privileges within central administration because SharePoint automatically adds a group called "BUILTIN\Administrators" to the Active Directory administrators group. You can use your account to become the Site Collection Administrator for all sites.

- **Site Collection Administrator:** You don't usually have access to the server, but you have full administrative rights to do anything you want within a single site collection that you are assigned to.

- **Site Owner:** You have top rights to configure and change just about anything within the site collection.

- **Site Designer:** Your primary role is to configure and change the site layout and design.

- **Site Contributor:** You are limited to editing site page content.

In general, if you have your own development environment there's no harm in using an account with server administration rights. If you don't have your own environment, determining the level of access you need depends on whether you'll be accessing the server files or simply using SharePoint Designer to create your own custom master page in the master page gallery. The next section describes different features that you'll need to account for within your SharePoint branding.

# Features That Affect Branding

Some SharePoint features directly affect the branding within your site. This could include navigation, page layouts, web parts, lists and library views, the ribbon, and any other custom elements added to the master page. For example, in SharePoint OOTB only the simple search bar is enabled by default. However, if you want custom search scopes, you have to change the settings in the site administration Site Settings page. Once you enable search scopes, the drop-down box is added to the left of the search box. Search and the top navigation share the same horizontal space, as shown in Figure 5-2. You might decide to alter the search controls using CSS to match your look and feel.

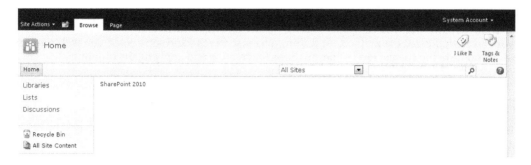

*Figure 5-2. SharePoint 2010 Search Scope*

The Tree view left navigation feature is another design element that is not enabled by default. You can turn on the Tree view by clicking on Site Actions ➤ Site Settings ➤ Look and Feel Grouping ➤ Tree View. Next you click on the "Enable Tree View" check box, and then click "OK." The Tree view allows you to expand the left panel to show all of the content that resides within that site, as shown in Figure 5-3.

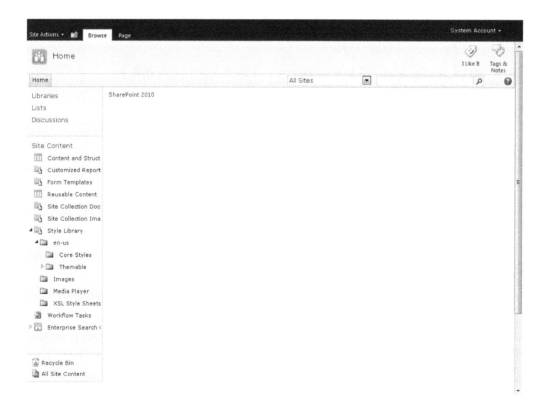

*Figure 5-3. SharePoint 2010 Tree view left navigation*

There isn't much you can do to stylize the Tree view other than a simple selected state for the current list or library that you have selected. The other type of left navigation and filtering for lists and libraries is the Metadata Navigation option (not available in the SharePoint Foundation edition). This allows you to view and filter lists or libraries by content type or through an advanced left-navigation control. The content type filter is located on the left navigation below the quick launch, as shown in figure 5-4. Also shown is the Key Filters component that allows you to easily filter out library content in a list or library. The background has an aqua blue gradient; you might need to change this if it doesn't match your color palette.

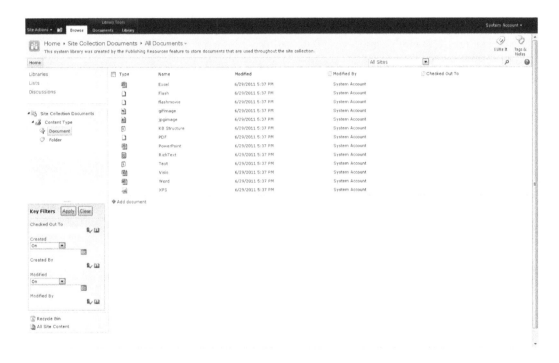

*Figure 5-4. SharePoint 2010 metadata navigation and filter*

The SharePoint 2010 profile pages are a unique design item in that they include shared pages that display unique profile information for each user and these pages include a custom tabbed navigation. All pages are shared for all users, and the content within each page is dynamic. If you make a change to the person.aspx page, you will be making the change across all pages. The profile pages also have the status update control that is made up of multiple CSS classes to give the input box the look of a status bubble. The next section covers a variety of tools and applications that you can use to brand SharePoint 2010.

# List of Required Applications

You only need a handful of tools to create a custom branding for SharePoint 2010. You can create and edit everything in a simple application like Notepad. However, SharePoint Designer 2010 provides better readability by adding color to the separate out code elements and auto suggestions for coding. In most cases, you don't need anything more advanced than that. If you plan to create a featured solution file, you will need to use Visual Studio to package up the files into a .wsp file. Here is a list of some helpful tools for branding SharePoint:

- **Adobe Photoshop or alternative:** You need some type of photo-editing software to create and modify images to be used for the visual design.

- **Microsoft SharePoint Designer 2010:** Designer will be your primary tool for editing CSS, Master Pages, Page Layouts, and XSLT, and adding and editing web part zones and other code formats with SharePoint. As its name suggests, this tool was designed specifically for SharePoint 2010. It is not backward-compatible, so you can't use it to modify any SharePoint 2007 environments. It is a free product that you can install on the same operating system as SharePoint Designer 2007.

- **Notepad:** It may sound silly to include this application in the list, but it comes in handy when you need to make a small edit to a master page file that is not in the database. There are some known issues with modifying a master page on the server, or anywhere external to SharePoint, using SharePoint Designer. To play it safe, always use Notepad to edit master pages that are not in a SharePoint master page gallery or on your local computer.

- **IE Developer Toolbar & Firebug:** As you start building out your site, you can use the CSS reference guide in this book, or you can use tools like the developer toolbar and Firebug to find and understand the CSS class names and properties that are being applied to each element within the site. Internet Explorer 8 and above have the toolbar built into the browser; all you have to do is hit Function F12 while browsing a site. Some people prefer Firefox's version, called Firebug, but it basically does the same thing. Both of these add-ons are free and either are built into the browser or can be downloaded as a plug-in.

- **Microsoft Visual Studio 2010:** This powerful application is a bit on the pricey side. If you aren't a developer, you can probably do without this application. For branding you would have your developer use Visual Studio to create a feature package that includes all of the custom files that support your custom branding. This includes CSS, Images, Master Pages, and Page Layouts. Code can then be written so that as a user creates additional sites, the custom master page gets uploaded to the gallery and is set as the custom master page to be used for the site.

Another aspect that you will want to consider is how you'll manage and keep track of all the changes you have made to the branding files. The next section describes some of the tools that you can use to effectively keep control over your files.

# Source Control

As you start building out your custom design files, you want to make sure they are not just sitting on your local machine's hard drive.

---

■ **Benefits**   Having some sort of source control not only keeps your files safe but it ensures that two people are not editing the same document at the same time.

---

This is especially important within larger based development teams. As with any SharePoint document, team members can check out these items and apply version control to them. I would recommend Visual Studio Team Foundation Server 2010 (TFS) for enabling version control on your custom branding files. TFS provides the following main features:

- **Version Control:** Allows you to check a document in and out, and easily track and manage your documents.

- **Work Item Tracking:** Allows you to track and document requirements, tasks, issues, bugs, and test cases.

- **Build Automation:** Allows you to schedule automated build cycles, and build and configure triggers for manual builds.

You can also get source control and version history on small branding projects when all of your support files are stored within the SharePoint style library. The next section describes the folder structure and file details for the files that support the default look and feel of SharePoint 2010.

# The 14 Hive

This term refers to the location of SharePoint 2010's application files, binaries, and data files on the server. It is also the root location for all of the branding support files. The full path to the 14 hive is: `C:\Program Files\Common Files\Microsoft Shared\Web Server Extensions\14`. Most developers and front-end designers could rattle off this path in their sleep. The directory contains two major folders that support the overall SharePoint branding.

- **SharePoint Images Folder:** Contains around 2,800 image files of the following types. The path to the images folder from the 14 hive is: `14\TEMPLATE\IMAGES`. With more modern browsers, such as IE8+ and above, .PNG files are more widely used than .jpg files based on quality and their ability to be fully or semi-transparent.

  - **Graphical Interchange Format (.GIF):** 1,889 files

  - **Portable Network Graphic (.PNG):** 849 files

  - **Joint Photographic Experts Group (.JPG):** 23 files

  - **Icon (.ICO):** 11 files

  - **Bitmap (.BMP):** 2 files

- **SharePoint Styles Folder:** Contains around 43 different CSS style sheets. The path to the styles folder from the 14 hive is `14\TEMPLATE\LAYOUTS\1033\STYLES`. The primary CSS files are:

    - **COREV4.CSS:** Includes all of the base CSS classes and properties that make SharePoint 2010 look the way that it does.

    - **SEARCH.CSS:** Includes the base styles for the search scope, search input, and button. It also includes all of the styles used for the search result pages.

    - **LAYOUTS.CSS:** Includes some of the base form and list view styles.

    - **CALENDARV4.CSS:** Includes all of the styles for branding the OOTB list calendar views.

    - **BLOG.CSS:** Includes all of the styles for branding the OOTB blog post styles.

    - **mysitelayout.CSS:** Includes all of the styles for branding the My Profile pages. The mysitelayout.css file has been renamed, and in Figure 5-5 you can see how much of the profile page style is being affected. The positioning, tabs, and background colors are all supported by that one single CSS file. When creating your own custom master page for My Site, make sure to include a reference to this file, or use the CSS classes and make the design your own.

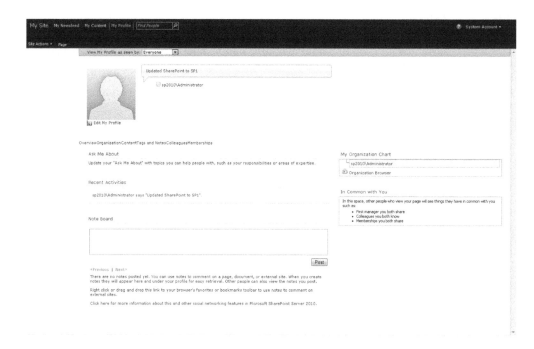

*Figure 5-5. SharePoint 2010 My Profile with mysitelayout.css removed*

# Summary

This chapter gave you helpful tips and definitions for setting up your development environment. You need to keep a few things in mind, but branding SharePoint 2010 doesn't require a lot of advanced configurations and, in most cases, a basic install gives you what you need to get started. A few tools like SharePoint Designer 2010 and IE Developer toolbar make branding SharePoint as simple as 1-2-3.

# CHAPTER 6

# Building the Design

## What's In This Chapter?

- Build Approach
- Connecting the Pieces
- Building a Custom Design
- Prepare a Basic Branding Solution in Visual Studio

This chapter walks you through the major front end development tasks for building your visual design, including optimizing images, creating CSS, master pages, page layouts, and other techniques to transform the approved visual designs into a functional SharePoint 2010 branded site. Building the design takes place within the development phase after the visual designer has received final approval of the visual design, as shown in step 7 of Figure 6-1. (This 7-step process was first introduced in Chapter 2.)

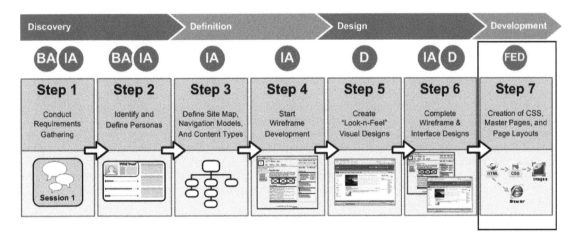

*Figure 6-1.* Step 7: Building the design

It is important to wait until the design has been fully defined and then approved before you start development. If you start the development too early, it's very likely that the design will change, which means you'll have some rework to do. However, if you wait for the designer to complete the design and deliver a visual style guide containing all of the necessary colors, widths, heights, padding, margins, and any other specifications, you can easily translate the visual design into the build. .

Here you'll learn an approach that will help streamline your design build, including creating optimized images for your backgrounds and icons and developing definitions around content placeholders and XSLT styling.

The last part of this chapter covers creating a basic branding feature in Visual Studio that can be activated manually by going to the feature activation page within site settings. This section also explains "Feature Stapling," where a feature is associated with a site definition and then enabled as a trigger when a new site is created.

# Build Approach

When it comes to building a production-based visual design in SharePoint 2010 requires time and patience, so you'll to be organized and fully dedicated to the process. I would recommend that you refrain from jumping in and hacking away at the v4.master master page or the corev4.css style sheet. You need to plan your build carefully, so that all of the pieces fall into place. With simple designs, you don't need to worry about managing a bunch of moving parts. A simple build might consist of CSS and images or a slightly modified master page based off of the v4.master that references your CSS and images. But as your design becomes more complex, with multiple master pages based on site templates and a variety of unique page layouts, you might find yourself lost in a web of confusion. You'll have many moving parts with dependencies that make your head spin. To guard against this, I usually create a diagram that maps out what master pages, page layouts, and CSS goes to what site collection, site template, or functional area. This way I don't have to keep it all in my head. Plus, everything is documented, giving anyone who might need to make modifications down the road something to reference.

The first part of building out the visual design is to convert any gradient, icon, or background image into web-ready files. The second part is to create a .CSS style sheet for storing all of your custom styles. The third part is to create custom master pages if you need to move any controls around within the page. The last part is to create custom page layouts if you need to have unique layouts within your site. This next section guides you through the first task: optimizing images.

## Optimizing Images

A flat visual design needs to be sliced up and broken out into multiple images. Background images or icons that are not a solid color or that cannot be replicated easily with CSS should be spliced out of the design and optimized for web viewing. The reason for optimizing background images instead of just saving them as full-fledged files is to reduce the time it takes for them to load. Given today's download speeds of 40-50MB per second, time is not as much of an issue as it was 10 years ago when some people were still using dialup modems. However, there are still many cases where your users might be accessing your site using a connection from a hotel, mobile phone tether, or even VPN. These speeds could range from .5MB to 5MB and up, which would be a reason to be cautious about the sizes of your image files. Be sure to keep your images under 100–150Kb. You have to make a choice between having high-quality images and fast loading speeds.

The more you compress and limit the amount of color in your image, the smaller it will be. For example, looking at the images in Figure 6-2, you see that the JPG versions provide image clarity. However, to get the GIF file to the same small file size as the 0% JPG, you would have to reduce the amount of colors to just 2. As you can see, this drastically affects the way your image looks. If you are optimizing an image with lots of gradients or lots of colors, use the JPG file format. The image is around 480 pixels in width and 400 pixels in height.

***Figure 6-2.*** *Comparison of image quality and file types*

The rule of thumb is to preserve as much of the quality of the image as possible while taking into consideration the size of the image. For example, the image in Figure 6-2 was medium to large in size and would probably be acceptable at a size of 40–50Kb. The final JPG quality might be somewhere around 60%. Looking at the image, it might be hard to see any major difference in the quality of the picture, but you can clearly see in the tree line in the back that the image quality degrades as the JPG number gets lower. Traditionally, GIF and JPG files were the only major supported files types that were used for the Web. But as technology grows, PNG files are becoming the new trend for Web-based image files. PNG files are far superior to GIF and JPG files. There are also 2 types of PNG files. The first is the PNG-8 format, which has indexed colors similar to a GIF. The second is the PNG-24 format, which is more like a JPG with millions of colors available, but with the addition of multiple levels of alpha transparencies.

## Working with Basic Images

When working with more simplistic images such as icons or images with a limited set of colors, you might be better off using a GIF file. Depending on the image dimensions, GIFs are usually less than 1Kb in size, and you can have pixels that are completely transparent, which allows you to position, overlay, and create unique patterns. The image shown in Figure 6-3 is a very basic icon that consists of about 64 colors. The image is 80 pixels wide and 38 pixels high. The checkered pattern is not part of the image; it is a setting in Photoshop that allows you to see what in the image is going to be transparent.

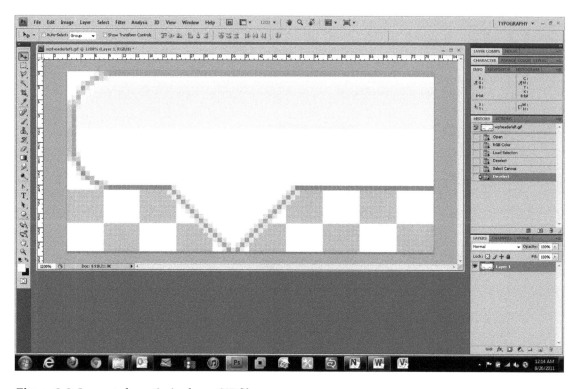

**Figure 6-3.** *Image to be optimized as a GIF file*

To save this image as an optimized GIF file in Photoshop, simply crop the image to fit within your full canvas area, and then press Ctrl+Shift+Alt+S, or click **File ➤ Save for Web & Devices**. This action brings up a screen (similar to the one shown in Figure 6-4) that allows you to choose a different optimizing format for each preview panel. This way, you can easily see differences in image quality as well as differences in size. With this particular image being so small, the choice of file type would not have been an issue except for the transparent background. For transparencies, use either a GIF or PNG file format. As stated earlier, the benefit of using a PNG is that it can handle more than 256 colors, and it also gives you a range of transparency percentages for each pixel.

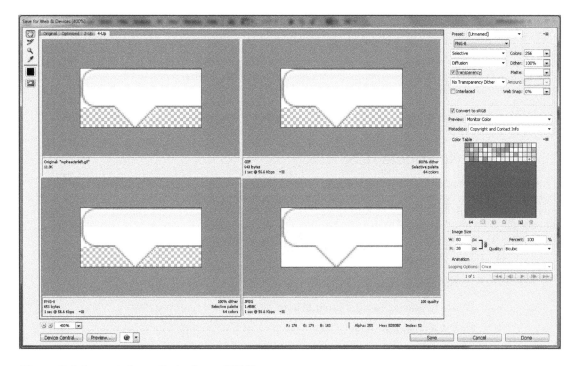

**Figure 6-4.** *Image to be optimized as a GIF file*

## Choosing the Right Format

It may be confusing at times knowing when to choose a particular format over another. The following is a list of the most frequently used image files.

- Joint Photographic Experts Group (**JPG**)
    - Images with lots of colors
    - Images with gradients
- Graphical Interchange Format (GIF)
    - Images with not a lot of colors (Less than 256)
    - Images that have full transparent backgrounds
- Portable Network Graphic (**PNG**)
    - Images that have multiple percentages of transparent pixels

As you start to save your image files, stick to a standard file-naming convention. You might want to try something like "portalname_imagename.gif." I would recommend that you use all lowercase in your file names; in some browsers the file name is case-sensitive, so accidently typing a reference to an image in your CSS with all lowercase when the image file name has uppercase and lower case might prevent the image from rendering. You can also create a "sprite" image, which includes multiple icons and images within a single file. You would then use CSS to target the specific area where the icon or background image is located within the sprite. For example, SharePoint 2010 uses sprites to display icons, social tags images, Site Actions arrow, and multiple other icons within the page. The benefit of sprite images is that you only have to load the image once on a page refresh and, with multiple elements using this image for display. The page load times will be slightly quicker than if you had them all as separate images.

The next step in preparing yourself to build your design is creating the base custom CSS files.

# Cascading Style Sheets (CSS)

As you learned in Chapter 1, CSS is the method used to centrally manage all of the styles attributes in SharePoint. For basic branding projects you might need only one CSS file. On larger projects you might consider breaking up the CSS classes into separate style-sheet files based on the function or template that uses those styles. By doing this you are limiting the amount of CSS that has to be compiled on specific sites. Here is an example of how you might want to break down your style sheets.

- Main Style Sheet: PortalName_Main.CSS

  - Global ribbon styles

  - Global header styles that include logo, site title, and search styles

  - Global navigation styles

  - Global web-part header styles

  - Global footer styles

- My Site Style Sheet: PortalName_MySite.CSS

  - My Profile pages styles

  - My Content site styles

- Community Based Site Style Sheet: PortalName_Communties.CSS

  - Unique styles for community-based sites

- Search Style Sheet: PortalName_Search.CSS

  - Search center styles

  - Search results styles

---

**Note**   You can use a variety of different approaches to add a CSS reference to your custom style sheet from your master page. Choosing the approach depends on where you plan to store your style-sheet files. These approaches are covered within this chapter, in a section called "Connecting the Pieces."

---

# Master Pages

SharePoint 2010 master pages play a very important role in your SharePoint branded site. They act as the backbone of the overall structure of the site. Depending on your design and approach, you might be able to just use the OOTB master pages without any customizations. One of the most common changes you would make to a master page is to reference your custom CSS, and possibly put in a footer that included your copyright and legal information. Some more advanced changes would be to move around controls and add your own custom HTML.

Part of the planning process is staying consistent with how you apply and name your custom CSS classes within the master page. As with the CSS style-sheet names, you want to stay consistent on how you name the classes or IDs that you are using. For example, if you wanted to add a class to a custom global navigation container, you might use this class name: `portalname-globalnavcontainer`. Another example of a good name for a custom footer link would be: "`portalname-footerlink`". You really don't have to use anything long and descriptive; as long as you choose a name with enough flexibility, you should be ok.

There are a handful of master pages that come standard with SharePoint 2010. I find that by creating the base master page first you will then be able to reuse some of the global components for the other master pages. This list includes some of the common OOTB SharePoint 2010 master pages.

- **v4.master**: The base master page used for both publishing and team collaboration sites. This is the most common master page that you copy and customize to make it your own.

- **mwsdefaultv4.master**: Specific to meeting workspace sites templates. This master page includes some unique code applied to the Site Actions to allow the user to create and manage pages specific to a meeting workspace.

- **minimal.master**: Used for the search center, search results, and also for the My Newsfeed page within My Site. The code within the master page basically consolidates a bunch of controls into mini headers and content areas. It also moves the breadcrumb feature control right above the content area that is directly tied to the search results.

- **mysite.master**: Used mainly for the profile pages within My Site. It has unique references to CSS style sheets to represent the unique look and feel for the OOTB profile pages.

If you are new to customizing master pages, you should start out by creating a copy of the v4.master. Give the new master page a new name, and apply it to your site through the user interface or with SharePoint Designer.

The next step is to make small changes like creating a reference to your custom CSS file within the header section of your custom master page. Once you've made all of your changes and tested them, you need to extend your custom master page to some of the other OOTB site master pages described above.

The next section takes a look at the process of copying your custom master page and making it work for meeting workspace sites.

# Creating a Meeting Workspace Master Page

Use the process described in this section only if you have a heavily customized base master page and you don't want to copy every piece into a copied mwsdefaultv4.master master page. For simple master page changes like CSS references and footers, you can save time by using a copy of the OOTB mwsdefaultv4.master and adding your changes directly to that file.

## Duplicating Your Custom Master Page

To convert your custom master page so that it works with all meeting workspaces, first you need to duplicate your customized master page and rename it something like this: "portalname_mwsv4.master." Then open the newly created master page and add the following registration tag to the very top of your master page, as shown in Listing 6-1:

*Listing 6-1. Meeting Workspace Registration.*

```
<%@ Register Tagprefix="Meetings" Namespace="Microsoft.SharePoint.Meetings"
Assembly="Microsoft.SharePoint, Version=14.0.0.0, Culture=neutral,
PublicKeyToken=71e9bce111e9429c" %>
```

There is a CSS registration called mws.css, which provides a little bit of styling to the meeting workspace sites. You can copy this registration but it is not mandatory. To include this registration, add the code in Listing 6-2 after the theme CSS reference in the header.

*Listing 6-2. Meeting Workspace CSS Reference.*

```
<SharePoint:CssRegistration Name="mws.css" runat="server"/>
```

To add in the "add and manage pages" functionality to the Site Actions within the meeting workspace master page, search within your master page for "MenuItem_CommitNewUI." This is the last menu item template within the Site Actions menu control. Copy the code from Listing 6-3 and paste it directly below the commitNewUI template, as shown in Figure 6-5.

*Listing 6-3. Meeting Workspace Add and Manage Page Site Actions Code.*

```
<SharePoint:MenuItemTemplate runat="server" id="MenuItem_AddPages"
      Text="<%$Resources:wss,siteactions_addpages%>"
      Description="<%$Resources:wss,siteactions_addpagesdescription%>"
      MenuGroupId="400"
      Sequence="410"
      UseShortId="true"
      ClientOnClickScript = "javascript:MtgTlPart_ShowToolPane('1');"
      PermissionsString="AddAndCustomizePages"
      PermissionMode="Any" />
<SharePoint:MenuItemTemplate runat="server" id="MenuItem_ManagePages"
      Text="<%$Resources:wss,siteactions_managepages%>"
      Description="<%$Resources:wss,siteactions_managepagesdescription%>"
      MenuGroupId="400"
      Sequence="420"
      UseShortId="true"
      ClientOnClickScript = "javascript:MtgTlPart_ShowToolPane('2');"
      PermissionsString="AddAndCustomizePages"
      PermissionMode="Any" />
```

■ **Note**  The OOTB meeting workspace template does not come standard with the create site menu item in the Site Actions like it does with the v4.master. It is up to you to keep it in or not.

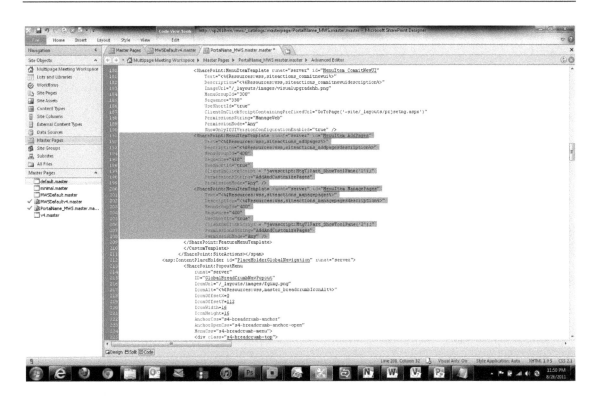

**Figure 6-5.** *Adding the "add and manage pages" to the site actions menu*

## Adding the Tool Pane Manager

The next step is to search for "s4-rp" in your custom master page. This brings you to an empty div that you want to populate with the code from Listing 6-4. This code places the pages Tool Pane Manager to the right of the page as shown in Figure 6-6 when you click on Site Actions ➤ Manage Pages.

*Listing 6-4.* *Meeting Workspace Add and Manage Page Site Actions Code.*

```
<Meetings:CustomToolPaneManager runat="server" __MarkupType="vsattributemarkup" WebPart="true"
Height="" Width="" __WebPartId="{FB6ACB46-6C56-4562-AEF3-964203B651AE}"
id="g_fb6acb46_6c56_4562_aef3_964203b651ae"/>
<Meetings:PropertyBag runat="server"/>
```

***Figure 6-6.*** *Meeting workspace page manager*

After you have added those three main code elements, you have a perfectly working meeting workspace site within your custom master page. If you chose not to add those code elements to your meeting workspace site, you would receive this not very helpful message in the left navigation area: "There are no more meeting occurrences to select from," as shown in Figure 6-7. You would also notice that clicking on the Site Actions menu does not display options for adding or managing your meeting workspace pages.

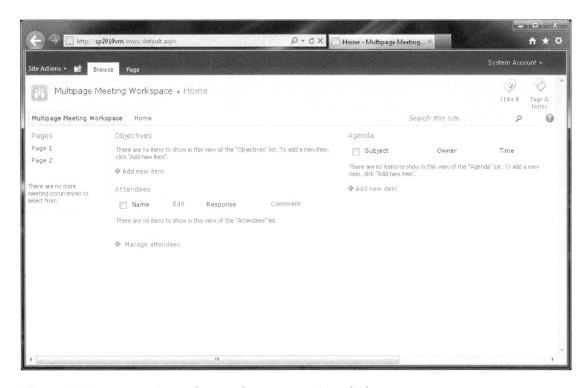

***Figure 6-7.*** *Error on meeting workspace when v4.master is applied*

This next section covers the steps needed to convert your custom master page so that it works with the SharePoint 2010 Search Center and result pages.

## Creating a Search Master Page

Like the meeting workspace process, you only want to create a search master page if you have a heavily customized base master page and you don't want to copy every piece of your custom code into a copied version of the minimal.master master page. If you aren't using a search center site to display your search results, SharePoint defaults all search results to a common search results page, called "osssearchresults.aspx", located on the server in the layouts directory. This page renders your search results within your custom master page.

If you are using the search center as your main search results page, then you only need to make a few changes to get search results to work correctly. If you apply your custom master page directly to the search center, you get a result like that shown in Figure 6-8. The search results are actually being displayed in the breadcrumb folder drop-down, and the positioning of the search results is pushed over to the right.

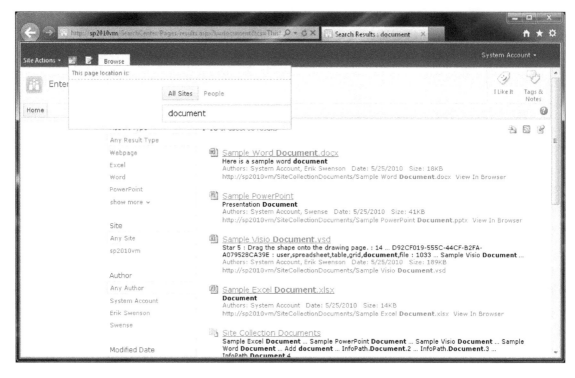

***Figure 6-8.*** *Display issue with search center results page when v4.master is applied*

To fix this problem you need to duplicate your customized master page and rename it something like "portalname_search.master." Then open up the newly created master page and at the end of the header simply add the code from Listing 6-5 to create a new CSS class reference. You should specify the "After" property to make sure your custom style sheet is being referenced after the main corev4.css or any other style sheet that you are using. This task is described in detail in the "Connecting the Pieces" section later in this chapter.

***Listing 6-5.*** *Search CSS Style Sheet Reference.*

```
<SharePoint:CssRegistration name="PortalName_Search.CSS" After="corev4.css" runat="server"/>
```

Within this new style sheet you want to use the CSS in Listing 6-6 to hide the left navigation and also to remove the left margins from the content area.

***Listing 6-6.*** *Search CSS Properties to Hide Left Navigation and Remove Left Margin.*

```
#s4-leftpanel{
display: none;
}
.s4-ca{
margin-left: 0px;
}
```

The next step is doing a search within the custom search master page for "PlaceHolderTitleBreadcrumb." In your custom search master page, remove the whole "SharePoint:PopoutMenu" control, as shown in Figure 6-9.

**Figure 6-9.** *Removing all of the pop-out menu control code from the custom search master page*

The search results are basically tied to this content placeholder control. I would recommend that you add a custom class to the div in case you need to make any specific style changes to the custom search results. After you have deleted this pop-out menu code, search within the file for "MSO_ContentDiv." Within this DIV tag, add the code from Listing 6-7.

**Listing 6-7.** *Code To Display Search Results.*

```
<div class="portalname-searchresults">
        <asp:ContentPlaceHolder id="PlaceHolderTitleBreadcrumb" runat="server" />
</div>
```

Now the search results are rendered directly above the main content placeholder. Your search results page should display your custom branding, as shown in Figure 6-10. The search results are centered on the page with no marginal space on the left.

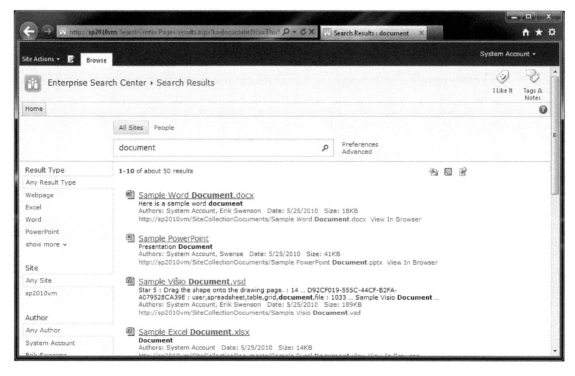

***Figure 6-10.*** *Correct display of search results with customized v4.master base master page*

The next step in the process is to create custom page layouts for publishing sites.

## Custom Page Layouts

SharePoint Publishing Page Layouts are available only with SharePoint Server Standard or Enterprise. Publishing cannot be enabled in SharePoint Foundation 2010. To create publishing pages, you need to enable the Publishing Infrastructure Site Collection Feature and the SharePoint Publishing Site Feature.

There are two main types of Page Layout Content Types: article pages and welcome pages. There are four unique page layouts within the Article Page Content type:

- **Body only:** This page layout includes a title, page content field control, and a roll-up image field control. You would use this for articles that are straight content and do not need additional images or links.

- **Image on left:** This type of page layout includes a title, page image, and caption on the left, article date, byline, page content, and rollup image. You would use this type of page layout for most news articles or announcements.

- **Image on left:** This type of page layout includes a title, article date, byline, page image and caption on the right, page content, and rollup image. You would use this type of page layout just like the image on the left page layout.

- **Summary links**: This type of page layout includes a title, article date, byline, summary links on the right, page content, and rollup image. You would use this type of page layout for articles that need additional links to support the content. The summary links might be useful for showing related news articles or links to documents for that particular news article.

The second type of Publishing Page Layout, the welcome page, includes nine different layouts. The first four listed below are used for landing pages or content pages with multiple web parts:

- **Blank Web-Part Page**: This type of Page Layout includes a title, Page Content field control, and eight web-part zones. This page layout would be used to add a variety of web parts on the page in many different layout configurations.

- **Splash**: This type of page layout includes a title, page image, two summary links web parts embedded in the page, and three empty web-part zones on the bottom. This page is unique as it includes some custom CSS within the page layout to hide the left navigation and remove the left margin in the content area. This page layout is useful on landing pages where you really need to use the horizontal space.

- **Summary Links**: This type of page layout includes a title, page image that is floating on the left side of the page content area, two summary links web parts embedded in the page, and three empty web-part zones at the bottom. Like the splash page, the left navigation has been hidden. This type of page layout is used for a more advanced type of landing page.

- **Table of contents**: This type of page layout includes a title, page image that is floating on the left side of the page content area, a top web-part zone that includes a table of contents web part, and two empty web-part zones at the bottom. This page layout could be used as a landing page to summarize content within its own site collection. However, in my opinion the OOTB table of contents web part does a poor job of summarizing the type of content that lives below this top landing page. It mixes in site content and site navigation, instead of using one or the other. This standard web part does not allow you to just show sites; it basically uses the content of the left navigation settings for the sub-sites below it.

These five welcome pages are used for custom search pages and results.

- **Advanced search**: Includes two top-left and right empty web-part zones and a bottom zone pre-filled with an advanced search web part.

- **People search results**: Includes the standard results page layout configuration with the people refinement web part in the left zone area and the people search core results web part within the bottom zone.

- **Search box**: One of the most basic page layouts. It includes only one web-part zone with nothing in it. You would use this page layout to add a search web part within this zone, to create something similar to the base search center page.

- **Search results**: The standard search center results page layout. This page includes a refinement web part in the left zone, a search statistics web part in the middle lower left zone, a search action link in the middle lower right zone, a related queries and people matches web part in the right zone, and in the bottom zone it includes a search core results, search best bets, top federated results, and search paging web part. You would use this search results page layout if you wanted to create a custom search results page with additional web parts and configurations.

- **Site directory home**: A bit unique page layout as it includes a multilined rich text comments field in the upper left, a contact details web part in the header zone, and three empty web-part zones on the bottom. A message is included on the page in edit mode that says, "This control depends on a Tabs list for its configuration, and is designed to work within an appropriate site template. To remove this control, edit the layout page." This page could be used for migrated SharePoint 2007 sites that do not have the visual upgrade enabled. SharePoint 2007 included a site template called Site Directory that used a tabs list for the top navigation of the page. After some investigation, it only seems like you can create a tabs list within the search center site templates. The problem with this is that even when you create this page layout in your search center it will produce a page error, if you have the new v4 visual upgrade enabled. I would recommend that you simply hide this page layout as it doesn't offer significant value to any new SharePoint 2010 sites.

As we saw in Chapter 4, page layouts can include a variety of different configurations. The OOTB blank web-part page layout provides a pretty good variety of zone configuration options, as shown in Figure 6-11. The nice thing about these web-part zones is that they have some custom JavaScript built in to them that prevents zone without web parts or content from taking up space on the page.

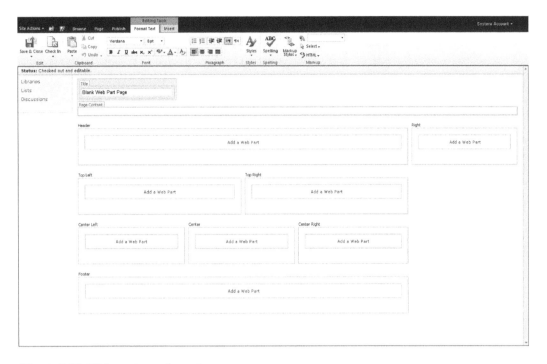

**Figure 6-11.** *Web-part page layout zones*

---

■ **Note**  The page content control on the page is normally a lot taller, but to include the whole web-part page layout zone items in Figure 6-11, I had to reduce the height of it. There is an inline style being applied that sets the height to a min-height of 400px. This min-height is used only in edit mode.

---

## Creating Your Own Page Layout

Now that you are familiar with the OOTB page layouts, it is time to create your own. The first step is to identify the OOTB page layout that most closely matches your needs. For a custom page layout that has just web-part zones and no embedded field controls, I normally start out with the basic blank web-part page layout.

### Selecting a Layout to Work With

The first step in creating your own custom page layout is to open up your site in SharePoint Designer 2010 and click on the page layouts tab in the left navigation, as shown in Figure 6-12. Then click on one of the existing page layouts to activate the options menu (also shown in Figure 6-12), and choose **Copy**. Once you have copied the file, you right-click within the page layout panel, and choose **Paste**.

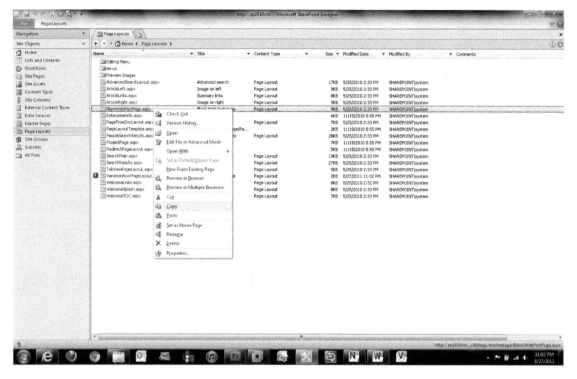

*Figure 6-12. Copying a page layout within SharePoint Designer 2010*

## Renaming the Page Layout

Now rename the newly copied page layout to something like: "portalname_communitylayout.aspx". To rename the file directly within SharePoint Designer, simply click on the arrow next to the file name, and choose **Rename**. After you have changed the name, press the Enter key on your keyboard. You'll want to change the metadata within your new page layout so that when you create a new page based off of it, the title and details will be unique. To change these properties, click on the page layout name in SharePoint Designer. This brings you to the summary page. Then click on Manage all file properties in the browser link within the Customization panel. This links you directly to the SharePoint page layout metadata properties page. Depending on your versioning settings within the master page gallery, you might need to click on the **Check Out** button first, and then click on the **Edit Item** button in the top left. Change the title and description to be specific about the type of page that you are creating. When you have finished, click the Save button, and check in your page layout as a major version.

## Customizing the Page Layout

To customize this page, go back into SharePoint Designer and click on the arrow next to the page title. If you have checked it back in, choose **Check Out**. If you have successfully checked out the document, a little green check mark appears next to the page, as shown in Figure 6-13.

*Figure 6-13. Newly copied page layout showing checked-out status.*

# Editing Your Document

The trick to editing a document is to avoid clicking on the document title that would navigate you to the summary screen and clicking on the text that says Edit File, as shown in Figure 6-14. This will open the file but will not allow you to make any changes. All of the code will be highlighted in a light orange color.

*Figure 6-14. Page layout summary page with edit file link*

The only way to customize the page layout is to go back to the list of page layouts in SharePoint designer, click on the document arrow next to the page layout title, and then click on **Edit File in Advanced Mode**, as shown in Figure 6-15.

---

■ **Note** If versioning is enabled and you have not checked out the file, you will be prompted to check it out. Clicking "Yes" will both check out the document and open the file for editing in SharePoint Designer.

---

*Figure 6-15. Edit page layout in advanced mode*

Now that you have the file open in advanced mode, you should be able to modify anything within the page layout. As an example, we will use the community wireframe in Figure 6-16 as our page layout model.

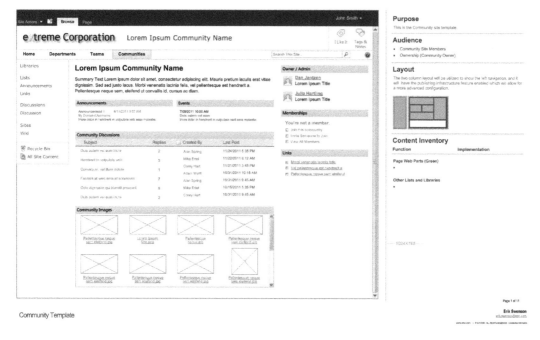

***Figure 6-16.*** *Example community wireframe with layout specifications in right panel*

This page layout has six different web-part zones. Each one of these zones can have more than one web part within it. Figure 6-17 shows this layout configuration in more detail.

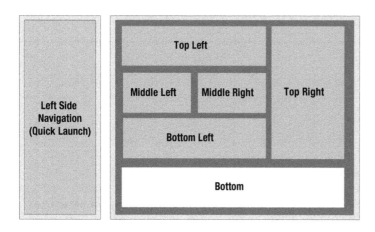

***Figure 6-17.*** *Community base page layout configuration details*

To transform your custom page layout into this configuration, it is helpful to first create a sample page and select your custom page layout that you created earlier. To create a new page, click on Site Actions ➤ View All Site Content, and then click on the Pages library. In the ribbon, within Library Tools, click on Documents ➤ New Document. On this page you will be able to supply a title, description, and URL (which automatically populates based on title), and choose a page layout. Hopefully, you will have your newly created page layout as an option to choose from in the list, as shown in Figure 6-18. If you don't see your custom page layout in the list, make sure that you have checked it in once as a major version. Once the page is created, simply click on the page title and it will navigate you to the page.

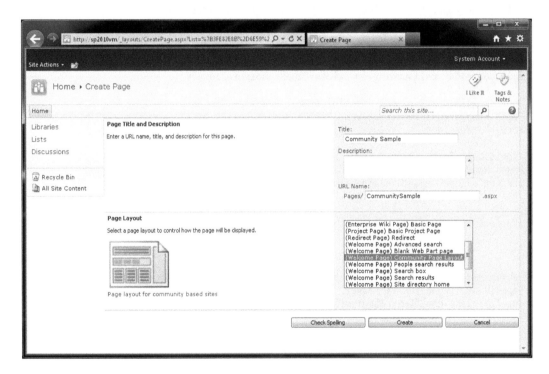

**Figure 6-18.** *Create a new page*

This is where the fun begins. To keep the process simple, you are going to use web-part zones and no field controls within the page. The first thing that you do is remove the rich text HTML field control from the page. Just search for "welcome" within the page layout. The first result should be a DIV tag with a class name of welcome. Select the whole content template and delete it. This will remove the tile field control from the page. Then delete the second content template within the first table to remove all rich text field controls within the page layout. The HTML for laying out these web-part zones is pretty simple. See Listing 6-8 for the basic layout.

**Listing 6-8.** *Community layout HTML.*

```
<table cellpadding="4" cellspacing="0" border="0" width="100%">
<tr>
<td valign="top" style="padding:0">
<table cellpadding="4" cellspacing="0" border="0" width="100%" height="100%">
<tr>
<td id="_invisibleIfEmpty" name="_invisibleIfEmpty" colspan="3" valign="top">
<WebPartPages:WebPartZone runat="server" Title="Top Left"
ID="TopLeft"><ZoneTemplate></ZoneTemplate></WebPartPages:WebPartZone>
</td>
</tr>
<tr>
<td width="100%" colspan="3" valign="top" style="padding:0">
<table cellpadding="4" cellspacing="0" width="100%" height="100%">
<tr>
<td id="_invisibleIfEmpty" name="_invisibleIfEmpty" valign="top">
<WebPartPages:WebPartZone runat="server" Title="Middle Left"
ID="MiddleLeft"><ZoneTemplate></ZoneTemplate></WebPartPages:WebPartZone>
</td>
<td id="_invisibleIfEmpty" name="_invisibleIfEmpty" valign="top">
<WebPartPages:WebPartZone runat="server" Title="Middle Right"
ID="MiddleRight"><ZoneTemplate></ZoneTemplate></WebPartPages:WebPartZone>
</td>
</tr>
</table>
</td>
</tr>
<tr>
<td id="_invisibleIfEmpty" name="_invisibleIfEmpty" colspan="3" valign="top">
<WebPartPages:WebPartZone runat="server" Title="Bottom Left"
ID="BottomLeft"><ZoneTemplate></ZoneTemplate></WebPartPages:WebPartZone>
</td>
</tr>
</table>
</td>
<td id="_invisibleIfEmpty" name="_invisibleIfEmpty" valign="top" height="100%">
<WebPartPages:WebPartZone runat="server" Title="Top Right" ID="TopRight"
Orientation="Vertical"><ZoneTemplate></ZoneTemplate></WebPartPages:WebPartZone>
</td>
</tr>
<tr>
<td id="_invisibleIfEmpty" name="_invisibleIfEmpty" colspan="3" valign="top" height="100%">
<WebPartPages:WebPartZone runat="server" Title="Bottom" ID="Bottom"
Orientation="Vertical"><ZoneTemplate></ZoneTemplate></WebPartPages:WebPartZone>
</td>
</tr>
<script language="javascript">if(typeof(MSOLayout_MakeInvisibleIfEmpty) == "function")
{MSOLayout_MakeInvisibleIfEmpty();}</script>
</table>
```

When you have added some sample content, the end result looks something like Figure 6-19. I would recommend that you change all of the web-part zone titles from the dynamic "`<%$Resources:cms,WebPartZoneTitle_TopLeft%>`" to plain text, like "Top Left." That way you are not restricted to using a particular zone title.

***Figure 6-19.*** *Custom page layout with modified web-part zones*

The next step in the process of creating a custom page layout is to learn about content placeholders and how they are connected between the master page and page layouts.

# Working with Content Placeholders

Content placeholders are used throughout SharePoint as a way to simplify the amount of HTML that is included in the master page. A content placeholder is basically a control with a unique ID that is specified in your custom master page and then can be referenced in a custom page layout. This referenced content placeholder in the page layout can then include any HTML that you want. To create a content placeholder, just add the code in Listing 6-9 within your master page.

*Listing 6-9.* *Basic Content Place Holder Specified in Master Page.*

```
<asp:ContentPlaceHolder id="PortalNamePlaceHolderName" runat="server" />
```

You then use the code in Listing 6-10 to call the content placeholder name and render the HTML or web part specified in the unique content placeholder element. Notice that the content placeholder ID matches the name that is used within the master page.

*Listing 6-10.* *Basic Content Place Holder Specified in Master Page.*

```
<asp:Content ContentPlaceHolderId="PortalNamePlaceHolderName" runat="server">
<div class="portalname-communitylinkedimage">
<a href="/communities">
<img src="/_layouts/images/portalname/communityimage.png" width="155" height="80" />
</a>
</div>
</asp:Content>
```

You can put anything you want in the content placeholder within the page layout. The only rule is that you cannot specify a content placeholder in a page layout if the master page that is being used does not include that placeholder. It will give an error and will not render the page. In addition, if you remove some content placeholders from within your custom master page, you will get errors as they are required to render the page correctly. Some of these required placeholders are described below.

- **Page Title**: Specifies the title of the page within the master page header and displays it on the top of the browser window. id="PlaceHolderPageTitle"

- **Page Title in title area**: Displays the page title on the page. id="PlaceHolderPageTitleInTitleArea"

- **Page Description:** Displays the description of the page. id="PlaceHolderPageDescription"

- **Search Control:** Displays the search input control on the page. id="PlaceHolderSearchArea"

- **Main Content:** One of the most important placeholders as it is used to display all of the content within the center of the page. id="PlaceHolderMain"

Now that you have the basics on optimizing images, CSS, master pages, and page layouts, you now need to connect all of these elements.

# Connecting the Pieces

There are a couple of decisions that you will need to make before you start throwing files on the server or within the style library within SharePoint. There are basically two main ways of connecting your master pages to your CSS and images. It comes down to where you are going to store your CSS and images. The first approach is to store them in the style library within SharePoint; the other is to store them in custom folders within the 14 hive on your servers.

# Storing Custom CSS and Images in the Style Library

For the first approach, you will store all of your custom files, like CSS and images, within the SharePoint style library. (The Publishing Infrastructure and Site Publishing Feature need to be enabled.) This approach gives you version control over your CSS and images. It also may be the only approach if you are dealing with a SharePoint installation that is hosted in the cloud without the ability to deploy features that will give you access to the server. These are typically referred to as sandbox solutions limiting your server-level access. Another thing to consider with this approach is that your files will need to be added to each site collection the branding will be applied to so if you have a lot of site collections there will not be a single source for your files. AKA if you update one it will not update the branding globally. This approach would be used if you are only going to be applying your custom branding to a few site collections. To setup this approach first you need to make sure that you have the publishing infrastructure and publishing feature activated within your site.

To verify that you have enabled them, click on Site Actions ➤ Site Settings ➤ Site Collection Administration ➤ Site collection features. Then, to verify the site feature, click on Site Actions ➤ Site Settings ➤ Site Actions ➤ Manage site features. Activating the publishing feature creates a style library at the root of the site collection where you can store and reference your custom CSS and images. You then navigate to the new style library. The URL of the style library is usually: http://sitename/Style%20Library/Forms/AllItems.aspx.

There are normally four folders: en-us, Images, Media Player, and XSL Style Sheets. Create a new folder at this root location that is either your company name or project name or whatever makes sense. After you have created this folder, you can then upload all of your optimized images. The other option is to store your images within a custom folder located in the images folder in the style library.

The next step is to create a new text document on your local machine in Notepad. Once you have opened up Notepad, save the file as "portalname_main.css", make sure you save as type "All Files" and Encoding "UTF-8". The second option is to store all of your files on your servers.

# Storing Custom CSS and Images on the Server File System

The second approach is more specific to larger implementations that, for the most part, will have one global look and feel. This approach allows you to store all of your CSS and images in a custom folder on the server within the 14 hive: "C:\Program Files\Common Files\Microsoft Shared\Web Server Extensions\14\TEMPLATE\LAYOUTS\1033\STYLES\customfolder". This approach gives you a single source for all of your CSS and images.

---

▪ **Note**  It is recommended that you create a solution package as described in the next section, with all of your files. This automatically deploys all of the files to the correct location on each web front end, so you don't have to do it manually.

---

The steps to manually add your files to the server are as follows:

1. Log into your web front end as an administrator.

2. Navigate to "C:\Program Files\Common Files\Microsoft Shared\Web Server Extensions\14\TEMPLATE\LAYOUTS\1033\STYLES."

3. Create a new folder within the styles library that is either your company name or project name or whatever makes sense. Upload all of your optimized images into this folder. Alternatively, you could upload all of your custom images to a new folder within the 14\TEMPLATE\LAYOUTS\IMAGES directory.

4. Right click and choose new text document.

5. Rename the file to something like "portalname_main.css." This will be your main custom CSS file for your design changes.

Once you have established where your files are being stored, you need to connect them to your custom master page. The next sections guide you through this process.

## Connecting Master Page to CSS

The most effective way to apply your custom CSS and images to your SharePoint 2010 site is by referencing them within the header section of a custom master page. To create this connection using the second approach, where all of your files are stored on the server, navigate to the master page gallery within the top-level site within the collection. If your site does not have publishing enabled, click on Site Actions ➤ Site Settings ➤ Galleries ➤ Master pages. If you have publishing enabled, click on Site Actions ➤ Site Settings ➤ Galleries ➤ Master pages and page layouts. Once you are in the library, hover over v4.master and click on Send To ➤ Download a Copy. Save this copy of v4.master onto your local machine. Rename it portalname_main.master. Open up the master page in Notepad.

---

■ **Note**  Do not try to open a master page file locally with SharePoint Designer 2010 as this will add some unnecessary references, and your master page will contain errors when you apply it to your SharePoint site.

---

After you have it opened the page in Notepad, locate the last line of the head tag and add the code in Listing 6-11.

*Listing 6-11. Alternate CSS on Server that is referenced after corev4.css.*

```
<SharePoint:CssRegistration name="client/portal_main.css" After="corev4.css" runat="server"/>
```

The After property within the CSS reference ensures that your custom master page will be referenced after the OOTB main CSS file called corev4.css. This will make sure that all of your CSS changes will override the OOTB classes that you are using. Depending on the approach you took for storing your CSS and images, Listings 6-12, 6-13, and 6-14 present a few more options for how to refreeze your CSS within your master page header.

*Listing 6-12. Alternate CSS In SharePoint Database For Sites Without Publishing Enabled.*

```
<SharePoint:CssRegistration name="<% $SPUrl:~sitecollection/Style
Library/client/portal_main.css %>" After="corev4.css" runat="server"/>
```

*Listing 6-13. Alternate CSS In SharePoint Database For Sites With Publishing Enabled.*

```
<SharePoint:CssRegistration name="<% $SPUrl:~sitecollection/Style
Library/~language/Themable/Core Styles/client/portal_main.css %>" After="corev4.css"
runat="server"/>
```

*Listing 6-14. Alternate CSS on Server That Is Using the Standard Link relationship - Does Not Need the After Attribute.*

```
<link rel="stylesheet" type="text/css"
href="/_layouts/1033/styles/customfolder/samplecustom.css"/>
```

When you have finished adding the reference code, save the master page and upload it to the master page gallery. Make sure that you publish the master page as a major version and approve it as needed. The next step is to apply your custom master page to SharePoint.

# Apply Custom Master Page to SharePoint 2010

To apply your custom master page when publishing has been enabled click on Site Actions ➤ Site Settings ➤ Look and Feel ➤ Master page. Click on the site master page and system master page drop-down, and change it to the custom master page that you just created. If publishing is not enabled, you won't see an option to choose a master page through the site setting pages. The first thing that you could do is use SharePoint Designer 2010 to set this custom master page manually. Open SharePoint Designer 2010 and connect it to your site. On the left panel click on Master pages, and then click on the arrow next to your custom master page. There will be two options within this drop down for you to set it as site and system master page. Alternatively, you could use PowerShell to apply your custom master page. To do this, modify the code in Listing 6-15 with your site name and URL.

*Listing 6-15. Powershell Script to Apply Master Page to All Sites Within a Collection.*

```
ForEach ($site in Get-SPSite http://sitename)
{
 ForEach ($web in $Site.AllWebs)
  {
    $web.MasterUrl   = "/_catalogs/masterpage/portalname_main.master";
    $web.CustomMasterUrl = "/_catalogs/masterpage/portalname_main.master";
    $web.update()
  }
}
```

Open the SharePoint Management Shell, paste the modified PowerShell script from Listing 6-15, and press Enter. This manually applies your custom master page to the specified master page. The next section walks you through the steps to creating a branding solution so that you don't have to use these manual options.

# Prepare a Basic Branding Solution in Visual Studio

I need to thank Matt Lally, an amazingly smart SharePoint developer and good friend, for providing all of the technical details around creating a SharePoint branding feature within Visual Studio 2010. In this section Matt describes the basics of adding your custom CSS, images, Master pages, Page layouts, and more within a Visual Studio solution. This solution is then compiled and built for deployment. The result of this build is a .WSP file, which can be deployed onto your server using PowerShell.

Developing a branding solution ultimately creates a feature in SharePoint that can be turned on or off as needed. This can include a feature receiver, which can be created to automate enabling your master page when the feature is activated. This will allow you to disable the custom branding for troubleshooting or for other reasons within the Manage Site Features administration page. Another benefit is that these files will automatically get added into TFS source control, and automatically upload your files directly to the server. So if for any reason you have to retract the branding solution the files will get removed from the server. This reduces the manual effort of adding and removing files to the server.

---

■ **Benefits**   Solution and feature receivers enable you to automate deployments. They also allow for easy retractions.

---

Visual Studio 2010 includes a number of Visual Basic and C# SharePoint templates. For these steps, we'll be working with the C# templates. (Most developers I've worked with prefer working with C# and many companies have selected C# as their SharePoint development language standard.)

Here we're using the **Empty SharePoint Project** template, which creates a SharePoint project with no project items. Also, your development machine must have SharePoint 2010 installed; otherwise you won't get past the New Project set-up screen. (You'll be able to open an existing solution to edit but you won't be able to build your solution and you'll get messages about missing references.)

## Getting Started

To start, open Visual Studio 2010 and create a New Project, as shown in Figure 6-20. From the SharePoint 2010 templates listed in the New Project window, select the Empty SharePoint Project and give it a name of your choosing.

*Figure 6-20. Creating a new Visual Studio project window*

When prompted, choose **Deploy as a Farm Solution**, as shown in Figure 6-21.

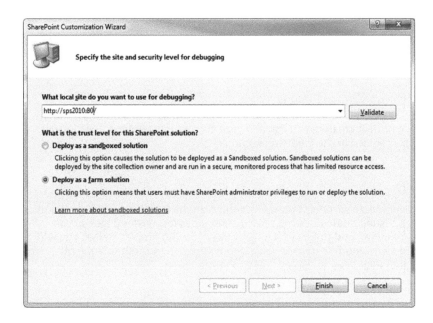

*Figure 6-21. SharePoint Customization Wizard*

With your project created, notice in Figure 6-22 that the Empty SharePoint Project gave you all the references you need to deploy a SharePoint solution, a Features stucture (the solution will need to create a feature you can activate in SharePoint), a Package structure which will build the XML manifest with instructions to deploy the solution (for the purposes of creating a basic branding solution, you won't need to touch the Package as Visual Studio will build it for you), and a unique default key file for signing your assembly.

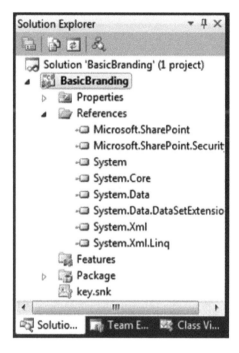

*Figure 6-22. Empty SharePoint Project Solution Explorer*

Now that you have your base project created, you can add your custom master page, CSS, images, and page layouts to the solution, as shown in the following sections.

## Adding a Master Page

With the master page as the core of most SharePoint branding solutions, the first thing you'll do is add one to your Visual Studio project. Visual Studio does not provide templates for master pages so you should build one in SharePoint Designer, and then add it to your Visual Studio project. Before you add the master page, you need to add a new module to your Visual Studio project. (A module is the file container which includes XML directives used to deploy files to SharePoint.)

Add a module by right-clicking on the project title, selecting Add a New Item from the list of SharePoint templates, selecting Module, and giving it a name of your choosing, as shown in Figure 6-23.

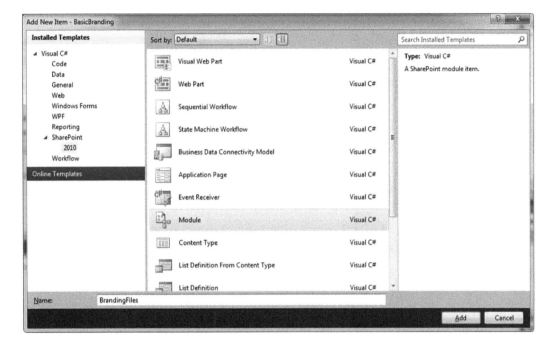

***Figure 6-23.*** *Creating a new module*

Notice in Figure 6-24 the Solution Explorer window now includes your new module called Branding Files and a Feature named Feature1.

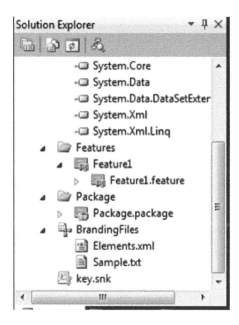

**Figure 6-24.** *Newly created module and feature*

Before going further, delete the Sample.txt file your module created. Now import the master page you created in SharePoint Designer (this file should be saved to your file system) by right-clicking on your module, selecting Add, and then selecting Existing Item. Instead of using the export feature from SharePoint Designer, it is recommended that you download it directly from the master page gallery by clicking on the document arrow, and choosing Send To ➤ download a copy. Saving the file this way will preserve the HTML formatting of the SharePoint master page. There have been some cases where the export feature in SharePoint designer messes up the formatting of the HTML.

You now need to change your module's XML directives to handle deploying the master page correctly. If it's not already open, open the Elements.xml file, and replace the markup so it's in the format shown in Listing 6-16.

**Listing 6-16.** *Master Page Deployment Code in elements.xml File.*

```
<Module Name=" BrandingFiles"  Url="_catalogs/masterpage" RootWebOnly="false">
   <File Path=" BrandingFiles\custom_V4.master" Url="custom_V4.master"
Type="GhostableInLibrary" IgnoreIfAlreadyExists="true" >
      <Property Name="Title" Value="Custom Master Page" />
      <Property Name="ContentType"
Value="$Resources:cmscore,contenttype_masterpage_name;"></Property>
   </File>
</Module>
```

Looking at Listing 6-16 above, the attribute **Type="GhostableInLibrary"** indicates that the item has been added to the content database. The **IgnoreIfAlreadyExists="true"** statement is used to provision the file without error even if the file already exists at the specified URL. The **Url** attribute of the module specifies where to store the file in the SharePoint content database. Lastly the **Name="ContentType"** indicates the localized master page content type.

You're also going to want to change the name of the Feature1 feature to a more appropriate name. If you double-click on the feature, you should also change the title and description (this is what appears in the SharePoint Feature Activation application pages). Also notice in Figure 6-25 the properties scope is set to Web, which means it will be activated in the Site Features. (You optionally could set it to Site, which means it would be activated for an entire Site Collection. We're not covering themes here, but if you are also deploying a theme, you must select the Site scope.)

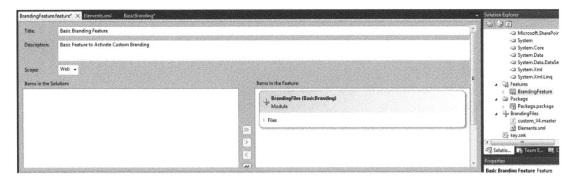

**Figure 6-25.** *Feature title, description, and scope*

Now that you have added your custom master page, the next step is to add your custom CSS and images to the solution.

## Adding CSS and Images

If you have any custom CSS and images as part of your branding, you need to add those files to your Visual Studio branding project.

Visual Studio 2010 SharePoint templates give you the ability to map directly to a SharePoint "14 Hive" folder. So, as referenced in the "Storing Custom CSS and Images in Style Library" section earlier in this chapter, all you need to do is map your project to these folders and add the files the same way you added the master page to the module.

To add the CSS, right-click on the project title, click Add, and choose SharePoint Mapped Folder. Select the English language root style folder TEMPLATE\LAYOUTS\1033\STYLES (if these files need to be deployed to a different language, choose the corresponding language folder), and click OK. It's a good idea to keep your style sheet in a separate, custom folder (make sure it's reflected in your master page's "SharePoint:CssRegistration" reference), as shown in Figure 6-26. Right-click on the Style folder in your project, click Add new folder, and name it appropriately. Now you can add your existing CSS files.

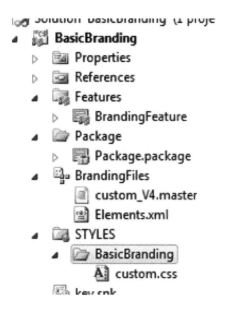

*Figure 6-26. Adding a custom styles folder and CSS files to your project*

To add images to your project, simply right-click on the project title, click Add, and choose SharePoint "Images" Mapped Folder. Notice in Figure 6-27 that this adds the mapping and a subfolder already named to match your project's name. Now you can add your existing image files.

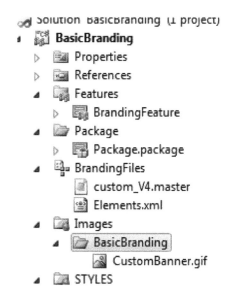

*Figure 6-27. Adding a custom image folder to your project*

The final step to getting all of your custom files within your branding solution is to add in all of your custom page layouts.

## Adding Page Layouts

If you have custom publishing page layouts (this requires the publishing feature) that you want to deploy, you can either add the files to the master page's module or to a new module. (A new module allows you to create a separate feature for activating the page layouts.) For this example, you'll just add the page layout files to the master page's module the same way you added the master page file.

If you started with a page layout from SharePoint designer, make sure to open the page layout you added in Visual Studio to remove the attributes shown in Listing 6-17. The code is located at the top of the page layout.

*Listing 6-17. Code to Remove From SharePoint Designer.*

```
meta:webpartpageexpansion="full" meta:progid="SharePoint.WebPartPage.Document"
```

If you leave this in, SharePoint shows your pages as having been customized in SharePoint designer, even though they were deployed via a feature. This causes problems in redeployment.

As with the master page file, you now need to change your module's XML directives to handle deploying the page layout correctly. Open the Elements.xml file, and replace the markup for your page layout file so it's in the format shown in Listing 6-18.

*Listing 6-18. XML Elements.xml Directives Code Changes to Deploy a Custom Page Layout.*

```
<File Path=" BrandingFiles\CustomPageLayout.aspx" Url="CustomPageLayout.aspx"
Type="GhostableInLibrary">
      <Property Name="Title" Value="Custom Page Layout" />
      <Property Name="ContentType" Value="$Resources:cmscore,contenttype_pagelayout_name;" />
      <Property Name="PublishingPreviewImage"
Value="~SiteCollection/_catalogs/masterpage/$Resources:core,Culture;/Preview
Images/ArticleBodyOnly.png,
~SiteCollection/_catalogs/masterpage/$Resources:core,Culture;/Preview
Images/ArticleBodyOnly.png" />
      <Property Name="PublishingAssociatedContentType"
Value=";#$Resources:cmscore,contenttype_articlepage_name;;#0x010100C568DB52D9D0A14D9B2FDCC9666
6E9F2007948130EC3DB064584E219954237AF3900242457EFB8B24247815D688C526CD44D;#" />
</File>
```

Notice the properties unique for the page layout. You can use your own preview image but the ArticleBodyonly.png is sufficient for this example. The Name="PublishingAssociatedContentType" property associates your page layout to the OOTB publishing feature Article Page content type, which allows you to set the same metadata properties as the article page when this page layout is used and is sufficient for our basic branding solution.

## Getting Fancy – Adding a Feature Receiver

Your master page solution is now ready to be built and deployed. From Visual Studio on your development machine, you can click Build and select Deploy, and the solution is automatically built, deployed, and activated on you target site. There is still a manual step you need to do. Go into the target site collection and from the Site Actions menu select Site Settings. Under Look and Feel, select Master page, and select your custom Master page as the Site Master Page.

If you like what you see on your target site, you can switch the Visual Studio Build Configuration from Debug to Release and redeploy your project. This is nice for deploying to your development machine, but if you want to deploy to other SharePoint installations, you need to go into the file system, browse to your project's "bin/release" folder, and grab the solution file (it's the file with the same name as your Visual Studio project and the ".wsp" extension) that was built. This file has to be placed on the file system of the target installation and can be deployed using either the PowerShell command line or the STSADM command line. With SharePoint 2010, PowerShell is preferred. (There's plenty of information on the Internet about deploying SharePoint 2010 solutions using PowerShell, so there's no need to get into the detail, but you can search for the command "Add-SPSolution" to get started.)

With all of this, the feature is activated, but you still have to manually go into the Site Settings and switch from the default master page to your new master page. To automate this, the SharePoint Visual Studio templates give you the ability to add a feature receiver," which allows you to add some custom code to act on a feature at various phases of activation. (For the master page, we only care about the "FeatureActivated" event and the "FeatureDeactivating" event.)

To add the feature receiver, from your Visual Studio Project's Solution Explorer, right-click on your feature name, and click Add Event Receiver. This automatically opens the receiver in the code window to edit. Replace the "FeatureActivated" and the "FeatureDeactivating" events with code in the following format in Listing 6-19. (This code is for deploying to the web scope; you need to use the SPSite object if deploying to the Site scope instead of the SPWeb object.)

***Listing 6-19.*** *Feature Receiver to Automatically Apply Custom Master Page.*

```
        // Uncomment the method below to handle the event raised after a feature has been
activated.
        public override void FeatureActivated(SPFeatureReceiverProperties properties)
        {
            SPWeb currentWeb = properties.Feature.Parent as SPWeb;
            Uri masterURI = new Uri(currentWeb.Url +
"/_catalogs/masterpage/custom_v4.master");
            currentWeb.MasterUrl = masterURI.AbsolutePath;
            currentWeb.CustomMasterUrl = masterURI.AbsolutePath;
            currentWeb.Update();
        }


        // Uncomment the method below to handle the event raised before a feature is
deactivated.
        public override void FeatureDeactivating(SPFeatureReceiverProperties properties)
        {
            SPWeb currentWeb = properties.Feature.Parent as SPWeb;
            Uri masterURI = new Uri(currentWeb.Url + "/_catalogs/masterpage/v4.master");
            currentWeb.MasterUrl = masterURI.AbsolutePath;
            currentWeb.CustomMasterUrl = masterURI.AbsolutePath;
            currentWeb.Update();
        }
```

The above code sets the master page to your custom master page when the feature is activated and sets it back to the default master page when it is deactivated.

You should now have all that you need for deploying your custom brand files to your portal sites. This next section describes how you can create a Visual Studio solution for branding the My Site pages.

# My Sites Branding Solution

My Sites are a little bit trickier when it comes to creating a branding solution. The navigation links and portal.css references for the My Site Host and My Content Sites are rendered via a separate DelegateControl rather than right on the master page where SharePoint Designer can't be used to set a reference to a custom stylesheet in your master page. Also, every user's My Content Site is a separate site collection which already uses a provisioning feature. Using Visual Studio 2010, a custom user control has to be used to modify the navigation and CSS, and a "Feature Staple" has to be used to attach to the existing my site provisioning feature.

As with the previous example, the template we'll use is the Empty SharePoint Project template.

## Creating the My Site Feature Staple

To start, open Visual Studio 2010 and create a New Project. From the SharePoint 2010 templates listed in the New Project window, select the Empty SharePoint Project shown in Figure 6-28 and give it a name of your choosing and deploy to your My Site host URL as a farm solution.

***Figure 6-28.*** *Empty SharePoint project within Visual Studio 2010*

With the Global Navigation Control holding the core of the My Site branding elements, you need to overwrite the out of the box one with a reference to your custom control. To do this, you need to add a new "Element" to your Visual Studio project which only contains the XML directives to declare your new control. Add a new Empty Element by right clicking on the project title, selecting Add a New Item, in the list of SharePoint templates, select Empty Element show in Figure 6-29, and then give it a name of your choosing.

***Figure 6-29.*** *Creating a new empty element*

Notice in Figure 6-30 the Solution Explorer window now includes your new element and a Feature named Feature1.

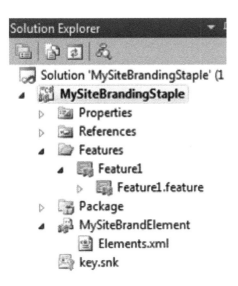

**Figure 6-30.** *New feature and element shown in Visual Studio 2010 Solution Explorer*

You'll now need to change your element's XML directives to handle deploying the control correctly. If it's not already open, open the **Elements.xml** file and replace the markup so it's in the format as shown in the below Listing 6-20.

**Important:** Note the 14 hive path and control name you use here for later steps where you'll add the folder and control to the Visual Studio project.

**Listing 6-20.** *Elements.xml Directives Code Changes to Deploy Control Correctly.*

```
<?xml version="1.0" encoding="utf-8"?>
<Elements xmlns="http://schemas.microsoft.com/sharepoint/">
  <Control Id="GlobalNavigation" Sequence="10"
ControlSrc="~/_controltemplates/custommysites/CustomMysiteNav.ascx" />
</Elements>
```

The attribute Id="GlobalNavigation" indicates that the item is overriding the My Sites Master page reference to the control with the name "GlobalNavigation", Sequence="10" is important in the loading of the control as to not conflict with other controls on the master page and ControlSrc is the location of your custom control in the "14 hive".

You're also going to want to change the name of the Feature1 feature to a more appropriate name. Double-click on the feature and change the title and description (this is what appears in the SharePoint Feature Activation application pages) also notice in Figure 6-31 the properties scope is set to **Web**. Switch the value to **Site** which means it will be activated for an entire Site Collection.

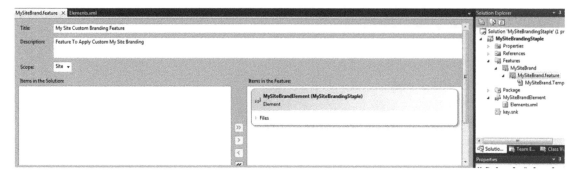

**Figure 6-31.** *My Site feature details with Title, Description, and scope*

## Stapling the Feature

In order to "Staple" this feature, we're going to need the GUID for the feature to be used in the next step. To do this, while still in the feature properties window, click the "Manifest" tab and note the "Id=" value in Figure 6-32.

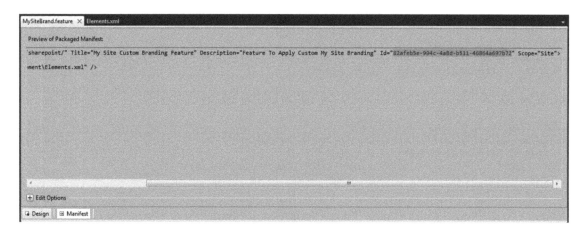

**Figure 6-32.** *Feature GUID id located in the manifest tab*

Now create a new "Staple" element with the XML directives to associate your feature to the existing My Sites site templates.

Just as with the first element, add a new Empty Element for stapling by right clicking on the project title, selecting Add a New Item, in the list of SharePoint templates, select Empty Element, and give it a name of your choosing as shown in Figure 6-33.

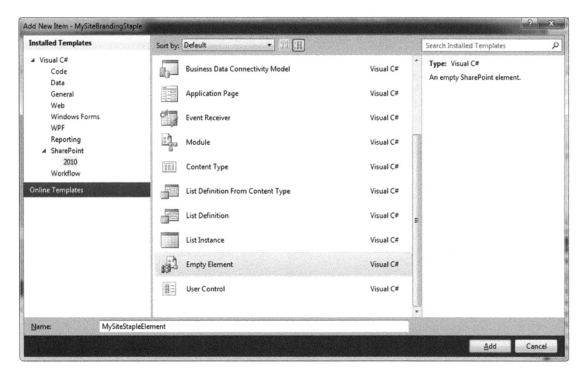

**Figure 6-33.** *Creating a new empty element for stapling*

Notice the Solution Explorer window now includes your new element.

You'll now need to change your staple element's XML directives to handle deploying the control correctly. If it's not already open, open the staple's **Elements.xml** file and replace the markup so it's in the format as shown in Listing 6-21 below.

**Listing 6-21.** *Elements.xml Directives Code Changes to Deploy Control Correctly.*

```
<?xml version="1.0" encoding="utf-8"?>
<Elements xmlns="http://schemas.microsoft.com/sharepoint/" >
  <FeatureSiteTemplateAssociation
   Id="82afeb5e-994c-4a8d-b511-46864a697b72"
   TemplateName="SPSMSITEHOST#0"/>
  <FeatureSiteTemplateAssociation
   Id="82afeb5e-994c-4a8d-b511-46864a697b72"
   TemplateName="SPSPERS#0"/>
</Elements>
```

Notice that in this markup you set the directive to associate the feature you created previously (by the feature's GUID) to the My Site Host and My Content site templates. This is how your feature will be stapled and "activated" when the My Sites site templates are used in provisioning.

## Creating a Web-Application Scoped Feature

To create a Web Application scoped feature, right-click on the Features folder in the Solution Explorer and select Add Feature.

Change the name of the feature to a more appropriate name. Double-click on the feature and change the title and description also notice the properties scope is set to Web. Switch the value to Web Application, which makes it available for any Site Collection within the Web Application. Add the Staple element you created previously to the Items in Feature column, as shown in Figure 6-34.

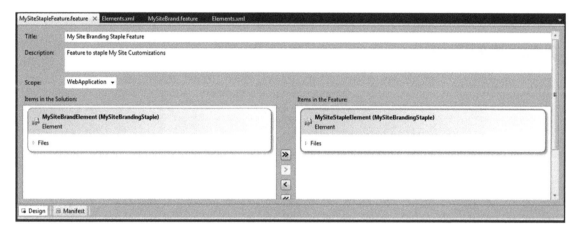

***Figure 6-34.*** *Edit custom staple feature title, properties, and description*

**Important:** Alternatively, return to the first feature you created (the one named MySiteBrand in this example), and remove the same staple element from the Items in Feature column, as shown in Figure 6-35. (You don't want the same element to be included in two separate features.)

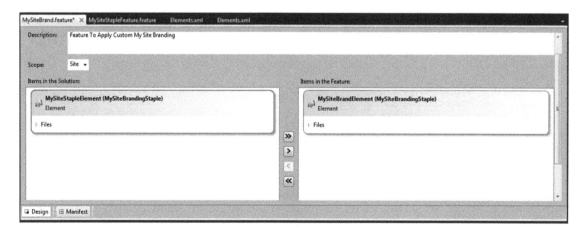

***Figure 6-35.*** *Edit custom apply feature title, properties, and description*

Now that you have created the feature, staple, and staple feature, the last step is to create a custom global navigation user control so that you can reference your custom CSS within My Sites.

## Reference My Site CSS with a Custom Control

To override references to classes within the portal.css stylesheet and add images to the top banner, you need to create a new global navigation user control copied from the existing GlobalNavigation user control.

To add this control, right-click on the project title, click Add, and then choose SharePoint Mapped Folder. Select the TEMPLATE\CONTROLTEMPLATES folder. It's important to keep your control in a separate, custom folder, so right-click on the CONTROLTEMPLATES folder in your project, click Add new folder, and name it appropriately. (Make sure this folder path is specified in the first element file that you created in this project.) Now you can add the OOTB user control to this new folder, which you'll rename and edit in the next step.

Right-click on the new folder, select Add, choose Existing Item, browse to C:\Program Files\Common Files\Microsoft Shared\Web Server Extensions\14\TEMPLATE\CONTROLTEMPLATES, and select the file named "MySiteTopNavigation.ascx," shown in Figure 6-36. (This is the control that generates the GlobalNavigation.) Rename this file to match the name specified in the first element file that was created in this project.

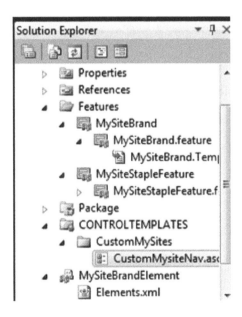

***Figure 6-36.*** *Rename file to the same name as the first element file created*

You can now add references to your custom style sheet by opening the renamed control file (CustomMySiteNav.ascx in this example) in the code window and adding in the code from Listing 6-22 directly under the last "<%@ Register…" tag.

*Listing 6-22. Custom Style Sheet reference in custom control file*

```
<SPSWC:MySiteCssRegistration ID="CustomMySiteCss" name="custommysites/custommysites.css"
runat="server"/>.
```

## Adding My Site CSS and Images

Use the same steps from the basic branding solution to add mapped folders where your image and stylesheet files will reside in the 14 hive.

## My Site Ribbon Considerations

The SharePoint 2010 Ribbon on My Sites appears below the global navigation. If you want the ribbon to appear above the navigation as it does on other site templates, you need to add a custom My Site master page to this project as you did for the basic branding solution, where you modify the OOB mysite.master master page to move the line in Listing 6-17 below the line starting with "<div id="s4-titlerow". (You'll notice this is after the Ribbon Row references in the mysite.master master page.)

*Listing 6-23. My Site Global Navigation Control.*

```
<SharePoint:DelegateControl runat="server" ControlId="GlobalNavigation" />
```

## My Site Feature Activation

Once the solution is deployed, the feature is automatically enabled on newly created personal My Content sites by virtue of the feature staple but for all existing sites, the feature has to be activated by going into Site Settings on each personal site and activating the feature or by running a script, as shown in Listing 6-24 below, from the SharePoint PowerShell Command prompt on any SharePoint server where the solution is deployed. (The script loops through all sites that use the personal site template and activates your feature.)

*Listing 6-24. PowerShell Command to Enable the Custom My Site Feature to Existing Sites.*

```
$personalSites = get-spsite | where {$_.RootWeb.WebTemplate -eq "SPSPERS"}
foreach ($site in $personalSites) {Enable-SPFeature -Identity "MySiteStapleFeature" -Url
$site.Url}
```

# Summary

This chapter gave you a number of helpful tips and instructions for how to take an approved visual design and splice it up into optimized images. You learned about cascading style sheets and where to place them so that they can be referenced by a custom master page. The chapter also showed you how to work with publishing page layouts and content placeholders. Once you connected your files, you learned the different ways that you can apply a custom master page to SharePoint 2010 including creating a custom branding solution in Visual Studio 2010.

# CHAPTER 7

# Testing the Visual Build

This chapter is all about the benefits to testing your SharePoint application. As you start building out the visual design, you need to conduct numerous tests on the site to ensure that it delivers the required content, functionality, and visual standards that have been defined by your users and stakeholders. Testing also helps you catch most of the bugs or defects prior to going live. In addition, you learn how to test your branding against the OOTB site templates and on multiple browsers. SharePoint has many features and functions, and you'll test them all to check that any of your customizations are not affecting functionality. There may be some cases where your stakeholders will want you to remove some standard features if they are not needed. However the visual design should not make the site perform slower or lose functionality.

The tests covered in this chapter provide critical information on how well your site performs to the standards and requirements that have been identified. The more time that you dedicate to testing, the better your site will be and the greater the chances of user adoption.

## Testing Types

You can perform four main types of testing on your site: unit, browser, performance, and user acceptance). At a minimum you want to conduct unit and browser tests on the visual design build before it gets added to a production system. This allows you to identify and fix any bugs before your users find them.

# Unit Testing

Unit testing happens during the build of the visual design elements. As you create your CSS, master pages, page layouts, and any other front-end development tasks, you should be checking the site constantly to make sure that what you are building matches the specific style-guide specifications that have been created. You can do these tests on the fly within your own development environment. In most cases, the results from your unit testing will have minimal documentation. Some of this documentation could include capturing screenshots and identifying any known issues or bugs. These issues can then be added to a list or spreadsheet for further testing or fixes. It's a good idea to communicate to your team and your project manager any major issues that you are having. This allows you to get help from others and document the issues before they are forgotten. The next type of testing that you will do while you are unit testing your development efforts is checking your customizations across different browsers.

# Browser Testing

Browser testing happens within the unit-testing phase and during system tests to make sure that all of the approved browsers look and perform the same. Microsoft provides multiple levels of browser support on its website: `http://technet.microsoft.com/en-us/library/cc263526.aspx`.

- **Supported**: Web browsers that are fully supported and include all features and functionalities:

    - Internet Explorer 9 (32-bit)

    - Internet Explorer 8 (32-bit)

    - Internet Explorer 7 (32-bit)

- **Supported with known limitations**: Web browsers that are supported, but have a few known limitations. Some features and functionality may not work or are disabled by design:

    - Internet Explorer 9 (64-bit)

    - Internet Explorer 8 (64-bit)

    - Internet Explorer 7 (64-bit)

    - Mozilla Firefox 3.6+

    - Safari 4.04+

- **Not tested**: Web browsers that have not been tested and may have some issues with common features and functionality of the site:

    - Internet Explorer 6 (32-bit)

- **Not supported**: Web browsers that are not supported:

    - Internet Explorer 5.01

    - Internet Explorer 5.5x

- Internet Explorer for Macintosh

- Earlier third-party Web browsers

During the process of building out your site's CSS and master pages, check each of the supported browsers to verify that they are displaying correctly. The older the browser that you have to support, the more time-consuming it is to test and fix. Internet Explorer 7 (IE7) and older versions are the hardest to support because they don't render floating DIVs and margins as well as the more modern browsers. The built-in developer toolbar in IE9 does a decent job of allowing you to view your site in IE7- or IE8-mode. In some situations the IE9 engine will display elements differently than a true IE7 browser. Setting up a separate virtual machine running XP with IE7 will give you the best results.

# Performance Testing

When conducting performance tests some pages may perform slowly because of complex calculations or a large amount of information being pulled from the server. These are not related to the branding and may be resolved using cache techniques not covered in this book. However, your branding may have some effect on performance if you have not optimized your images for web viewing. As an example, if you have a very large background image on your site and you have not compressed the image, it might take a couple of seconds longer to render the page. Another way to make your sites load faster is to break your CSS into multiple files so that you are rendering only the CSS needed for that page or site type, for example, if you have a separate style sheet for each page layout or site template.

# User Acceptance Testing (UAT)

Doing UAT tests is an effective way to get truly unbiased results from your users, but the tests require a significant amount of time. This type of test allows users to perform predetermined tasks on the site. Some of these tasks are as simple as navigating the site, while others are more complicated and require multiple steps. If the system is an upgrade from a current system, these tests are critical because they give you insight into how your users will adapt to changes. For example, if you have a new navigation model, you need to check that users understand the groupings of information and can find what they need with little to no effort. When it comes to design, you may want to ask your users what they think of the new visual design. Don't expect to get highly detailed feedback on the design unless there is something that users clearly do not like or that prevents them from performing a particular task.

As an example, if you modified the site header to include a large image, users might provide feedback about the new header taking up too much space and causing some of the important information on the page to fall below the fold, which requires them to scroll down to see it.

It is recommended that you have at least 10 participants perform the same tasks to identify any patterns on how users interact with the site. If the majority of people click on an element expecting to view more details but the current system does not allow for that, you might consider modifying it so that users clearly know if something is clickable or not. This is related to the branding since you want to always strive for consistency within your branding. You will want to make sure that all of your links follow a particular style and color. This gives your users a predefined expectation that a piece of text is a link if it is light blue and changes to underlined when they mouse over it. The results of these tests give your stakeholders confidence that the final production site will perform as intended.

The next step in testing your design is to test it against all of the standard SharePoint 2010 templates that users will create within the system.

# Testing Out Of The Box (OOTB) SharePoint Templates

These site templates should be created and tested against your design to make sure that all of the standard layouts, features, and functionality will still work with your custom design.

## Publishing Site Template

Publishing site templates differ from other site templates in that they utilize the publishing infrastructure feature. The site owner can use this site collection and site feature to create pages with different page layouts. It also allows the site owner to add to the page unique web parts such as the content query web part and summary links web parts. Both of these web parts have unique display styles that you can modify to match the look and feel of your design. Publishing pages include additional Ribbon commands for when you are doing such tasks as editing the page and uploading documents that have to be accounted for within your design, as shown in Figure 7-1. The tall editing Ribbon tabs force the Ribbon to a height of 43 pixels. Removing the top label bar for each tab would save you about 20 pixels in height.

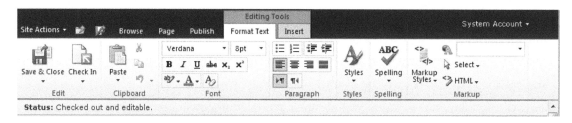

***Figure 7-1.*** *Publishing page Ribbon toolbar*

To reduce the height of the Ribbon you have to add the code in Listing 7-1 to your custom style sheet. This basically removes the top headers on all of the Ribbon tabs. These headers are used just to group the tabs together and have no real functionality. You might need to do some extra testing on IE7 to make sure it behaves consistently with other modern browsers.

***Listing 7-1.*** *Code to Reduce the Height of the Ribbon Bar*

```
.ms-cui-cg-i{display: none;}

body #s4-ribbonrow{min-height: 23px; height: auto; margin-bottom: -20px;}

.ms-cui-topBar2{height: 23px;}

.ms-cui-tts{height: 24px;}

.ms-cui-tt, .ms-cui-cg{height: 22px;}

.ms-cui-TabRowLeft{margin-top: 0px;}
```

```
.ms-cui-tt-a{margin-top: 0px;}
```

```
.s4-trc-container-menu{margin: 3px 0px 0px 0px;}
```

Adding this code reduces the Ribbon height in your designs, as shown in Figure 7-2.

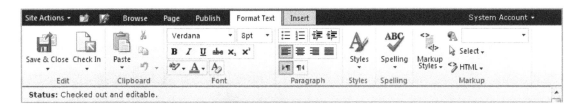

**Figure 7-2.** *Ribbon with reduced height from adding custom CSS*

You'll want to test other aspects of the publishing pages, to make sure the page layouts still work and display correctly.

- **Body only**: Verify that the body content is displayed on the page.

- **Image on left**: Verify that the page image is shown on the left, and the title, byline, date, and body content are displayed on the page.

- **Image on right**: Verify that the page image is shown on the right, and the title, byline, date, and body content are displayed on the page.

- **Summary links**: Verify that article title, date, byline, and summary links are on the right, and the body content is displayed on the page.

## Team Site Template

The standard SharePoint 2010 team site template includes the Quick Launch left navigation shared document library view and a placeholder image in the right column. You create the standard team site using a unique site feature called "Wiki Page Home Page," which transforms the site into a wiki-based page layout that does not include any web-part zones. This page layout does not work well with center fixed-width designs since the overall content area exceeds 980 pixels, as shown in Figure 7-3.

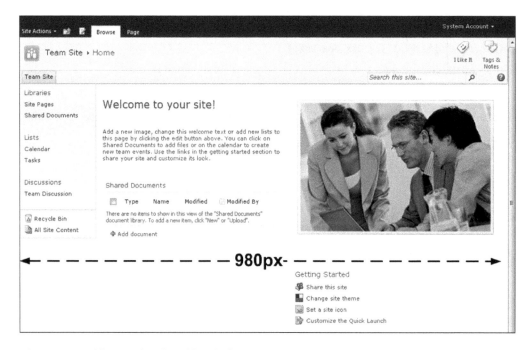

**Figure 7-3.** *Ribbon with reduced height from custom CSS*

The content area is a floating DIV, so depending on the size of your fixed width, the image might display outside of the fixed content area, as shown in Figure 7-4.

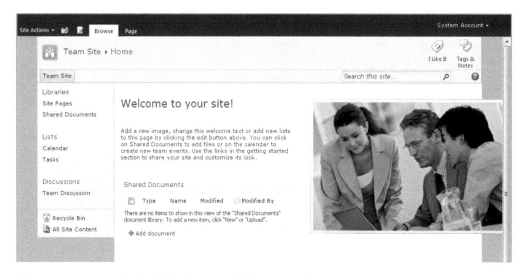

**Figure 7-4.** *Center fixed-width of 900px with image overlap*

To convert the team site to a more traditional site layout with web-part zones, you simply have to disable the Wiki Page Home page site feature. To do this, click on Site Action ➤ Site Settings ➤ Manage Site Features, as shown in full view in Figure 7-5.

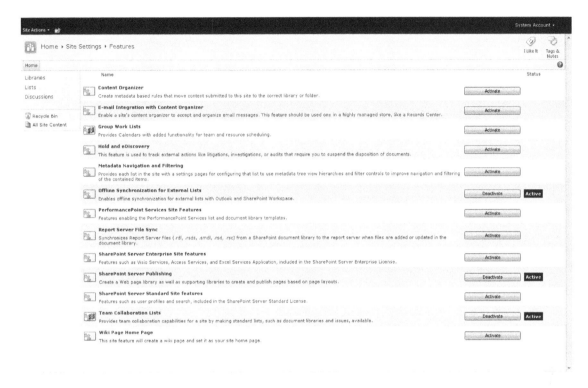

**Figure 7-5.** *Manage Site Settings Features page*

Scroll down to the bottom of the list and click on the **Deactivate** link next to the feature called "Wiki Page Home Page," as shown in Figure 7-6. Another page appears with a confirmation that you want to deactivate this feature. Simply click on **Deactivate this feature**.

**Figure 7-6.** *Deactivate team site wiki page layout*

Once you have disabled the feature, navigate back to the team site and edit the page. You will now notice in Figure 7-7 that, in edit mode, the team site has two web parts on the page. The left column is fixed at a 70% width, and the right column is fixed at 30%. These widths are specified in the default.aspx page. The basic team site layout includes an announcement, calendar, and links list web part on the page by default.

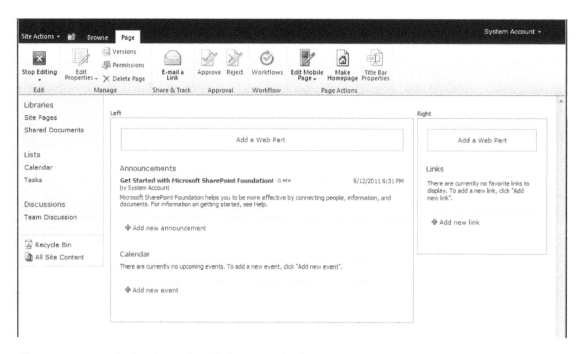

*Figure 7-7. Team site in edit mode with deactivated wiki page feature*

## Blog Site Template

The blog site template has quite a few unique design elements that you should test to ensure that your branding is applied correctly to these types of sites. The first main element that you need to check is the blog post title and date graphic, as shown in Figure 7-8. These styles can be easily modified to fit within your design theme. The left Quick Launch on blog sites are unique and have their own classes. Make sure that you check these styles for consistency.

***Figure 7-8.*** *Blog site template*

## Meeting Workspace Template

The meeting workspace site templates are unique since they require their own master page. This unique master page provides a feature that allows the site owners to create and manage pages within the site. Each one of these pages can include different web parts. You will want to make sure that if you have made any master page changes (described in the previous chapter), they are replicated into your new meeting workspace master page. Figure 7-9 shows what a standard multipage meeting workspace site template looks like when you are managing the site pages. To get the page manager, simply click on Site Actions ➤ Manage Pages. From here you can change the order of the pages.

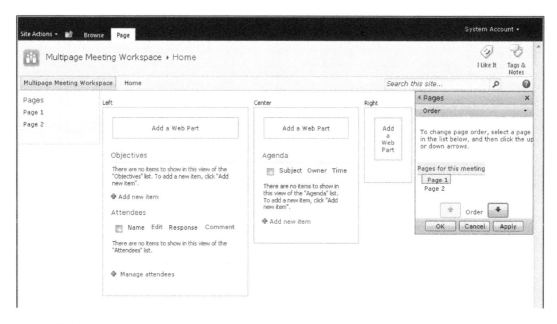

*Figure 7-9. Multipage meeting workspace site template*

You can test some other templates, including the Search Center pages or database templates. Now that you have tested all of the standard site templates with your design, you need to unit test your visual design build against some additional feature and functions within SharePoint 2010.

# Testing SharePoint Features and Functions

Following is a list of some of the standard features and functions of SharePoint 2010 that you should check against your visual design build. All of these components have their own unique CSS and styles. Testing these features and functions helps you find and change any out-of-the-box styles.

## Ribbon

The Ribbon can be a complex element to test against. At minimum you will want to make sure the Ribbon does not display any unnecessary extra space above and below it. Figure 7-10 shows the default look and feel of the Ribbon.

*Figure 7-10. SharePoint 2010 Ribbon*

- **Browse Tab**: The browse tab has three states. The first is the selected state, the second is the hover state, and the third is the non-selected state. All of these can be modified with CSS.

- **Page Tab**: The page tab is similar to the browse tab but is available only on publishing sites with pages.

- **Other Tabs**: These tabs include the item, library, and other tabs that show up based on what you have clicked on with the SharePoint site.

## Fly-Out and Drop-Down Menus

All of the drop-down menus can be stylized and rebranded if necessary. They have the same or similar classes, so be sure to style them accordingly. The default SharePoint top Navigation drop-down looks similar to what is shown in Figure 7-11.

*Figure 7-11. SharePoint 2010 navigation drop down*

- **Top or Global Navigation**: If you have publishing enabled, you can create top navigation drop-down menus that show up if you hover over the top navigation parent link. Test to make sure the links within the drop-down are consistent with your branding.

- **Site Actions**: Verify that the site actions drop-down menu is consistent with your branding

- **Modify Web Part**: Verify that the icon to modify the web parts is displaying correctly. Sometimes when you customize the web-part header and title area, the icon element does not get updated.

- **Quick Launch if enabled:** If you have modified the master page to allow the left navigation to have fly-outs, make sure that the display of these fly-outs is correct.

## Dialog Windows

SharePoint 2010 has a few different types of dialog windows, and each one should be tested with your custom branding. A sample New Item dialog window is shown in Figure 7-12.

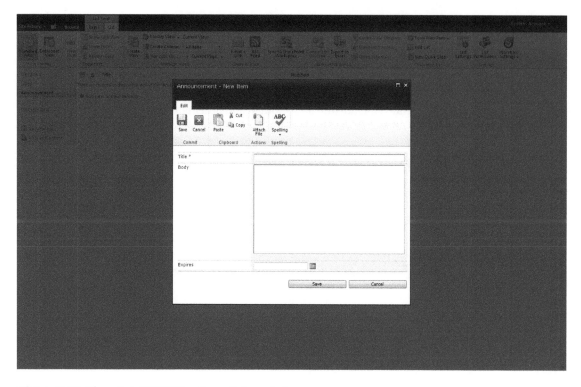

*Figure 7-12. SharePoint 2010 New Item dialog window*

- **New Item:** Open up any SharePoint list in your site and add a new item. Verify that the dialog window does not include any unintended custom elements. You can hide custom elements within the dialog windows by just adding the s4-notdlg class to them. Also verify that the Ribbon in the dialog window is displaying correctly.

- **View Item:** Click on the list item, and then choose to view properties to display the list item in a dialog window. Verify that the window content does not include unintended scroll bars, that the content is not hidden, and that the dialog window includes some branding style that matches the rest of your site branding.

- **Create Site/List:** This unique dialog window uses Silverlight, if you have it installed. This window allows you to create a list, library, or site. Verify that the look of this window is consistent with the overall branding of your site.

- **Upload Document:** This dialog window has a couple of different views. The first is the standard document upload view, and the second is the multiupload screen.

# Quick Launch

You need to test the left navigation or Quick Launch on all site templates. By default, the Quick Launch displays a list of headers and links vertically on the left side of the standard SharePoint templates. These elements should be tested for consistency. The default Quick Launch for a team site is shown in Figure 7-13.

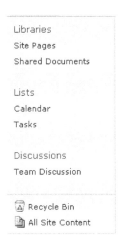

*Figure 7-13.* SharePoint 2010 Team Site Quick Launch

- **Headers:** The Quick Launch headers can be easily customized to fit within your design specifications. Test to make sure that a header that is also a hyperlink displays correctly.

- **List Items:** Verify that the list items are spaced correctly and have the correct hyperlink color.

- **Selected headers/Items:** By default, the Quick Launch headers and links have a predefined, selected state style. Verify that the selected state look-and-feel is appropriate for your design.

- **Tree View:** The Quick Launch tree-view control is enabled by the site owner to show the content that resides within the site. Users will be able to expand and collapse the menu, so verify that the control is displaying correctly with your custom branding applied.

- **Metadata Navigation:** This unique navigation control also allows users to expand and collapse it as needed. Test that as a user expands the navigation, it does not break your custom designs.

# Breadcrumbs

There are two types of breadcrumbs within SharePoint 2010. Figure 7-14 shows an example of the Site breadcrumb.

*Figure 7-14.* *SharePoint 2010 Site breadcrumb*

- **Site:** The site breadcrumb is located in the upper-left corner of your SharePoint site in that little folder icon. If you have created a couple of levels of sites, navigate down to the lowest one, and then click on the folder icon. This displays a tree view of the top parent site within that site collection, all the way down to your current site.

- **Page:** By default, the page breadcrumb is located within the site header next to the page title. Verify that it displays correctly as you navigate to other pages on the site.

# Calendar

The calendar in SharePoint 2010 also has multiple views, and you will want to verify that all of the standard features and components are working and displaying correctly. Figure 7-15 shows a default SharePoint 2010 Month Calendar view.

*Figure 7-15.* *SharePoint 2010 Month Calendar view*

- **Date Picker:** Verify that all of the calendar picker pop-ups display correctly. Any custom JavaScript that you have added to your master page might conflict with the OOTB date picker and not display it correctly, if at all.

- **Month View:** Ensure that all of the days of the month and the ability to create a new event item are available when you hover over a day of the week.

- **Week View:** Verify that the spacing and colors of the week view are consistent with your branding style.

- **Day View:** Verify that the page loads this view correctly.

- **Current Day Indicators:** There is a default style that indicates what the current day is. Verify that the correct day is being displayed and with the correct style.

## Lists and Libraries

The lists and library views have a few unique design elements that you should test for consistency within your design build. Figure 7-16 shows an example of a simple announcement list.

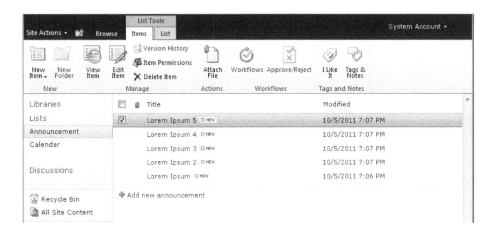

***Figure 7-16.*** *SharePoint 2010 Full Announcement list view*

- **Datasheet View:** The datasheet view is visible when a content author is viewing a list or library and clicks on this view within the Ribbon. In SharePoint 2007 the background of the datasheet view was tied to the body class, so if you made any background changes to the body of your site, it would be reflected in the datasheet view. In SharePoint 2010 you no longer have to worry about the datasheet view background color getting colors applied by accident, as it is included on the page as an object and not through an IFRAME.

- **Alternating item shade:** When viewing a list or library with multiple list items, every other item will have a very light-gray background that represents an alternating color. Verify that the color works with your design.

- **Libraries with a lot of columns:** A common branding issue with lists and libraries that include many columns is that they may display incorrectly within a site if it has a fixed width within the content area. Verify that when viewing a list or library with a lot of columns (eight or more), the list does not flow outside of your center fixed-width design or that the top header does not get disconnected when scrolling.

## Web Part

Since your design will have many different types of web parts, you need to check a set of elements for consistency. Figure 7-17 shows a document library web-part style.

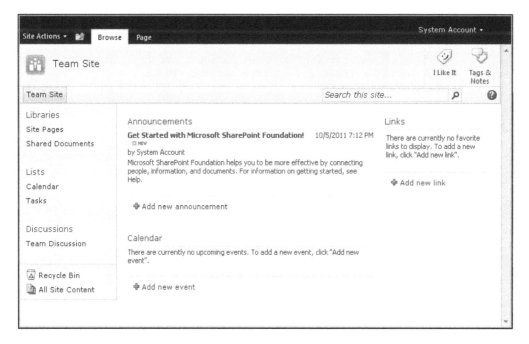

*Figure 7-17. SharePoint 2010 Document Library web-part style on the page*

- **Chrome/Title:** Test the title and web-part headers to make sure they are consistent with the branding style.

- **Border color:** If you have modified the web part to change the Chrome Type to "Border and Title" or "Border Only," you will want to make sure that the border width and color are consistent with your design.

- **Separator Lines:** Some list view or document library view web parts display the summary toolbar below the web part. Verify that the separator line is consistent with the colors and line weight of your design.

# Edit Page

When the page is in Edit mode there are a few styles that get added around the current web parts that you should check for consistency. Figure 7-18 shows an example of what a team site template looks like in Edit mode.

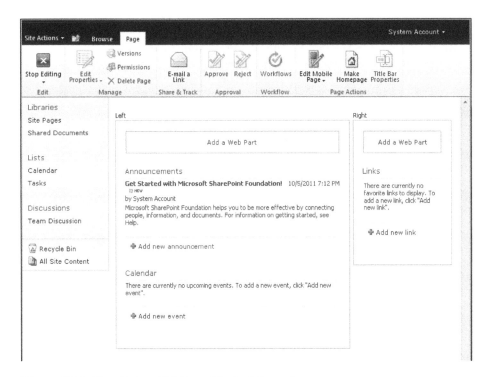

**Figure 7-18.** *SharePoint 2010 Team Site in Edit mode*

- **Web Part Zone Colors:** By default, when the page is in edit mode some additional padding and margins are added to the web parts that help define the different zone areas. This might cause a problem if the zone areas are floating and require a specific width. Verify that the zone areas display correctly in Edit mode.

- **Drag and Drop Style:** As you drag and drop web parts from one zone to another, verify that the location indicator is showing up in the correct location and that you can successfully move web parts around.

- **Web part Chrome/Titles:** The web-part header and title might look different in Edit mode. Verify that it is consistent with your branding style.

- **Add Web Part Panel:** If you have made modifications to the height of the Ribbon toolbar, verify that the Add Web Part panel displays correctly and does not hide the Add or Cancel buttons.

# Admin Pages

In SharePoint 2010 all of the administration pages have your custom master page and design applied automatically. In SharePoint 2007 you were forced to modify two server-side master pages (Application.master and Simple.master) or create a theme to apply your custom branding to those pages. Now that they inherit your chosen master page, you should verify that the following pages display correctly.

- **Site Settings:** Verify that the Site Settings landing page and subpages within it all display correctly, as shown in Figure 7-19. The Site Information panel can sometimes be out of place.

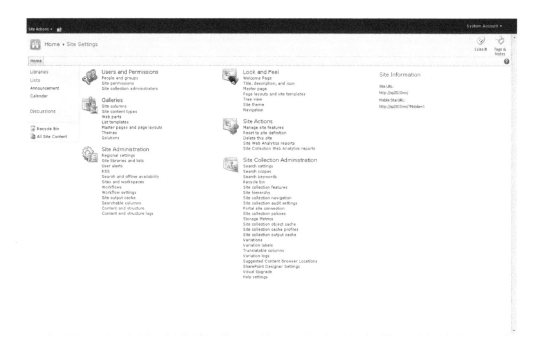

*Figure 7-19. SharePoint 2010 Site Settings page*

- **Error Pages:** The error pages use the corev4.css as the only CSS reference file. The main class for the error window is `body #s4-simple-card`. Verify that the error pages fit within the design style of your site. Figure 7-20 shows an example of a standard SharePoint 2010 error page.

**Figure 7-20.** *SharePoint 2010 error page*

# Themes

SharePoint 2010 themes are much more simplistic than SharePoint 2007 themes. To create your own theme, simply click on Site Actions ➤ Site Settings, and within the Look and Feel section, click on Site Theme. On this page you can choose from a variety of predefined theme colors or build your own.

- If you are going to allow OOTB themes you will have to test, test, and triple test that all themes work and function as expected with your custom design…

# Fonts

By default, SharePoint uses the following font types within the base SharePoint UI.

- **Verdana**: 63% of the site uses this font for displaying small labels, description text, web-part titles, and body content,

- **Tahoma**: 24% of the site uses this font for general elements like left-navigation list items or page titles.

- **Segoe UI**: 12% of the site uses this font for the site actions and social notification labels, and within the Ribbon.

- It is recommended that you stick with system fonts (Verdana, Tahoma, Arial, for example), so that everyone gets the same experience. Also, you'll want to specify a font family (Tahoma, Arial, Helvetica, San-serif, for example) for your CSS elements to provide alternate fonts for users who do not have the initial font you specify.

## Images

Images within the site branding should be tested for web optimization. If an image file size is too large, the page will load slower and performance is affected.

- **Custom Logo:** Verify that the logo fits the specific specifications for size, color, usage, and spacing as defined within your style guide.

- **Background Images:** If you have background images, verify that they work with smaller and larger browser sizes. Some images might look good on smaller browsers but do not display correctly on larger ones.

- **Consistent Icons and Bullets:** Ensure that you are using a consistent style for all icons and list bullets.

## Customized and Third Party Web Parts

It's kind of a given, but it is recommended that when you apply styles to custom web parts, third party web parts, or custom controls that you test for functionality and brand consistency before you deploy it onto production servers.

The next section focuses on testing your design for mobile devices and print styles.

## Mobile Views

Testing your visual design for mobile devices varies depending on the type of device that you plan to support for user access to the system. Almost any type of phone that includes a built-in browser can get the standard mobile view. Most tablets display the website in the standard full web-browser view. To view your site in a mobile view within your browser, you can simply type **?Mobile=1** after your site's URL, for example: `http://siteurl/?Mobile=1`. Your mobile view will look similar to the image in Figure 7-21.

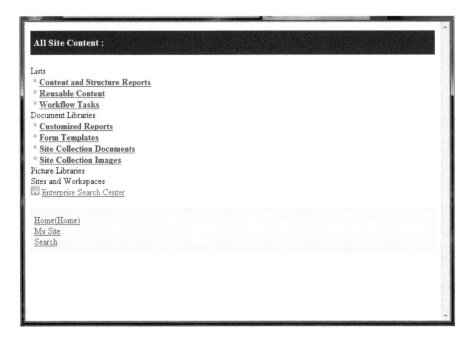

**Figure 7-21.** *SharePoint 2010 mobile view in a browser (screenshot 800x600)*

As you can see, the visual interface for mobile devices has been greatly simplified. There's no easy way to modify the look and feel of these OOTB mobile page views since no master page or CSS is referenced. Inline style properties were used to create the layout and design of these mobile pages.

## Printing Styles

You need to test how your branding affects the print quality of your site. The CSS print styles have stripped out all of the unnecessary elements of the page, as shown in Figure 7-22. This includes the Ribbon, social tags, top navigation, search, and Quick Launch.

**Figure 7-22.** *SharePoint 2010 print preview*

The elements that are hidden by default and any other elements like footers can easily be hidden from printing views by using the `@media print` class. The OOTB print styles are shown in Listing 7-2. Note that the classes in the first `@media print` all have the property **display: none** when the page is being printed. Use the second set of `@media print` classes to format and position the elements for the best printing experience.

**Listing 7-2.** *Standard CSS Print Styles*

```css
@media print{
        .ms-globallinks,.ms-siteaction,.ms-areaseparatorcorner,.ms-titlearealeft,
        .ms-searchform,.ms-banner,.ms-buttonheightwidth,
        .ms-areaseparatorright,.ms-titlearearight,.ms-rightareacell,.ms-leftareacell,
        .ms-areaseparatorleft{
        display:none;
        }
}

@media print{
        body #s4-ribbonrow{
        display:none;
        }
        body #s4-titlerow{
        display:block !important;
        }
        body #s4-workspace{
        overflow:visible !important;
        width:auto !important;
```

```
height:auto !important;
}
body.v4master{
overflow:visible !important;
}
body #s4-topheader2{
display:none;
}
body #s4-leftpanel{
display:none;
}
.s4-ca{
margin-left:0px !important;
margin-right:0px !important;
}
.s4-clust{
display:none !important;
}
}
```

If you removed all of the print styles, the print preview would look similar to Figure 7-23. You will notice that the left navigation pushes the image on the right almost off the printable page.

***Figure 7-23.*** *SharePoint 2010 print preview with all elements visible*

Verify and test that your branding displays correctly when printed, by using the `@media print` class within your custom style sheet.

## Summary

This chapter provided examples and procedures on how to test your visual design build. By unit testing the standard site templates, you can ensure that all standard and custom features with the SharePoint 2010 site display and function as intended. The next chapter focuses on some of the top tips and tricks for branding SharePoint.

# CHAPTER 8

# Tips and Tricks

What's In This Chapter?

- Creating a Sub-Brand
- Photoshop Tips
- Creating a Center Fixed-Width Design
- Customizing Dialog Windows
- Changing Logo Globally With Just CSS
- Hiding Quick Launch (Left Navigation)
- Displaying Small Social Tag and Notes Icons
- Working with Web Part Zones
- SharePoint 2010 Themes
- Basics of CSS3

This chapter introduces a few tips and tricks that you can use as you design and build out your SharePoint 2010 visual design. Some of these tips help you define the visual look and feel of a site while others are more specific to building a site. For more tips and tricks on SharePoint branding and customization, you can check out the following sites:

- **http://erikswenson.blogspot.com**: My blog focuses on SharePoint branding, design, and customization. You'll find many blog posts that provide solutions to some of the most common branding issues that you might encounter.

- **http://blog.drisgill.com**: Randy's blog has some handy tips on creating a minimal starter master page and a few other tips and tricks on mobile views.

- **http://www.thesharepointmuse.com**: Marcy Kellar's blog site has some great topics on SharePoint branding strategy and theory.

- **http://www.sharepoint911.com/blogs/john:** John's blog is more focused on the developer side but provides a lot of great resources and tips for SharePoint 2010 customization.

This chapter also gives you the basics on SharePoint web-part zones, themes, and extending the OOTB breadcrumbs. The first topic is specific to the design process, where there could be requirements that indicate a need for divisional or departmental sites having their own brand look and feel.

# Creating a Sub-Brand

As you go through the process of gathering the design requirements, you might come across some requirements for sub-sites or site collections that require their own branding. The definition of sub-branding is the process of creating an alternate or child brand identity. These brands could be used to indicate a separation of functionality, content ownership, or other criteria. You still want to keep the core branding elements like the header, corporate logo, and footer. The benefit to users is that they will be able to clearly identify that they are in a separate section of the site. I am not recommending that all sites have sub-branding, but it is a great way to extend the visual brand to create a separation based on different site types. For example, in Figure 8-1 the parent brand is the "eXtreme" corporation. This includes a corporate blue color scheme. The sub-branding for the divisional project site called "Fusion" includes a custom logo, color palette, and customized web-part title bars.

The following sections provide some examples of these types.

***Figure 8-1.*** *Example of sub-branding*

# Sub-Branding Types

The following sub-branding types describe why someone would want to have a child brand within a SharePoint 2010 site.

- **Departmental/Divisional**: Some departmental sites need to be more than just a title. They might include their own logo, imagery, or color scheme. Some corporate divisions, like HR, prefer to make their sites more about the people and tie their brand identity to the type of content that they are providing to their users. The IT department might want to more of a cutting-edge or retro style to the site to express innovation and knowledge.

- **Functional**: Adding Sub-branding to sites that provide unique functionality can help your users navigate and identify what type of site they are on just based on the branding. For example if you were to apply the same look and feel for community sites, blogs, My Sites, and other social areas your users would understand that these sites all have a similar function and are tied to each other. There are other portal areas like news and department sites that could have their own unique branding to indicate more static and corporate information.

- **Navigation/Hierarchy**: Another way that you can effectively create sub-branding is by applying different brand styles to specific sections within your site hierarchy. For example, collaboration sites could have a slightly different color scheme than department sites or my sites. Each main navigational section within your global navigation could include a different color scheme.

- **Template**: Using templates to define sub-branding can be an effective way of connecting similar sites and functionality for your users. An example of this would be project sites that would all share the same site template and functionality. The benefit to this approach is that your end users will be able to identify what type of site it is by the unique branding theme applied.

- **Language**: Creating a separate theme based on the language pack installed for each site collection is another way to include sub-branding. For example all English sites could have a blue theme, while all Spanish sites could have a green theme applied.

There are also a variety of different levels of sub-branding that you can implement to get the visual separation that is required.

# Sub-Branding Levels

As you define the different types of sub-branding, you also need to identify how much the branding will be different. It might be important in your portal to have all of your sites carry the exact color scheme and branding across all sites and in that case you would not create a separate design but you could use the content within those sites as ways to make them stand out. I would not recommend that site owners deviate from the global visual design just to make their site stand out. The following list describes some of the ways that you can create sub-branding within your site.

- **None**: In general, most SharePoint sites will not include any sub-branding. This could be because of the level of support needed and the time it takes to establish an effective secondary brand.

- **Icons/Imagery**: You can connect sites together with icons, images, and other types of visual indicators.

- **Themes/Colors**: Using color schemes are effective, but you need to consider accessibility. You should not rely only on color for navigation. Some of your users might be color-blind and therefore are unable to identify the difference between color types.

- **Custom**: This type of sub-branding could include custom master pages, images, background colors, and even layouts.

It is important to work with your business stakeholders to clearly identify what the ultimate need for the sub-branding is and what levels you will support. There are also a few tips within Adobe Photoshop that may help you save time during the creation of your visual design.

# Photoshop Tips

Adobe Photoshop is a very useful tool for creating the visual design composition, as described in Chapter 4. However, it is very complex and takes some time to get used to. In this section you learn some quick techniques for speeding up the creation of the visual design.

## Layer Mask

You use a layer mask if you need to blend an image with the background or section off an area to not be affected by an effect or color change. To blend an image into the background you click on the layer that you want blended. Then you make a selection around the area where you want your image appear. In this example, we want to add a large image to the header section within the design, as shown in Figure 8-2.

**Figure 8-2.** *Header area selected where image should be shown*

Once the area is selected you click on the layer mask icon shown in Figure 8-3.

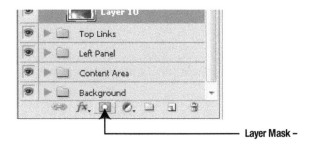

**Figure 8-3.** *Layer mask icon*

Once the icon is clicked it automatically crops out the entire image except for the elements inside of the selected area. The great thing about using masks is that you are not modifying the image at all. In fact, you can actually resize, move, and adjust the image by just clicking on the link icon in between the mask and the layer thumbnail, as shown in Figure 8-4.

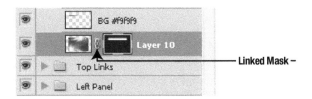

**Figure 8-4.** *Linked layer mask icon*

The mask itself uses the black areas to hide the image and the white areas to show the image. You can modify the mask by transforming or even painting it with black or white to hide specific areas that are not needed. You can also use the gradient tool to create a fading effect from black to white, as shown in Figure 8-5, where the image on the right is full opacity and then fades to nothing on the left.

**Figure 8-5.** *Using the gradient tool within a layer mask*

Another useful tip when working with Photoshop is to use layer styles to create unique effects.

# Layer Styles

Layer styles are used to stylize the selected layer with shadows, borders, and other effects. These types of styles can come in handy when you want to stylize multiple layers with the same effect such as a drop shadow. To create a drop shadow on a layer, simply click on the layer that you want to style, and then click on the layer style icon, as shown in Figure 8-6.

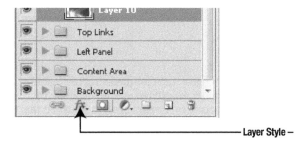

**Figure 8-6.** *Layer style icon*

Once you click on the icon it will present you with the following layer styles. See Figure 8-7 for an example of what some of these could look like applied to a simple gray box.

- **Blending Options**: The blending options allow you to configure and customize the blending features of the selected layer. As you choose different options it will change how the layer below it will look.

- **Drop Shadow**: The drop shadow style will allow you to configure the drop shadows color, opacity, angle, distance, spread, and size.

- **Inner Shadow**: You have the same amount of options as the drop shadow but the shadow is directed within the objects inner boundaries.

- **Outer Glow**: The outer glow is similar to a drop shadow but it does not allow you to have the glow displaced on an angle. The glow is displayed equally on all sides.

- **Inner Glow**: Same as outer glow but the direction of the glow is towards the center of the object.

- **Bevel and Emboss**: You can customize an object to look like it has some depth.

- **Satin**: The satin is not used very often but allows you to overlay a grid like pattern on top of the layer.

- **Color Overlay**: This allows you to place a color over the selected area of a layer. You can set the transparencies and the specific color to be used.

- **Gradient Overlay**: This helpful style allows you to add a gradient on top of the selected area within a layer.

- **Pattern Overlay**: This style is used for when you want to apply a patter on top of an existing image layer. You could use patterns that come with Photoshop or create your own.

- **Stroke**: The stroke style allows you to add a border around the layer. You can choose the stroke size, position, opacity, color, width, and style. You can even create strokes that have a gradient fill.

**Figure 8-7.** *Photoshop layer styles*

As you start working with stylizing the layers using filters and effects, you might also want to set the layers opacity or fill. In the next section you will learn the difference between them.

## Opacity vs. Fill

Some design effects require that a layer be somewhat transparent. There are two layer options that you can use. The first option is to use Opacity, and the second option is to use Fill (both shown in Figure 8-8). They are very similar but based on the type of layer selected they can provide a variety of different effects.

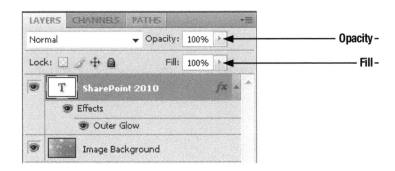

**Figure 8-8.** *Opacity and fill layer options*

For example, if you wanted to make a layer 50% transparent, all you would have to do is click on the layer and change the opacity to 50%. Opacity basically takes the whole layer and all of the layer styles and makes it transparent to the layer below it. However, fill does not change the transparencies of the layer styles. For example, in Figure 8-9 the text is black with a white outer glow layer style applied. There is also an image in the background one layer down.

**Figure 8-9.** *Text over image with 100% opacity and fill*

If you were to change the opacity of the text layer to 30%, it would look something like what is shown in Figure 8-10. As you can tell, the text looks washed out and does not give you the result that you want.

**Figure 8-10.** *Text over image with 30% opacity and 100% fill*

Instead of using opacity to change the transparency, if you set the fill to 0%, the layer style will still be visible at 100%, and you get a nice ghosting effect on the text layer, as shown in Figure 8-11. The great thing is that this text layer did not have to be flattened and is still editable.

**Figure 8-11.** *Text over image with 100% opacity and 0% fill*

The next Photoshop tip is a simple way of using hue and saturation to colorize elements within your design.

# Hue and Saturation

The hue and saturation image adjustment settings allow you to colorize or change the hue, saturation and brightness of a layer by using the shortcut CTRL + U or by clicking on Image ➤ Adjustments ➤ Hue and Saturation. This brings up a dialog window, as shown in Figure 8-12.

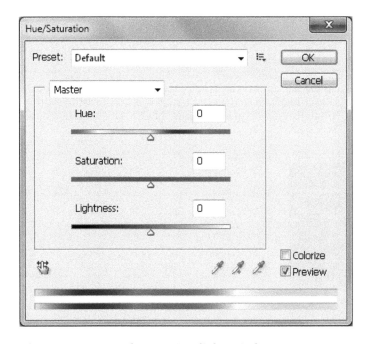

**Figure 8-12.** *Hue and Saturation dialog window*

This window allows you to configure the following settings for a single layer. If used properly you can effectively change the look of layers to help match the overall color palette and theme of the design.

- **Hue**: Use this slider to change the color of the selected layer by sliding the arrow back and forth through the color spectrum.

- **Saturation**: This slider allows you to increase the amount of selected color to the layer. If you move the slider all the way to the right, no color will be included, and it will be grayscale.

- **Lightness**: With this slider, you can slide the arrow to the right to make the image brighter and moved it to the left to make it darker. You can control the brightness and contrast better by clicking on Image ➤ Adjustments ➤ Brightness and Contrast.

- **Colorize**: If you click on the colorize option checkbox it will take the foreground color and adjust the hue and saturation to match it. This can be very useful if you want to change the look of a background image to a mono-type color that will match your color palette.

- **Preview**: If unchecked, this box allows you to see what the original layer looks like before the hue and saturation updates are applied. Checking the box displays a preview of the changes.

The next Photoshop design tip comes from a design trend that is still popular. This trend is to apply rounded corners to elements to give them a soft and attractive look and feel.

## Rounded Corners

The following sections describe the different techniques you can use to create rounded corners in Photoshop. For all of these techniques the end result is shown in Figure 8-13. Some of the challenges with this example are the checkered pattern in the background and the 2px wide border. Both of these add to the complexity of the design build. As described later in this chapter, browsers compatible with CSS3 can get rounded corners on elements with borders with just a few lines of CSS. This section focuses on how to create them in Photoshop.

***Figure 8-13.*** *Example of Photoshop rounded corner*

# Elliptical Marquee Tool

Let's assume that you are starting out with a corner that is squared off, as in Figure 8-14. You would like to add a corner radius of about 12 pixels.

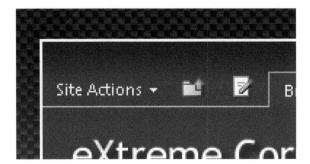

**Figure 8-14.** *Example of Photoshop squared-off corner*

The first step is to select the elliptical marquee tool by typing "M" or choosing the marquee tool from the Tools panel. Once you have selected it, move your mouse to the top-left side of the square corner. Click and then press the Shift key to make a selection that is perfectly round. Use your info bar to get the selection to 25 pixels, double the size of the radius that you want. Create a new layer and fill it with white. Use the arrows on your keyboard and move the selection down 2px and to the right 2px. Then press the Delete key, and it will remove part of the white circle. Hide the layer with the 2px solid border, and then select the outer edges of the circle to remove the excess, as shown in Figure 8-15.

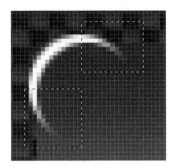

**Figure 8-15.** *Selected areas to remove excess white*

Next you should use the rectangular marquee tool and draw a box around the remainder of the circle shown in Figure 8-16. Unhide the 2px border layer and delete the corner area with the selection that you just made.

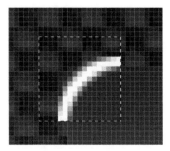

***Figure 8-16.*** *Selected area to remove 2px line*

The final result should look like the model example shown earlier in Figure 8-13. The next technique shows how to create rounded corners in Photoshop by using the rounded rectangle tool.

## Rounded Rectangle Tool

Another technique is to use the rounded rectangle tool. To get the rectangle tool, type "U" on your keyboard within Photoshop, or choose it from the Tools panel, as shown in Figure 8-17.

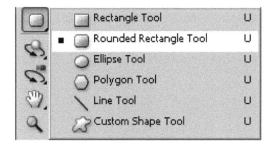

***Figure 8-17.*** *Rounded rectangle tool*

Once you have the tool selected in the top options window, change the radius to 12px. Change your foreground color to the color that you want the background of the box to be. You can then draw the box to the size that you want it. To add a border, click on the newly created button later and add a stroke layer style. Choose the stroke size of 2px and color of white, as shown in Figure 8-18.

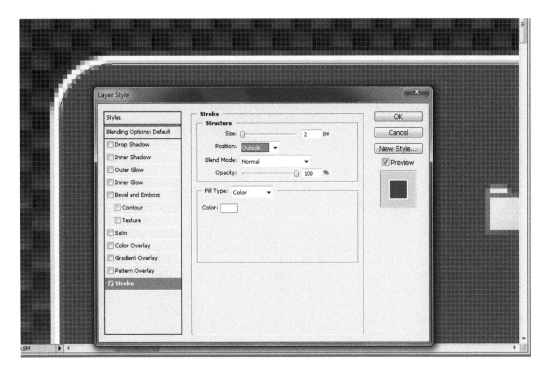

**Figure 8-18.** *Stroke layer style options*

These are just a couple of ways that you can create rounded corners in Photoshop. The next few tips focus on the build aspect of the visual design, which includes CSS, web-part zones, themes, and CSS3 properties.

# Creating a Center Fixed-width Design

Another design trend that is holding strong is converting the standard SharePoint 2010 design from a fluid or liquid design to a fixed width. The default fluid design allows the content to expand and contract with the browser window as it gets larger or smaller. A fixed-width design applies a specific width to the outer container of the content area. This keeps the content at a consistent size no matter what size the browser is. The fixed width can then be centered on the page, which gives equal distance on the left and right side of the fixed area. This frames the content area and provides more focus on it. See Figure 8-19 for the difference between fluid and fixed width.

***Figure 8-19.*** *Fluid and fixed-width designs*

To get the content area fixed you want to add the CSS in Listing 8-1 to your custom style sheet. The s4-bodycontainer ID is the first child DIV within the s4-workspace ID. The s4-workspace is unique as it is tied to JavaScript that detects the browser width and height and sets its width and height accordingly. By adding CSS to set the width to the body container as shown in Listing 8-1, it will reduce the size of the header and the body area width as shown in Figure 8-20.

***Listing 8-1.*** *CSS to Center Content Area*

```
#s4-bodyContainer{
width: 960px !important;
margin: 0px auto;
}
```

Adding the width to the body container reduces the size of both the header and the body area, as shown in Figure 8-20.

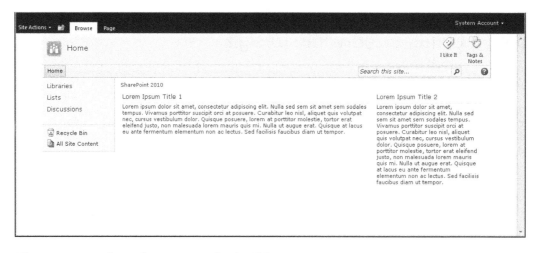

***Figure 8-20.*** *Header and content area fixed width*

To make the top Ribbon a fixed width, and to frame in the body area a little, use the CSS in Listing 8-2 within your custom CSS.

*Listing 8-2.* *Starter CSS and a More Stylized Centered Fixed-Width Design*

```
/* Ribbon 980 pixels centered */
.ms-cui-ribbonTopBars{
width: 960px !important;
margin: 0px auto;
}

/* Removes bottom Line in ribbon */
.ms-cui-ribbonTopBars > div{
border:none !important;
}

/* Fixes width issue and hides borders */
#s4-titlerow{
width: auto !important;
border: none !important;
}

/* Adds background color behind fixed content area */
#s4-workspace{
background-color: #EEE;
}

/* Header and Content area 960px centered */
#s4-bodyContainer{
width: 960px !important;
margin: 0px auto;
height: 100%;
background-color: #FFF;
border-left: 1px #BBB solid;
border-right: 1px #BBB solid;
}
```

The result of this starter center fixed CSS is shown in Figure 8-21. You can then modify the CSS to add background images, borders, and other CSS properties to further stylize the look and feel.

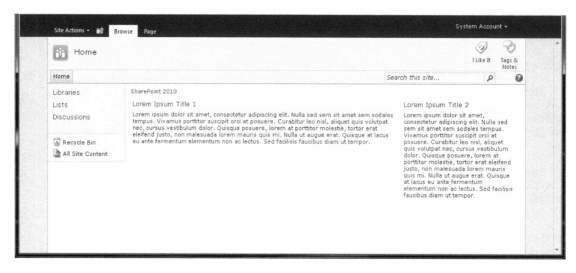

**Figure 8-21.** *Starter centered fixed-width design*

The next tip is for customizing SharePoint 2010 dialog windows. These are new to SharePoint 2010 and provide users and content authors a cleaner and more professional page for adding and viewing list items.

# Customizing Dialog Windows

There are a variety of different dialog widows within SharePoint 2010 that you can customize with just some CSS. The New Item dialog window is the most basic and common that you will see within SharePoint 2010. To display this dialog window, simply create a new custom list, and click on the "Add new item" link. All dialog windows will display centered on the page and will gray out the background, as shown in Figure 8-22.

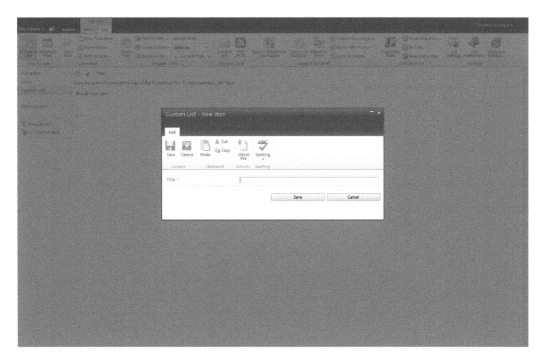

**Figure 8-22.** *Basic New Item dialog window*

There are a variety of different things that you can customize within these windows using just CSS. The first customizable element is the background color behind the dialog window.

## Dialog Window Background Color

The default CSS class for this is `.ms-dlgOverlay`. It has an absolute position at the top-left and has a width and height of 100%. It uses CSS transparencies to make the background color 70% transparent. There is also a background color of #182738, which is a dark blue. See Listing 8-3 for the default CSS properties.

**Listing 8-3.** *Dialog Window Transparent Background*

```
.ms-dlgOverlay{
position:absolute;
top:0px;
left:0px;
width:100%;
height:100%;
filter:alpha(opacity=70);
-ms-filter:"alpha(opacity=70)";
opacity:0.7;
background-color:#182738;
```

```
display:none;
}
```

You can add this base CSS to your custom style sheet and change the properties, such as the amount of transparency or background color, to get the look and feel that matches your brand. For example, Listing 8-4 I shows a dialog background color of a dark green with a more transparent background to allow more of the background to show through.

**Listing 8-4.** *Custom Dialog Window Background Color*

```
.ms-dlgOverlay{
filter:alpha(opacity=60);
-ms-filter:"alpha(opacity=60)";
opacity:0.6;
background-color:#030;
}
```

■ **Note**   You do not have to specify all of the properties of the original CSS properties. You just need to add the ones that you want to override.

The dialog window is structured in a unique way. It contains a base container element and an IFRAME to represent the content. This next section describes how these work together.

## Dialog Window Structure

All SharePoint dialog windows are constructed the same. They have a base container that includes a variety of DIVs that make up the dialog window's shell, title, and close buttons. The other component to the dialog window is the IFRAME, which contains the dialog content. See Figure 8-23 for more details on the modal window structure and some of the main classes that you could target.

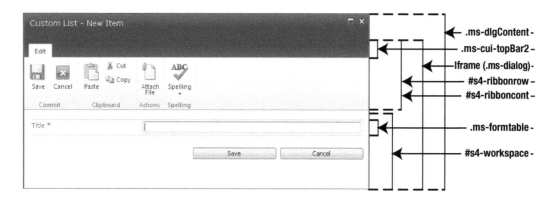

**Figure 8-23.** *Dialog window structure and base classes*

# Dialog Window Container

The default CSS class for this container is `.ms-dlgContent`. This is the outer shell that includes some basic borders. The sub-class within the container is the `.ms-dlgBorder` class. This class also has borders specified within the corev4.css file. The next element that you can customize is the dialog title class made up of two classes: `.ms-dlgTitle` and `.ms-dlgTitleText`. The `ms-dlgtitle` class has a background image and color that you can modify or change to be more specific to your brand. Listing 8-5 shows an example of some CSS that you can use to change the look of the dialog window container and title.

*Listing 8-5.* *Custom CSS for Dialog Container and Title*

```
.ms-dlgContent{
border: none;
border-top: 8px #030 solid;
}
.ms-dlgBorder{
border: none;
}
.ms-dlgTitle{
background-image: none;
background-color: transparent;
height: 45px;
}
.ms-dlgTitleText{
margin-top: 5px;
margin-left: 7px;
font-family: Arial, sans-serif;
font-size: 16pt;
color: #444;
font-weight: bold;
text-transform:uppercase;
letter-spacing: -.8pt;
}
.ms-dlgTitle{
background-image: none;
background-color: transparent;
height: 40px;
}
```

The custom CSS from Listing 8-5 produces a simplified design for your modal window, as shown in Figure 8-24, that removes all borders around the dialog window except for an 8px border on top and title text that is clean, bold, and easy to read.

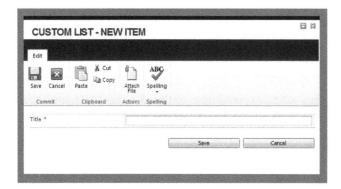

**Figure 8-24.** *Custom dialog container and title look and feel*

However, the dialog window looks a bit weird with the Ribbon background color and image. In this next section you learn how to target specific elements just within dialog windows.

## Changing Ribbon background just for dialog windows

One of the greatest things about the dialog windows having their own unique container class is that you can target elements within that container by using the **.ms-dialog** class specified within the HTML of the IFRAME. In this example, we want to keep the OOTB standard Ribbon look and feel but have it look different for dialog windows. All you have to do is specify the **.ms-dialog** class first, and then include the element ID or class name after it. The CSS properties within Listing 8-6 remove the background image and color from the Ribbon toolbar within the dialog window.

**Listing 8-6.** *Removing the Ribbon Background Color and Image for Dialog Windows*

```
.ms-dialog  #s4-ribbonrow{
background-color: #FFF;
}
.ms-dialog .s4-ribboncont{
background-image: none;
}
```

The combined CSS changes shown in Listing 8-7 give you a decent base to work from. This starter CSS allows you to customize and provide branding for your dialog windows that matches the overall look and feel of your branded site.

**Listing 8-7.** *Combined CSS Properties for a Custom-Looking Dialog Window*

```
.ms-dlgOverlay{
filter:alpha(opacity=50);
-ms-filter:"alpha(opacity=50)";
opacity:0.5;
background-color:#030;
}
.ms-dlgContent{
```

```
border: none;
border-top: 8px #030 solid;
}
.ms-dlgBorder{
border: none;
}
.ms-dlgTitle{
background-image: none;
background-color: transparent;
height: 45px;
}
.ms-dlgTitleText{
margin-top: 5px;
margin-left: 7px;
font-family: Arial, sans-serif;
font-size: 16pt;
color: #444;
font-weight: bold;
text-transform:uppercase;
letter-spacing: -.8pt;
}
.ms-dlgTitle{
background-image: none;
background-color: transparent;
height: 40px;
}
.ms-dialog  #s4-ribbonrow{
background-color: #FFF;
}
.ms-dialog .s4-ribboncont{
background-image: none;
}
```

The CSS supplied from Listing 8-7 and added to your custom style sheet should display like Figure 8-25.

**Figure 8-25.** *Custom dialog window look and feel*

If you have modified your master page to include additional elements such as header links or a custom footer, this next section will give you a way to remove them from the dialog windows.

## Removing custom master page code from dialog windows

If you have ever added custom elements to your master page above or below the standard DIV tags, you will notice that they start appearing in the SharePoint 2010 dialog windows when you don't want them to. The simple fix is to add the **s4-notdlg** class to your custom element to hide it from showing in the dialog windows. For example, if you were to place a DIV tag at the bottom of the page for a footer, and did not include the **s4-notdlg** class name, it would look something like what is shown in Figure 8-26. The footer element is displaying on the bottom of the dialog window.

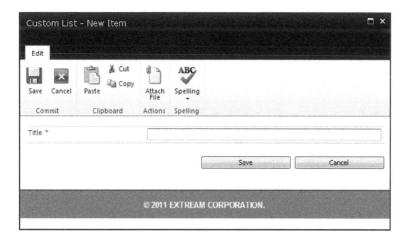

***Figure 8-26.** Dialog window with custom footer showing*

To remove this element from just the dialog windows, you need to add in the **s4-notdlg** class, as shown in Listing 8-8. Now when a new dialog window is opened, it no longer has the footer element included, as shown in the original dialog window in Figure 8-25.

***Listing 8-8.** HTML with **s4-notdlg** Class Added*

```
<div id="clientname-footer" class="s4-notdlg">
       © 2011 eXtream Corporation.
</div>
```

This next section describes a method for easily replacing your site's logo, using only CSS.

# Changing the Logo Globally Using Only CSS

In most cases, your site's logo is the corporate logo and should always be visible for every site and page. The manual way of changing it is to click on Site Actions ➤ Site Settings ➤ Title and description ➤ Type in URL path to the logo ➤ Click on Ok. You could create some script to do this through code but why waste all of that time when you can just do it with CSS. The first step is to create your logo and optimize it for the web. It should be saved as a GIF, JPG, or PNG file. Once you have created the image, depending on your implementation method, upload the file to where all users have read access. Then simply update the following CSS in Listing 8-9 with your own path and logo name. You also need to change the height and width to match the image dimensions of your logo.

***Listing 8-9.*** *CSS to Change the Site Logo*

```
.s4-titlelogo{
background-image: url(/_layouts/images/centraladmin_security_48x48.png);
background-position:left center;
background-repeat: no-repeat;
}
.s4-titlelogo > a > img{
visibility: hidden;
width: 48px;
height: 48px;
}
```

If you used the example CSS in Listing 8-8 as is you will see that the site logo has changed from the standard SharePoint logo icon to what is shown in Figure 8-27.

***Figure 8-27.*** *Site logo modifed using only CSS*

The next tip is used quite frequently to hide the left-side navigation and provide a full space for the content to expand into.

# Hiding Quick Launch (Left Navigation)

The Quick Launch side navigation is contained within a DIV tag that is set to float to the left side of the content area. To hide the Quick Launch, you just need a few lines of custom CSS, as shown in Listing 8-10.

**Listing 8-10.** *CSS to Hide Quick Launch*

```
#s4-leftpanel{
display: none;
}
.s4-ca{
margin-left: 0px;
}
```

The first CSS property sets the Quick Launch or left panel to not display. But if you used that as your only CSS there would be a large blank spot where the Quick Launch was. This is because the `s4-ca` class has a margin set to the left of 155px. If you change the margin to "0px", it will take up the whole content area, as shown in Figure 8-28.

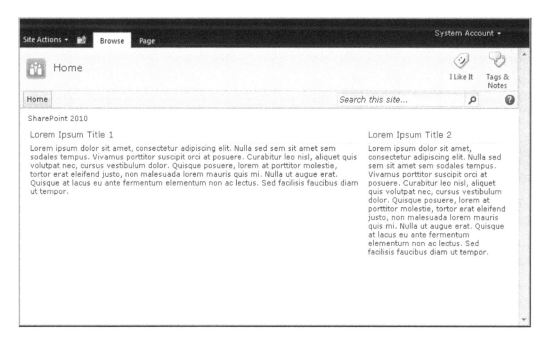

**Figure 8-28.** *Blank site with Quick Launch hidden*

You can use another quick tip to reduce the size of the social tags. This requires some modifications to the master page.

# Displaying Small Social Tag and Notes Icons

The default sizes of the social tags and notes icons are quite big, as shown earlier in Figure 8-26. One way to reduce the size of the icons without losing any functionality is to make a very small change to the SharePoint Delegate Control within your custom master page. With your master page open, search for "GlobalSiteLink3". Once you have found this control ID, add "-mini" to the end of that ID so that it now displays as "GlobalSiteLink3-mini". Save your custom master page, and check it in to see the difference. It should now display similar to Figure 8-29.

***Figure 8-29.*** *Small social tags and notes icons*

As you can see in Figure 8-28, the icons are stacked on top of each other. This orientation might work well for some designs, but for others you might want to conserve vertical space and have the icons be displayed horizontally. To fix this, you just need to add a width to the class that contains the icons. See Listing 8-11 for the CSS to make them horizontal and aligned to the top.

***Listing 8-11.*** *CSS to Make Small Social Icons Horizontal and Aligned to the Top*

```
.s4-socialdata-notif{
vertical-align: top;
}
.ms-mini-socialNotif-Container{
width: 50px;
}
```

Figure 8-30 shows what it would look like when they are positioned horizontally.

***Figure 8-30.*** *Small social tags set to horizontal orientation and aligned to the top*

One of the core elements that make up a SharePoint page layout is web-part zones. The following tips help you create your own zones and layouts.

# Working with Web-part Zones

Web-part zones allow content authors to add and arrange web parts on the page within the browser. Each web-part zone can include multiple web parts. By default, SharePoint blank templates and Team Site templates come with only two zones: a left and a right, as shown in Figure 8-31.

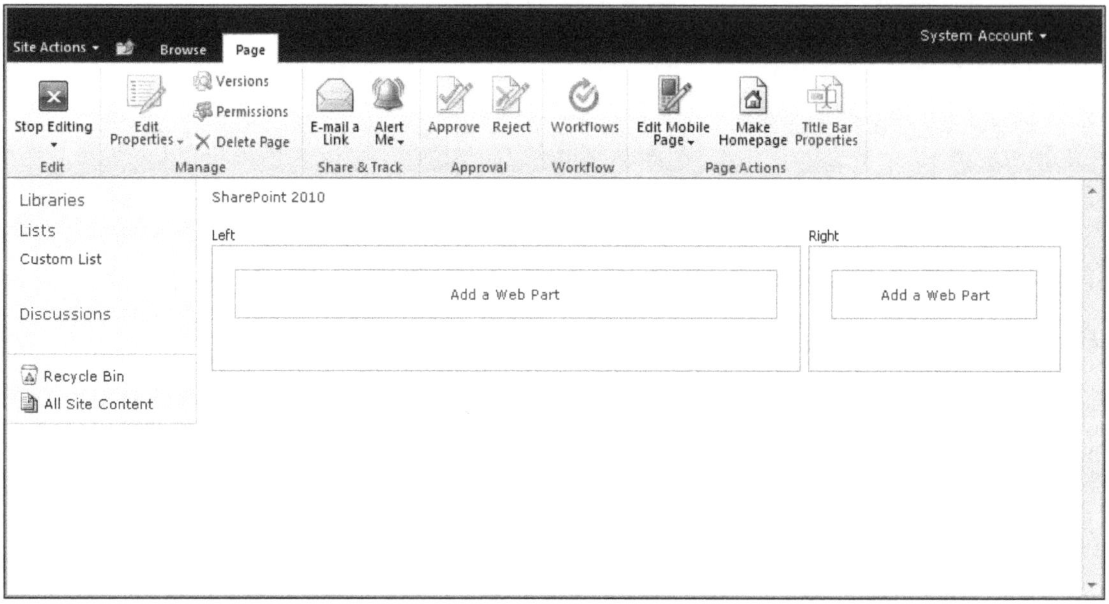

**Figure 8-31.** *Blank site web-part zones*

If you need a different type of layout, you have the following options described in this section. It is not recommended that you modify the default.aspx file directly as this is not supported by Microsoft. However, you could create a new web-part page by clicking on Site Actions ➤ More Options, and then clicking on Page in the left toolbar area. Choose the web-part page icon, and then click on Create. You then just need to add a title, choose an appropriate layout that best fits your needs, and choose a destination library for your page.

If you need additional web-part zones or a different layout, you can open SharePoint Designer 2010, click on "All Files," and navigate to the library that you saved your web-part page into. Right-click on the page, and choose to edit it in advanced mode. This opens up your page so that you can add or change the web-part layout. The one drawback to web-part pages is that they do not include the left-side navigation control. The other option is to enable publishing within your site and create a new page layout, as described in Chapter 6. To create your own web-part zone, you just need to include in your page the following basic elements, as shown in Listing 8-12.

**Listing 8-12.** *Structure of a Web-part Zone*

```
<td id="_invisibleIfEmpty" class="tlzone" name="_invisibleIfEmpty" valign="top" height="100%">
<WebPartPages:WebPartZone runat="server" Title="Top Left" ID="tlzone" Orientation="Vertical">
        <ZoneTemplate></ZoneTemplate>
</WebPartPages:WebPartZone>
</td>
```

The containing TD has a unique ID that is tied to some JavaScript within the page. The JavaScript is written so that if there is nothing within the web-part zone, it will not display on the page. You can also add in your own custom class to this TD to stylize the web parts in that zone differently. The web-part zone itself has the following properties.

- **Title:** This zone property allows you create a unique label that will be displayed above the web-part zone area.

- **ID:** This property requires you to have its own unique ID. The zone ID also cannot include spaces.

- **Orientation:** This property allows you to set the zone to display web parts stacked vertically or horizontally. To have them stacked vertically, use the "Vertical" value. To set them to display side by side, use the "Horizontal" value.

Once you have finished adding the web-part zones, save the page layout or web-part page. Then create a new page and apply the page layout or edit the web-part page. You should now see all of the zones that you have created. Click on the "Add a web part" button to start adding web parts to your page.

The next section will focus on tips around creating SharePoint 2010 themes.

# SharePoint 2010 Themes

Themes in SharePoint 2010 have been simplified so that they really only change background colors and font types within a site. If you are familiar with creating themes in PowerPoint, Word, and Visio creating a SharePoint theme is very similar. To create your own custom theme simply click on Site Actions ➤ Site Settings, and then click on "**Site Theme**" within the look and feel section. This brings you to a new page, as shown in Figure 8-32.

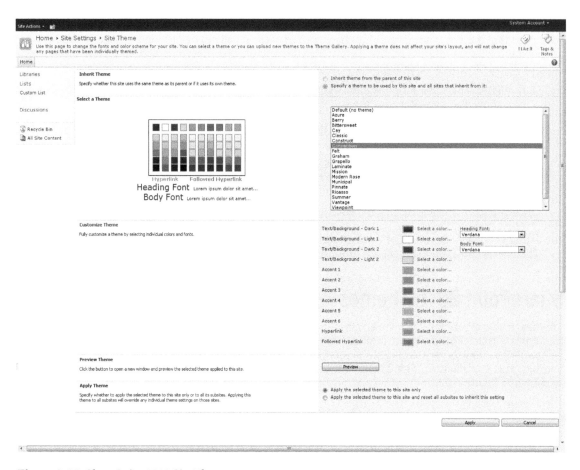

**Figure 8-32.** *SharePoint 2010 Site Theme creator page*

On this page you can choose from a variety of predefined themes. Once you have chosen a theme, you can click on the "Preview" button to see what it would look like, without actually applying it to the site. You also have the option to reset all sub-sites to have the selected theme. If you want to create your own theme manually, you can simply start from an existing theme or click on Default (no theme), to start from scratch. To start creating your own theme, you just have to click on the color boxes next to the label "Select a Color". This will bring up a dialog window, as shown in Figure 8-33.

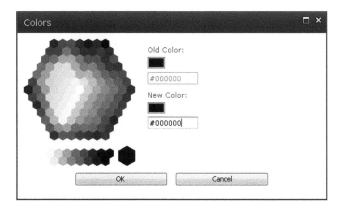

*Figure 8-33. SharePoint 2010 Theme dialog window color picker*

You can type in a hex color or use the color picker on the left to choose your color. When you click on the "OK" button the list selector changes from "Default (no theme)" to "Custom". Each time you choose a color you can preview what it will look with the new color choice. You can also change the font family used for heading fonts and body fonts by using the drop-downs on the right. Once you are happy with the look of your theme, simply just click Apply. The site theme will be applied and bring you back to the Site Settings page.

---

■ **Note** There is no way to save your manually created theme if it was created through the SharePoint interface.

---

If you go back to the Site Theme page, your custom applied theme will display as "Current theme (Custom)". However, once you choose a different theme, your custom theme will be lost. To create your own custom theme you will need to have an office 2010 product like PowerPoint or word. If you have Word 2010 open up a new document and click on the "Page Layout" tab within the top ribbon. Then click on the colors drop down located on the left side of the ribbon and choose "**Create new theme colors**". You will notice that the labels for these colors are the same as what you would see in the theme creator in SharePoint 2010. If you are using PowerPoint 2010, click on the Design Tab within the top Ribbon area, and then click on the colors drop-down. Choose the "create new theme colors" option, and you will get the same window as you would in Word 2010. Once you have chosen your colors, simply provide a name for your new theme, and click Save. Then choose the fonts drop-down and choose "Create new theme fonts". Choose your fonts, give them a name, and then click Save. The theme effects are not used within SharePoint 2010, so you do not need to define those. Once you have finished selecting your theme colors and fonts, click on the themes button within the Ribbon, and choose "**Save Current Theme**". Provide a unique name for your theme, and save it to your desktop. You can now import your saved THMX theme file into SharePoint 2010. Within your SharePoint site click on Site Actions ➤ Site Settings, and then click on Themes within the galleries section. In the Ribbon click on the documents tab, and then click on Upload Document. Browse to the location where you save the file, and then click on Open and Ok. This opens a new dialog box, where you can change the name of the theme and also provide a description for it. Next, click Save. Navigate back to the Site Settings page, and click on the Site theme link within the look and feel section. You should be able to see your custom theme within the list. Select your theme and then click on Apply.

Within the next section I will cover some basic tips when working with the new CSS3 properties.

# Basics of CSS3

SharePoint 2010 default master pages are configured to display in IE8 Standards document mode. As you can see from the list below, Internet Explorer 8 does not support CSS level 3 specifications. Below is a basic list of CSS levels and what web browser versions they support.

- **CSS3**:
    - Internet Explorer 9+
    - Firefox 3+
    - Safari 3+
    - Google Chrome
- **CSS2**:
    - Internet Explorer 8
    - Internet Explorer 7
        - CSS2 is not fully supported by IE7. There are some selectors that are not recognized. No max/min-width/height support. No CSS table display support.
    - Firefox 1 & 2
    - Safari 1 & 2
- **CSS1**:
    - Internet Explorer 6

To change the display mode within your master pages to IE9, do a search within your custom master page for "X-UA-Compatible". This is located at the top of the standard SharePoint master page. The default content value is "IE=8". Simply change the 8 to a 9; if your users are viewing the site with an Internet Explorer browser version 9 or greater, the SharePoint site will default to IE9 Standards document mode. This allows you to use the following CSS3 properties within IE9.

## Rounded Corners

The **border-radius** CSS3 property allows you to make rounded corners on elements. The rounded corners will also be created with elements that include background images. So say goodbye to those transparent GIF or PNG files, and say hello to border-radius. For the first example shown in Listing 8-13, the border radius of the ID #s4-topheader2 is being applied to the top navigation control. Both the background and the borders are being rounded.

*Listing 8-13. CSS3 Border-Radius Example*

```
#s4-bodyContainer{
width: 960px !important;
margin: 0px auto;
}
.ms-titlerowborder,
#s4-leftpanel-content{
border: none !important;
}
#s4-topheader2{
border-radius: 10px;
padding-left: 10px;
}
```

> **Note** Earlier versions of Firefox, Chrome, and Safari utilize different methods for rounded corners.
>
> -moz-border-radius: 10px; /* Firefox */
>
> -webkit-border-radius: 10px; /* Safari, Chrome */
>
> border-radius: 10px; /* CSS3 */

The look and feel of rounding the top navigation container is shown in Figure 8-34.

*Figure 8-34. Top navigation container with rounded corners*

## Drop Shadows

CSS3 also allows you to create drop shadows on elements using the **box-shadow** property. As shown in Listing 8-14, the box shadow has the following properties: the first 5px moves the shadow to the right, the second moves it down, and the third sets how large the spread of the shadow will be. You can also use negative values to position the shadow differently. The second RGBA value sets the red, green, and blue to "0," which is black. The "A" is for alpha, and that allows you to set the transparency level.

***Listing 8-14.*** *CSS3 Border-Radius Example*

```
#s4-bodyContainer{
width: 960px !important;
margin: 0px auto;
}
.ms-titlerowborder,
#s4-leftpanel-content{
border: none !important;
}
#s4-topheader2{
border-radius: 10px;
box-shadow: 5px 5px 5px rgba(0,0,0,.35);
padding-left: 10px;
}
.s4-ca, #s4-leftpanel-content{
background-color: transparent !important;
}
```

The result of what this will look like is shown in Figure 8-35. With the combination of rounded corners and drop shadow, the top navigation container is starting to look pretty stylish with just a few lines of CSS code. Doing this with images and standard CSS would require changes to the master page and a lot of CSS and image support.

***Figure 8-35.*** *Top navigation container with rounded corners and drop shadow*

## Object Transformations

The object transformation CSS3 "-ms-transform" property allows you to move, rotate, and scale elements within your site. The example used within Listing 8-15 is not something I would recommend for any top site navigation but gives you a good impression of what this CSS3 property can do. This could be used effectively on elements such as images or diagrams within your site. See Figure 8-36 for an example of what it would look like if applied to your top navigation.

***Listing 8-15.*** *CSS to Move, Rotate, and Increase the Size of the Top Navigation*

```
#s4-bodyContainer{
width: 960px !important;
margin: 0px auto;
}
.ms-titlerowborder,
```

```
#s4-leftpanel-content{
border: none !important;
}
#s4-topheader2{
border-radius: 10px;
box-shadow: 5px 5px 5px rgba(0,0,0,.35);
-ms-transform:translate(170px,30px) scale(2) rotate(-7deg);
padding-left: 10px;
z-index: 1;
width: 600px;
}
.s4-ca, #s4-leftpanel-content{
background-color: transparent !important;
}
```

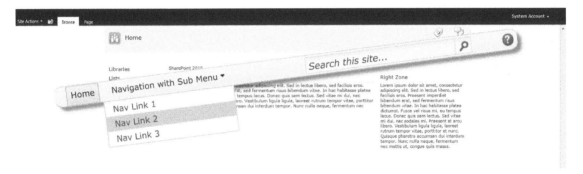

***Figure 8-36.*** *Top navigation container with rounded corners, drop shadow, and transformation*

What is interesting about the transformation is that the object is still fully functional. The drop-down still works and so does the search input box. Within this property, the translate property is what moves the element. Of course, the scale is what increases its size, and rotate, just as it sounds, allows you to rotate the element by degrees.

## Multiple background images

With CSS3 you can now have multiple background images for a single element. In this example I am going to have a background image that covers the whole workspace area. The second image is a repeating semi-transparent PNG file that will repeat across the top of the area. And the third image is the SharePoint Server 2010 logo that is positioned within the center of the page. It is important to note that the order in which you specify the images determines the layer they are displayed in. For example, the first background image is the SharePoint logo, which will be on top; the large background image is specified third, so that will be on the bottom. See Listing 8-16 for the CSS and Figure 8-37 for the preview.

*Listing 8-16. CSS to Display Multiple Background Images within a Single Class*

```
#s4-bodyContainer{
width: 960px !important;
margin: 0px auto;
}
#s4-workspace{
background: url(/_layouts/images/clientname/sharepoint2010.png) no-repeat center center,
url(/_layouts/images/clientname/contentbgrepeat.png) repeat-x top left,
url(/_layouts/images/clientname/contentbg.jpg) no-repeat top left,;
background-size: auto, auto, cover;
}
.s4-ca{
background-color: transparent;
}
.ms-WPBody{
background-color: rgba(255, 255, 255, .7);
padding: 10px;
}
```

*Figure 8-37. Workspace container with multiple background images*

These are just a few of the most popular CSS3 properties that you can start to use within your SharePoint branding site. However, support for CSS3 is still not that widespread, especially within large corporations that might run only IE7 and IE8. Make sure that you know who your users are and build your design for the majority of users.

# Summary

In this chapter you learned a few tips and tricks for defining and creating your visual designs. You also learned how to create rounded corners within Adobe Photoshop and how to create a fixed-width design using just a few CSS classes. This chapter also provided tips for quickly changing the look and feel of dialog windows and logos, and tips for hiding the left-side navigation. The last section of this chapter showed the process of creating a SharePoint theme through a browser and also with PowerPoint and Word 2010.

# CHAPTER 9

# Tools and Resources

This chapter includes a brief overview of a variety of tools and resources that will help support you with designing and building your custom SharePoint visual design.

## Microsoft SharePoint Designer 2010

SharePoint Designer is a free tool that you can use to help build and customize your SharePoint site. It can be used to create CSS, master pages, page layouts, and a variety of other file types. This version of SharePoint Designer requires you to have a connection to a SharePoint 2010 site to make any modifications to HTML, CSS, or other types of code. It will not work with SharePoint 2007, so if you are supporting multiple sites in both 2007 and 2010, you can install both versions on the same workstation. However, SharePoint Designer 2007 only comes in a 32-bit version, so if you choose to install both applications side by side, you must download the 32-bit version of SharePoint Designer 2010. You should also install the 2010 version after you have already installed SharePoint Designer 2007. I would recommend that you install the 32-bit version of Office, SharePoint Designer 2007, and 2010, just to be safe.

- **SharePoint Designer 2010 (32-bit):**
  http://www.microsoft.com/download/en/details.aspx?displaylang=en&id=16573

- **SharePoint Designer 2010 (64-bit):**
  http://www.microsoft.com/download/en/details.aspx?displaylang=en&id=24309

After you have installed SharePoint Designer 2010, open the application and connect it to your site.

# SharePoint Designer 2010 Basic Tour

With SharePoint Designer open, you see a starting screen similar to what is shown in Figure 9-1.

***Figure 9-1.*** *SharePoint Designer 2010 starting screen*

To open a site, click on the Open Site button; if you have already opened a site, you will see those sites in the Recent Sites list. Once you have successfully opened your site, you are presented with a newly designed page, as shown in Figure 9-2. The components within the figure are described in detail below.

**Figure 9-2.** *SharePoint Designer 2010 site details*

The page shown in Figure 9-2 gives you a lot of information about the site and its content. This version includes the Ribbon toolbar, left-side navigation, multiple tabs, the breadcrumb, and the active working content area.

- **Ribbon**: Consistent across all Office 2010 applications including SharePoint 2010, the Ribbon is a toolbar that includes helpful tools and actions that you can use based on the page or element that you have selected.

- **Navigation**: This panel provides you with all the major site objects that are specific to the site that you have opened. This is your primary way of viewing all of the sub-sites, lists, libraries, and workflows with the site. You can also click on the All Files link at the bottom of the left navigation to see a listing of all the lists and libraries. If you wish to see how the file structure is presented within SharePoint, you can right click on All Files and choose "Pin" from the drop down.

- **Tabs**: The tabs display the folder or file that you are actively working on. This allows you to work on multiple files at one time. You can rearrange and close these tabs as needed.

- **Forward/Back Arrows**: Initially inactive, the forward and back arrows will become active and useful once you start navigating through various lists and libraries. Similar to the buttons of a web browser, they are used to go forward and back through the navigation history as you move through SharePoint. These arrows are located to the left of the breadcrumb.

- **Breadcrumb:** A nice feature about this breadcrumb is that it not only tells you where you currently are and allows you to go back, but it also allows you to see what is available within this section by clicking on the arrow to the right of the breadcrumb title.

- **Content Area:** This panel on the summary screen provides you with some very helpful information about your site and its configurations. This panel is used in multiple ways to display lists, item detail, site preview, and code.

SharePoint Designer 2010 also provides great contextual menus. For example, if you click on a document row, the Ribbon displays specific actions for the item that you selected, as shown in Figure 9-3. With the item selected, the Ribbon allows you to perform some of the following actions: cut, copy, paste, edit, delete, rename, and check out. The drop-down menu has pretty much the same actions but also includes the ability to edit the document in Advanced Mode.

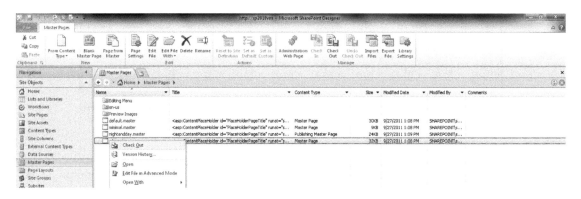

***Figure 9-3.*** *SharePoint Designer 2010 contextual menus and the Ribbon*

Once you have a document open, you see additional panels, indicators, and tools that will help you with your customization. For example, if you have opened a master page, you are able to switch between the following views, as shown in Figure 9-4. All of the panels can be resized to your own personal preference.

- **Design:** This view allows you to edit the site in what is called the WYSIWYG (What You See Is What You Get) editor. This view is not intended for very detailed modifications since you will not be able to see the code. This could be used for previewing what the site looks like or for quick content authoring.

- **Code:** In this view, the entire content panel is filled with code. This allows you to focus only on the code and not be distracted with the preview.

- **Split:** The split view is useful because it shows both the design and code view at the same time. Clicking on an element in the design view highlights the code within the code view. This reduces the time that it takes to search for code elements.

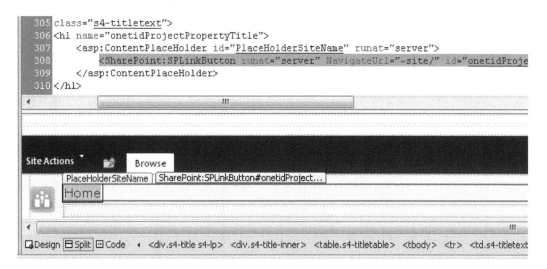

**Figure 9-4.** *Design, Split, and Code views*

If you are new to SharePoint Designer, another helpful feature is the code breadcrumb. As shown in Figure 9-4 above, the elements to the right of the Design, Split, and Code views allow you to click and highlight the entire code listing for that particular element, so you're able to see where the tags are open and closed. It also helps if you need to copy, delete, or move an entire block of code.

This next section gives a brief overview of Visual Studio 2010 and where you can get it.

# Microsoft Visual Studio 2010

Visual Studio is a very powerful tool. For most SharePoint branding design projects, you will only scratch the surface of what this application can really do. Some express versions of Visual Studio are free, but they don't provide the rich application features that are in the full version of Visual Studio 2010. You can compare the different versions at the following site: `http://www.microsoft.com/visualstudio`. You can download a trial version of Visual Studio 2010 ultimate or buy a version from the links below.

- **Visual Studio 2010 (Ultimate Trail)**:
  `http://www.microsoft.com/download/en/details.aspx?displaylang=en&id=12752`

- **Visual Studio 2010 (Full Purchase Version)**:
  `http://www.microsoft.com/visualstudio/en-us/buy`

After you have installed Visual Studio 2010, open the application.

## Visual Studio 2010 Basic Tour

With Visual Studio open you will see a starting screen similar to what is shown in Figure 9-5.

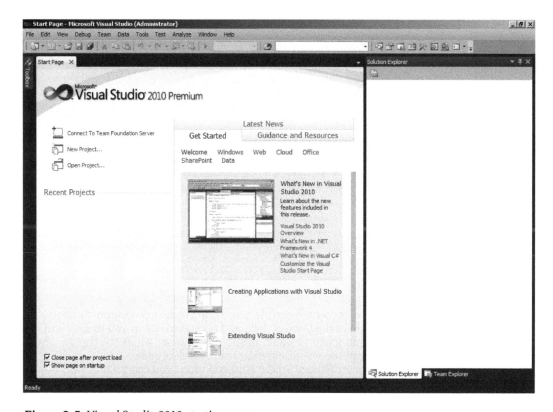

**Figure 9-5.** *Visual Studio 2010 starting screen*

From this screen you can create a new project, open an existing project, or open any recent projects. Once you have a project open, you will use the solution explorer to view all of the files within your project, as shown in Figure 9-6.

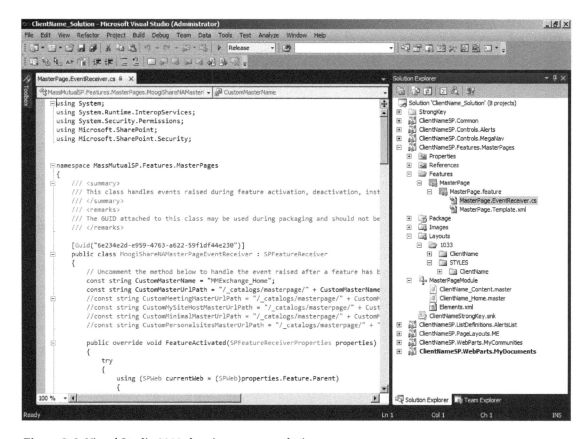

**Figure 9-6.** *Visual Studio 2010 showing an open solution*

To deploy a feature to your local site, you need to change the site URL property for that feature. To do this, simply click on the View menu at the top, and choose the Properties window. This displays a window below the solution explorer where you can specify the URL to which you deploy and activate each project, as shown in Figure 9-7.

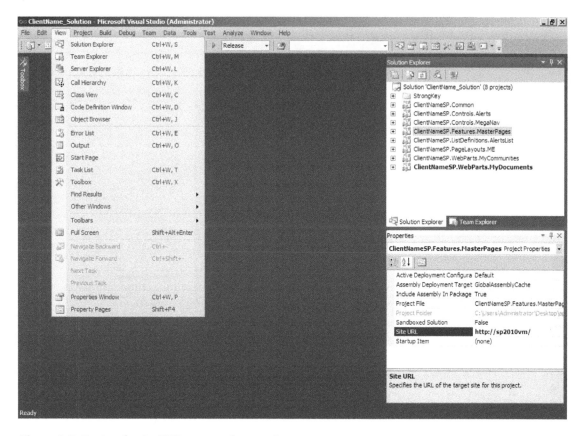

**Figure 9-7.** *Setting the site URL property for a project*

Right-click on either the solution title or on each project, and choose to build, rebuild, deploy, clean, package, or retract, as shown in Figure 9-8.

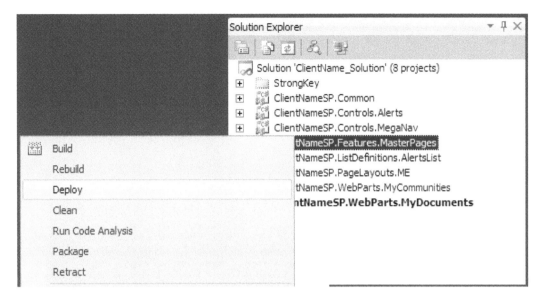

**Figure 9-8.** *Contextual menu for the solution or project*

These are just some of the basic features within Visual Studio 2010. Next we cover some of the free browser add-ons that help guide you through testing and debugging your SharePoint branding visual design builds.

# Browsers and Add-ons

Use the following tools and browser add-ons to help identify class names and any issues with the performance or display of the SharePoint 2010 site.

## Internet Explorer Developer Toolbar

This toolbar is a free tool that is built into Internet Explorer 8 and 9. You can also download and install it for workstations using Internet Explorer 7. To display the IE Developer Toolbar, simply press F12 on your keyboard at any time, or on the menu bar click on Tools ➤ F12 Developer Tools. The first time you display the toolbar it might be unpinned from the browser window, but you can dock it to the bottom of your browser window by pressing Ctrl+P when the window is selected. A Pin icon is located under the (X) Close icon to pin it to the parent browser window as well. Figure 9-9 shows that you can click on the white arrow on the left, and then select any element on the site to show the code for that element in the DOM explorer window. In cases where content is rendered through AJAX or renders after the page has loaded, you may need to click the Refresh icon.

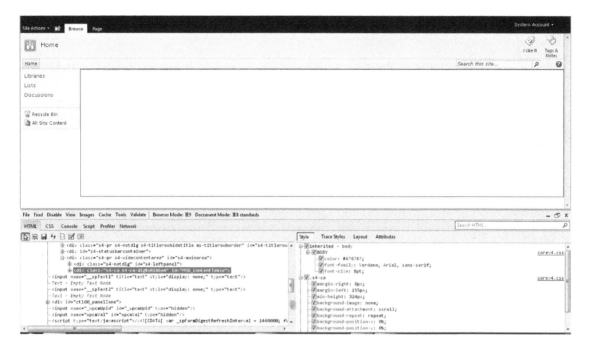

***Figure 9-9.*** *IE Developer Toolbar*

Other tools within the IE Developer Toolbar allow you to do the following:

- **Disable**: From this menu you can disable the pop-up blocker and disable CSS from displaying on the page.

- **View**: From this menu you can view elements on the page such as class and ID information, link paths, link report, and page source.

- **Images**: From this menu you are able to disable images on the page, view image dimensions, file size, paths, and a full detailed report for every image on the page.

- **Cache**: From this menu you can specify to only get the latest files from the server, and clear browser and cookies.

- **Tools:** This menu allows you to resize the browser window in case you want to see how the site looks at different window sizes. There are preset sizes based on common resolution settings. You can also choose a different user agent such as IE6, Firefox, or Opera. The tools tab allows you to use a ruler and a color picker.

- **Validate:** From this menu you can check the HTML, CSS, links, and other accessibility options with the W3C validator site.

- **Browser Mode:** This menu will allow you to choose which browser you want the site to render with.

- **Document Mode**: This menu will allow you to choose between the types of IE document modes that the site will display with. By default, SharePoint 2010 uses IE8.

You can use the IE Developer Toolbar to find a CSS class or update an existing class style property without having to modify your custom CSS file. This helps you make quick changes in your own browser without affecting other users.

# Firefox Firebug

Firebug is very similar to the IE Developer Toolbar, as shown in Figure 9-10. It can be downloaded from the following link: `http://getfirebug.com/`.

**Figure 9-10.** *Firefox Firebug*

Firebug includes a feature that lets you see search results for elements as you type. (This isn't available in the IE Developer Toolbar.) This allows you to easily see the results without having to hit the Submit button. It also changes to red if there are no results for what you have typed. You also have the ability to select the CSS on the right and copy and paste entire CSS snippets within Firebug. However, the CSS viewer is harder to understand, so I usually end up using the IE Developer Toolbar over Firebug when dealing with CSS issues.

There are add-ons for Firebug that take you even further, some of which are shown in Figure 9-11.

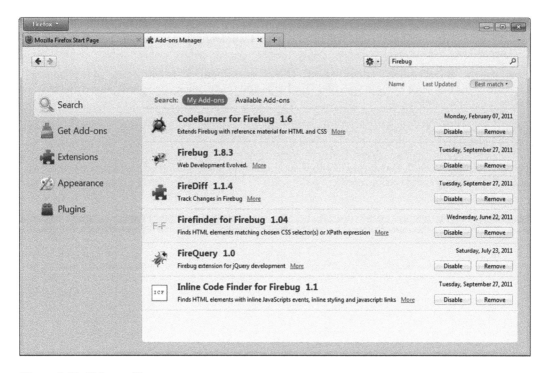

*Figure 9-11. Firbug add-ons*

# HttpWatch

This application is very helpful when you need to view what elements are loading within your site and how long it takes to fully render the page. Download this add-on from the following URL: http://www.httpwatch.com/download/. See Figure 9-12 for an example of what the results would be when using it against a blank SharePoint site.

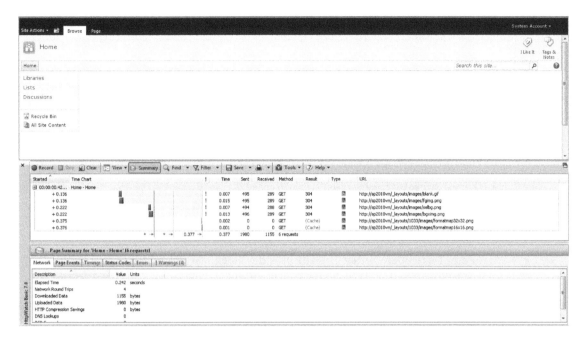

*Figure 9-12.* *HttpWatch*

Simply by pressing the Record button and then refreshing the page, you get a time chart indicating how long it took the site to load and which items took the longest to load. For example, if I had a very large image on the page, as shown in Figure 9-13, it would capture that the image took the longest to load.

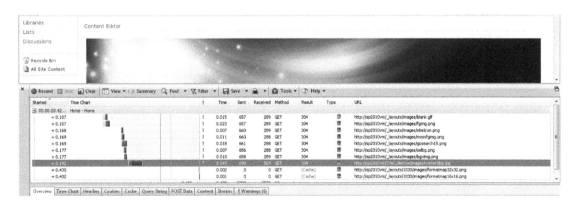

*Figure 9-13.* *HttpWatch showing the length of time to load a large image*

This tool can also be helpful for identifying if any JavaScript or other external files take long to load. The next section lists some additional resources that help with branding and customizing SharePoint 2010.

## Additional Resources

The following resources are included to provide additional support for your SharePoint customization project.

- **SharePoint 2010 Software Development Kit (SDK)**: The SDK provides a huge amount of helpful development information.
  http://msdn.microsoft.com/en-us/library/ee557253.aspx

- **SharePoint Server 2010 Download**: You can download a trial version of SharePoint at the following link.
  http://sharepoint.microsoft.com/en-us/Pages/Try-It.aspx

- **SharePoint Developer Center**: This site provides blogs, learning material, resources, and a community of people to help through the forums.
  http://msdn.microsoft.com/en-us/sharepoint/default.aspx

- **MSDN Real World Branding Technical Article**: This article provides some additional great resources about SharePoint branding.
  http://msdn.microsoft.com/en-us/library/gg430141.aspx

- **960 Grid System**: As described in detail in Chapter 4, this site includes some great information about grid systems.
  http://960.gs

## Summary

In this chapter you learned about SharePoint Designer 2010 and Visual Studio 2010 and a variety of tools and resources that can help you with your SharePoint 2010 project customizations.

# APPENDIX

# CSS Reference Guide

## What's In This Chapter?

- The Ribbon Container
- Site Actions
- Site Breadcrumb
- Welcome Menu
- Content Containers
- Site Logo
- Page Breadcrumb
- Social Tags & Notes
- Top Header 2
- Top Navigation
- Search and Help
- Status Bar
- Quick Launch (Left Panel)
- Content Area
- Web-Part Elements
- Dialog Windows
- Blog Posts
- My Profile
- Search Results

This chapter includes the top most visible CSS classes used within SharePoint 2010. You can take the following CSS classes and use them to override the OOTB look and feel by changing the CSS properties. This can include making changes to background images, fonts, padding, margins, and other properties. Figure A-1 is a guide to the visual elements that are being covered in sections 1-13. Sections 13-19 have their own figure images. The majority of these classes come from the main SharePoint 2010 CSS file called "**corev4.css**" located on the server at: `C:\Program Files\Common Files\Microsoft Shared\Web Server Extensions\14\TEMPLATE\LAYOUTS\1033\STYLES\COREV4.CSS`.

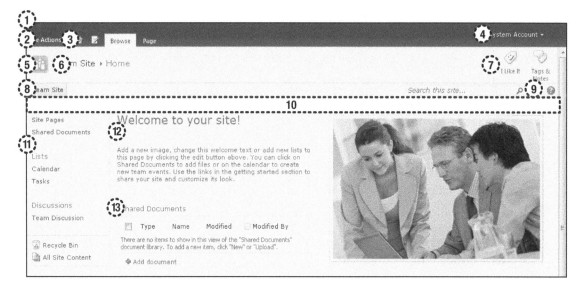

***Figure A-1.*** *Team Site CSS reference guide*

For all of the elements listed within this chapter I will provide the following details:

- **Class Title:** Label used to identify element

- **Description:** Brief description of the class/ID properties and how they are used

- **Preview Image:** Visual image showing what the element looks like (not all classes will have a preview image)

- **Style Sheet:** What style sheet the class/ID is referenced in

- **ID/Class Name:** The unique class/ID name

- **Listing of Standard Class Properties:** Listing of the CSS code properties used within the referenced style sheet

The first main section that I will cover is the Ribbon container area. The Ribbon control is new to SharePoint 2010 and has a lot of CSS classes.

# #1: The Ribbon Container

The Ribbon shown in Figure A-2 includes the following CSS elements.

***Figure A-2.*** *SharePoint 2010 Ribbon*

- Ribbon Row/Ribbon Hide Title
- Ribbon Cont DIV Tag
- Ribbon Container
- Ribbon CUI
- Ribbon CUI Top Bar 2
- Ribbon CUI Tab Container (Ribbon Control)
- Tab Row Left (Site Actions and Breadcrumb)
- Ribbon Tabs
- Tab Row Right (Welcome Menu)

---

■ **Note**  I have removed some of the CSS comments that are used for the standard SharePoint 2010 themes in the listings below to keep the display of the CSS properties simple and easy to read.

---

## Ribbon Row/Ribbon Hide Title

This is the container for all of the items in the top Ribbon. It is the first DIV element that can be used to hide the whole Ribbon element if needed. This applies the background to the main Ribbon and also sets the vertical overflow to hidden so if the height goes beyond 43 pixels it will not show. There is also a CSS reference that is used to hide the whole Ribbon when you are printing out the page based on the @ media Print Element. Listing A-1 shows the standard CSS properties.

- **Style Sheet:** COREV4.CSS
- **ID:** s4-ribbonrow
- **Class:** s4-ribbonrowhidetitle

*Listing A-1. Ribbon Row Base CSS*

```
body #s4-ribbonrow{
min-height:43px;
background-color:#21374c;
overflow-y:hidden;
}
@media print{
body #s4-ribbonrow{
display:none;
}
```

## Ribbon Cont DIV Tag

This is the second-level DIV that includes the repeating background image Sprite PNG file. Listing A-2 shows the standard CSS properties.

- **Style Sheet:** COREV4.CSS
- **ID:** s4-ribboncont

*Listing A-2. Ribbon Cont DIV Tag CSS*

```
body #s4-ribboncont{
padding:0px;
background:url("/_layouts/images/bgximg.png") repeat-x -0px -565px;
}
```

## Ribbon Container

This is the third-level nested DIV that includes a CSS property of setting the height of the DIV to auto. Listing A-3 shows the standard CSS properties.

- **Style Sheet:** COREV4.CSS
- **ID:** RibbonContainer

*Listing A-3. Ribbon Container CSS*

```
body #RibbonContainer.loaded{
height:auto !important;
}
```

## Ribbon CUI

This is the third-level nested DIV that includes a CSS property of setting the height of the DIV to auto. Listing A-4 shows the standard CSS properties.

- **Style Sheet:** COREV4.CSS
- **ID:** Ribbon
- **Class:** ms-cui-ribbon

*Listing A-4. Ribbon CUI CSS*

```
.ms-cui-ribbon,.ms-cui-menu,.ms-cui-toolbar-toolbar{
font-family:"Segoe UI",Tahoma,Verdana,sans-serif;
font-size:8pt;
color:#6c6e70;
}
```

# Ribbon CUI Top Bar 2

This class is used to add height to the Ribbon area and also provides a border color. This bottom border and other border colors might get changed depending on the Ribbon tab that you have selected. For example, if you are in an announcement list and you click on the Items or List tabs within the list tools container, as shown in Figure A-3, the border on the bottom gets added automatically. Listing A-5 shows the standard CSS properties.

*Figure A-3. SharePoint 2010 list tools with added border colors*

- **Style Sheet:** COREV4.CSS
- **Class:** ms-cui-topBar2

*Listing A-5. Ribbon CUI CSS*

```
.ms-cui-topBar2{
border-bottom:1px solid #cad2db;
height:43px;
}
```

# Ribbon CUI Tab Container (Ribbon Control)

This class is used for the containing DIV tag, as shown in Figure A-4. This class is not referenced in any style sheet but can be used if you need to stylize the container DIV element.

*Figure A-4. SharePoint 2010 Ribbon tab container*

- **Style Sheet:** No Reference Used
- **Class:** ms-cui-tabContainer

## Tab Row Left (Site Actions and Breadcrumb)

This class is used to float the site actions, breadcrumb, and Edit icon to the left of the Ribbon area, as shown in Figure A-5. Listing A-6 shows the standard CSS properties.

*Figure A-5. SharePoint 2010 Ribbon tab row left elements*

- **Style Sheet:** COREV4.CSS
- **ID:** RibbonContainer-TabRowLeft
- **Class:** ms-cui-TabRowLeft ms-siteactionscontainer

*Listing A-6. Ribbon Tab Row Left CSS*

```
.ms-cui-TabRowLeft,.ms-cui-QATRowCenter{
float:left;
}
.ms-cui-TabRowLeft{
margin-top:19px;
font-size:0px;
}
```

## Ribbon Tabs

This class is used to set the height of the Ribbon tabs and also float it to the left. There is a property to set the element to not wrap and hide the overflow for both horizontal and vertical. This element is shown in Figure A-6. Listing A-7 shows the standard CSS properties.

*Figure A-6. SharePoint 2010 Ribbon tabs*

- **Style Sheet:** COREV4.CSS
- **Class:** ms-cui-tts

*Listing A-7. Ribbon Tabs*

```
.ms-cui-tts,.ms-cui-tts-scale-1,.ms-cui-tts-scale-2{
display:block;
float:left;
white-space:nowrap;
height:44px;
overflow-y:hidden;
overflow-x:hidden;
margin:0px 0px -1px 0px;
padding:0px;
list-style-type:none;
}
```

# Tab Row Right (Welcome Menu)

This class is used to float the Welcome Menu text container that displays your name to the right. It also sets the top margin to zero and vertically aligns the element in the middle, as shown in Figure A-7. Listing A-8 shows the standard CSS properties.

*Figure A-7. SharePoint 2010 Welcome Menu container*

- **Style Sheet:** COREV4.CSS
- **ID:** RibbonContainer-TabRowRight
- **Class:** ms-cui-TabRowRight s4-trc-container

*Listing A-8. Ribbon Welcome Menu Container*

```
.ms-cui-TabRowRight,.ms-cui-QATRowRight{
float:right;
}
.ms-cui-TabRowRight{
margin-top:0px;
```

```
vertical-align:middle;
}
.s4-trc-container{
padding-right:0px;
}
```

The next section that I will cover is based around the Site Actions menu button and icon, and also its drop-down menu that shows when you click on Site Actions.

## #2: Site Actions

The site actions shown in Figure A-8 include the following CSS elements:

- Site Actions Menu Container
- Site Actions Menu Inner
- Site Actions Menu Text
- Site Actions Menu White Arrow Icon
- Site Actions Menu Hover
- Site Actions Menu Drop-Down Container
- Site Actions Menu Drop-Down Icon
- Site Actions Menu Drop-Down Icon IMG
- Site Actions Menu Drop-Down Title
- Site Actions Menu Drop-Down Description

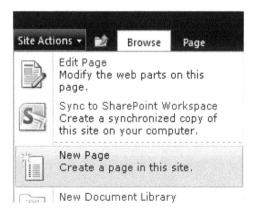

***Figure A-8.*** *SharePoint 2010 site actions*

# Site Actions Menu Container

This class is used to vertically align the elements within it to the top and set the font size of its child elements, as shown in Figure A-9. Listing A-9 shows the standard CSS properties.

***Figure A-9.*** *SharePoint 2010 Site Actions menu container*

- **Style Sheet:** COREV4.CSS
- **ID:** siteactiontd
- **Class:** ms-siteactionsmenu

***Listing A-9.*** *Site Actions Menu Container CSS*

```
.ms-siteactionsmenu{
display:inline-block;
vertical-align:top;
font-size:8pt;
}
```

# Site Actions Menu Inner

This class is within a SPAN tag that is used to display a placeholder border spacing and background color for when the item is hovered over, as shown in Figure A-10. Listing A-10 shows the standard CSS properties.

***Figure A-10.*** *SharePoint 2010 Site Actions menu inner*

- **Style Sheet:** COREV4.CSS
- **ID:** zz9_SiteActionsMenu_t
- **Class:** ms-siteactionsmenuinner

***Listing A-10.*** *Site Actions Menu Inner CSS*

```
.ms-siteactionsmenuinner,.ms-siteactionsmenuhover{
border-width:1px;
border-style:solid;
```

```
margin-right:3px;
padding:3px 4px 0px 2px;
height:18px;
display:inline-block;
font-family:"Segoe UI",Tahoma,Verdana,sans-serif;
}
.ms-siteactionsmenuinner{
border-color:#21374C;
border-top-color:#394f63;
background:url("/_layouts/images/bgximg.png") repeat-x -0px -467px;
background-color:#21374c;
}
.v4master .ms-siteactionsmenuinner{
border-color:transparent;
background:transparent none no-repeat;
}
```

■ **Note** When you see the class `.v4master` in a style sheet, it will work only if you have the `v4master` class applied to the body tag of your master page. If you create a custom master page from scratch, you may need to either alter your CSS to use your own class applied to the body in your master page or add this class to the body in your master page.

## Site Actions Menu Text

This class is used to stylize the site actions hyperlink text. This "A" tag includes inline CSS that forces it to not wrap and also have the cursor set to Pointer. The Site Actions menu "A" element font color is set to white with a margin on the right of 4px and its child SPAN tag includes some margins. Figure A-11 shows just the site actions text. Listing A-11 shows the standard CSS properties.

**Site Actions**

***Figure A-11.*** *SharePoint 2010 Site Actions menu text*

- **Style Sheet:** COREV4.CSS
- **ID:** zz9_SiteActionsMenu
- **Class:** ms-menu-a

***Listing A-11.*** *Site Actions Menu Text CSS*

```
.ms-siteactionsmenu > span > a{
color:#fff;
}
```

```
.ms-siteactionsmenu > span > a > span{
display:inline-block;
margin:1px 0px 0px 2px;
}
.ms-siteactionsmenuinner .ms-menu-a,.ms-siteactionsmenuhover .ms-menu-a{
margin-right:4px;
}
```

## Site Actions Menu White Arrow Icon

This class is used to include the white arrow next to the site actions text. There is some inline CSS used to give it a width of 5px and height of 3px. The class contains styles that give it some margins and vertically aligns its image element to the middle, as shown in Figure A-12. Listing A-12 shows the standard CSS properties.

**Figure A-12.** *SharePoint 2010 Site Actions menu icon*

- **Style Sheet:** COREV4.CSS

- **Class:** s4-clust ms-viewselector-arrow

**Listing A-12.** *Site Actions Menu Icon CSS*

```
.ms-siteactionsmenu .ms-viewselector-arrow{
display:inline-block;
margin:7px 0px 1px 0px;
vertical-align:top;
}
.ms-viewselector-arrow{
vertical-align:middle;
}
```

## Site Actions Menu Drop-Down Icon IMG

Listing A-13 shows the inline CSS properties used to position the sprite image in the correct position to be viewed. If you change the background color for the Ribbon container to a lighter color, you might want to add in the CSS from Listing A-14. You cannot simply change the top position of the FGIMG.PNG image since the inline CSS has the `!important` tag within the code. So, you have to hide the IMG with CSS, and then use the same sprite PNG file as a background image and position it differently to make the image a dark arrow, as shown in Figure A-13.

- **Style Sheet:** Inline CSS

*Listing A-13. Site Actions Menu Icon Image Inline CSS*

```
.ms-siteactionsmenu .ms-viewselector-arrow IMG{
position: absolute;
left: 0px !important;
top: -491px !important;
border: none;
}
```

*Listing A-14. Site Actions Menu Icon Image CSS for Light Ribbon Backgrounds*

```
.ms-viewselector-arrow{
background-image: url(/_layouts/images/fgimg.png) !important;
background-position: -1px 381px;
}
.ms-viewselector-arrow img{
visibility: hidden;
}
```

*Figure A-13. SharePoint 2010 Site Actions menu icon on light Ribbon colored background*

## Site Actions Menu Hover

This class is used to add a style to the site actions once you hover over the control. The CSS adds the border color, repeating background image, and a background color, as shown in Figure A-14. Listing A-15 shows the standard CSS properties.

*Figure A-14. SharePoint 2010 Site Actions menu hover*

- **Style Sheet:** COREV4.CSS
- **Class:** ms-siteactionsmenuhover

*Listing A-15. Site Actions Menu Hover CSS*

```
.ms-siteactionsmenuhover{
border-color:#8b929a;
background:url("/_layouts/images/bgximg.png") repeat-x -0px -489px;
background-color:#21374c;
}
```

# Site Actions Menu Drop-Down Container

The following classes are used to specify the outer drop-down borders, background color, and the background image that repeats vertically and displays that light line between the image and the label, as shown in Figure A-15. Listing A-16 shows the standard CSS properties.

*Figure A-15. SharePoint 2010 Site Actions menu drop-down container*

- **Style Sheet:** COREV4.CSS

- **Container Class:** ms-MenuUIPopupBody ms-MenuUIPopupScreen

- **Inner Class:** ms-MenuUIPopupInner

- **Large Menu Class:** ms-MenuUILarge

***Listing A-16.*** *Site Actions Menu Drop-Down CSS*

```
.ms-MenuUIPopupBody{
border:1px solid;
border-top-color:#a4aab4;
border-left-color:#a4aab4;
border-right-color:#7895ac;
border-bottom-color:#7895ac;
margin:0px;
padding:0px;
}
.ms-MenuUIPopupInner{
border:1px solid;
border-color:#ececec;
border-top-color:transparent;
border-left-color:transparent;
}
.ms-MenuUI,.ms-MenuUILarge,.ms-MenuUIRtL,.ms-MenuUILargeRtL
{
background-color:#fff;
background-repeat:repeat-y;
cursor:pointer;
}
.ms-MenuUI,.ms-MenuUILarge{
background-position:left;
}
.ms-MenuUILarge{
background-image:url("/_layouts/images/MGradLarge.png");
width:250px;
}
```

# Site Actions Menu Drop-Down Icon

The following classes are used to set the width and height to 40 pixels and also add some padding, as shown in Figure A-16. Listing A-17 shows the standard CSS properties.

*Figure A-16.* *SharePoint 2010 Site Actions menu drop-down icon*

- **Style Sheet:** COREV4.CSS
- **Container Class:** ms-MenuUIIconLarge
- **Image Class:** ms-MenuUIULImg

*Listing A-17.* *Site Actions Menu Drop-Down Icon CSS*

```
div.ms-MenuUIPopupScreen div.ms-MenuUIPopupInner ul.ms-MenuUIUL a span.ms-MenuUIIconLarge{
height:40px;
width:40px;
}
.ms-MenuUIIcon,.ms-MenuUIIconLarge{
padding:0px 6px 0px 2px;
}
div.ms-MenuUIPopupScreen div.ms-MenuUIPopupInner ul.ms-MenuUIUL a img.ms-MenuUIULImg{
border-style:none;
}
```

## Site Actions Menu Drop-Down Title

The following classes are used to set the font size, width, and padding of the Site Actions menu title, as shown in Figure A-17. Listing A-18 shows the standard CSS properties.

Edit Page
Modify the web parts on this

*Figure A-17.* *SharePoint 2010 Site Actions menu drop-down title*

- **Style Sheet:** COREV4.CSS
- **Class:** ms-MenuUILabel

*Listing A-18.* *Site Actions Menu Drop-Down Title CSS*

```
.ms-MenuUILabel,.ms-MenuUILabelRtL,.ms-menuuilabelcompact,.ms-menuuilabelcompactRtl{
font-size:8pt;
width:100%;
}
```

```
.ms-MenuUILabel{
padding:2px 0px 3px 6px;
}
```

## Site Actions Menu Drop-Down Description

The following classes are used to set the width and height to 40 pixels and also add some padding, as shown in Figure A-18. Listing A-19 shows the standard CSS properties.

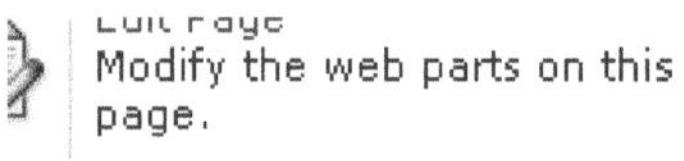

Edit Page
Modify the web parts on this
page.

***Figure A-18.*** *SharePoint 2010 Site Actions menu drop-down description*

- **Style Sheet:** COREV4.CSS

- **Class:** ms-menuitemdescription

***Listing A-19.*** *Site Actions Menu Drop-Down Description CSS*

```
.ms-menuitemdescription{
color:#545454;
}
div.ms-MenuUIPopupScreen div.ms-MenuUIPopupInner ul.ms-MenuUIUL a span.ms-menuitemdescription{
color:#4c535c;
font-weight:normal;
white-space:normal !important;
}
```

The next section that I will cover is the little site breadcrumb that allows you to navigate back up to a higher parent site.

# #3: Site Breadcrumb

The site breadcrumb shown in Figure A-19 includes the following CSS elements. To display the breadcrumb in a more traditional way, similar to how it was done in SharePoint 2007, follow the steps within this blog post: http://erikswenson.blogspot.com/2010/11/convert-folder-breadcrumb-to.html.

- Site Breadcrumb Container

- Site Breadcrumb Icon

- Site Breadcrumb Pop-Out Menu Container

- Site Breadcrumb Pop-Out Menu Header

- Site Breadcrumb Pop-Out Menu Item

- Site Breadcrumb Pop-Out Menu Arrow

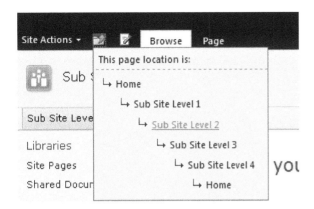

*Figure A-19. SharePoint 2010 site breadcrumb*

# Site Breadcrumb Container

This class is used to add margins and spacing around the breadcrumb image and also vertically align it to the bottom, as shown in Figure A-20. Listing A-20 shows the standard CSS properties.

*Figure A-20. SharePoint 2010 site breadcrumb container*

- **Style Sheet:** COREV4.CSS

- **Class:** s4-breadcrumb-anchor

*Listing A-20. Site Breadcrumb Container CSS*

```
.s4-breadcrumb-anchor,.ms-qatbutton{
margin:0px 3px 0px 0px;
padding:2px 5px 0px;
display:inline-block;
text-align:center;
border:1px solid transparent;
vertical-align:bottom;
}
```

# Site Breadcrumb Icon

This icon is displayed by using the "fgimg.png" sprite image and having inline CSS set the position of it, as shown in Figure A-21. Listing A-21 shows the inline CSS properties.

**Figure A-21.** *SharePoint 2010 site breadcrumb icon*

- **Style Sheet:** Inline CSS

**Listing A-21.** *Site Breadcrumb Icon Inline CSS*

```
left: 0px !important;
top: -112px !important;
border: none;
position: absolute;
```

# Site Breadcrumb Pop-Out Menu Container

The following classes are used to set the minimum and maximum width, padding, word wrap, horizontal overflow, border size, font size, background image, and background color. The inline CSS is used to set the positioning and z-index of the menu, as shown in Figure A-22. Listing A-22 shows the class and inline CSS properties.

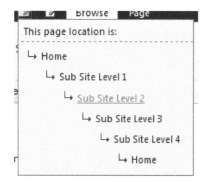

**Figure A-22.** *SharePoint 2010 site breadcrumb pop-out menu container*

- **Style Sheet:** COREV4.CSS & Inline CSS
- **ID:** GlobalBreadCrumbNavPopout-menu
- **Class:** ms-popoutMenu s4-breadcrumb-menu

**Listing A-22.** *Site Breadcrumb Pop-Out Menu Container CSS*

```
.s4-breadcrumb-menu{
max-width:400px;
min-width:142px;
```

```
padding:1px 15px 5px 1px;
word-wrap:break-word;
-ms-word-wrap:break-word;
overflow-x:hidden;
border:1px solid;
font-size:8pt;
}
.v4master .s4-breadcrumb-menu{
background:url("/_layouts/images/selbg.png") repeat-x left top;
-color:#f8f8f8;
border-color:#94989f;
}

/* Inline CSS on DIV */
left: 89px;
top: 40px;
display: none;
visibility: visible;
position: absolute;
z-index: 1002;
```

## Site Breadcrumb Pop-Out Menu Header

The following classes within the container set the margins, padding, and dashed border on the bottom. The header class sets the text to be displayed inline and also sets the color, as shown in Figure A-23. Listing A-23 shows the standard CSS properties that are used for both elements.

*Figure A-23. SharePoint 2010 site breadcrumb pop-out menu header*

- **Style Sheet:** COREV4.CSS
- **Container Class:** s4-breadcrumb-top
- **Header Class:** s4-breadcrumb-header

*Listing A-23. Site Breadcrumb Pop-Out Menu Header CSS*

```
.s4-breadcrumb-top{
display:block;
margin-bottom:5px;
margin-right:-15px;
padding:5px;
border-bottom:1px dashed;
}
```

```
.v4master .s4-breadcrumb-top{
border-bottom-color:#a7b0ba;
}
.s4-breadcrumb-header{
display:inline;
}
.v4master .s4-breadcrumb-header{
color:#3b4f65;
}
```

## Site Breadcrumb Pop-Out Menu Item

The following classes are used to set the padding and margins of the item to zero, sets the color, and adds in a margin to the left, as shown in Figure A-24. Listing A-24 shows the standard CSS properties.

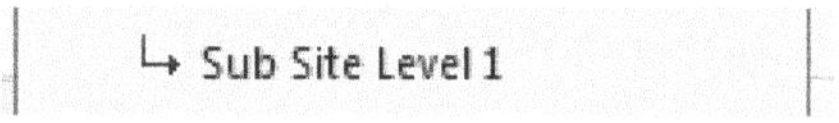

↳ Sub Site Level 1

*Figure A-24. SharePoint 2010 site breadcrumb pop-out menu item*

- **Style Sheet:** COREV4.CSS
- **Class:** s4-breadcrumbNode

*Listing A-24. Site Breadcrumb Pop-Out Menu Item CSS*

```
.s4-breadcrumbNode,.s4-breadcrumbCurrentNode,.s4-breadcrumbRootNode{
list-style-type:none;
padding:0px;
margin:0px;
}
.v4master .s4-breadcrumbNode,
.v4master .s4-breadcrumbCurrentNode,
.v4master .s4-breadcrumbRootNode{
color:#3b4f65;
}
ul.s4-breadcrumbNode{
margin-left:21px;
}
```

## Site Breadcrumb Pop-Out Menu Arrow

This icon is displayed by using the "fgimg.png" sprite image and having inline CSS set the position of it, as shown in Figure A-25. Listing A-25 shows the inline CSS properties.

*Figure A-25*. *SharePoint 2010 site breadcrumb pop-out menu arrow*

- **Style Sheet:** Inline CSS

*Listing A-25*. *Site Breadcrumb Pop-Out Menu Arrow Inline CSS*

```
left: 0px !important;
top: -353px !important;
border: none;
position: absolute;
```

The next section that I will cover is the text that displays the logged-in user's name in the top right of the Ribbon.

# #4: Welcome Menu

The Welcome Menu shown in Figure A-26 includes the following CSS elements. The drop-down element uses the same classes as the Site Actions menu. Refer to those classes specified earlier in this chapter as needed.

- Welcome Menu Container
- Welcome Menu Inner Container
- Welcome Menu Text
- Welcome Menu Icon

**Figure A-26.** *SharePoint 2010 Welcome menu*

## Welcome Menu Container

This class is used to float the element to the left and add in some margins, as shown in Figure A-27. Listing A-26 shows the standard CSS properties.

**Figure A-27.** *SharePoint 2010 Welcome menu container*

- **Style Sheet:** COREV4.CSS

- **Class:** s4-trc-container-menu

**Listing A-26.** *Welcome Menu Container CSS*

```
.s4-trc-container-menu{
float:left;
margin:12px 3px;
}
```

## Welcome Menu Inner Container

The first class is used to add padding, margins, font size, and font family, as shown in Listing A-27. The second class within Listing A-27 adds the border and background image styles for when you hover over the user's name.

- **Style Sheet:** COREV4.CSS

- **Class:** ms-welcomeMenu

- **Hover Class:** ms-welcomeMenu.ms-SpLinkButtonActive

***Listing A-27.*** *Welcome Menu Inner Container CSS*

```
.ms-welcomeMenu{
padding:2px 5px 3px;
margin:0px 3px;
font-size:1em;
font-family:Verdana,sans-serif;
border:1px solid transparent;
display:inline-block;
}
.ms-welcomeMenu.ms-SpLinkButtonActive{
border-color:#8b929a;
background:url("/_layouts/images/bgximg.png") repeat-x -0px -489px;
background-color:#21374c;
}
```

# Welcome Menu Text

This class is used to add margins, text color, and text decoration, as shown in Figure A-28. Listing A-28 shows the standard CSS properties.

Erik Swenson ▾

***Figure A-28.*** *SharePoint 2010 Welcome menu text*

- **Style Sheet:** COREV4.CSS

- **Class:** ms-menu-a

***Listing A-28.*** *Welcome Menu Text CSS*

```
.ms-welcomeMenu .ms-menu-a{
margin-right:5px;
}
.ms-welcomeMenu a:link{
color:#fff;
}
.ms-welcomeMenu a:hover{
text-decoration:none !important;
}
.ms-welcomeMenu.ms-SpLinkButtonActive a:link{
color:#fff;
}
```

## Welcome Menu Icon

This is the same icon and style used for the site actions menu. It is displayed by using the "fgimg.png" sprite image and having inline CSS to position the icon as shown in Figure A-29. Listing A-29 shows the inline CSS properties.

*Figure A-29. SharePoint 2010 Welcome menu icon*

- **Style Sheet:** Inline CSS

*Listing A-29. Welcome Menu Icon Inline CSS*

```
left: 0px !important;
top: -491px !important;
border: none;
position: absolute;
```

Within this next section I will describe the main container elements that frame the header and content areas.

# #5: Content Containers

The content area shown in Figure A-30 includes the following CSS elements.

- Workspace
- Body Container
- Title Row
- Title Area
- Title Inner
- Title Table

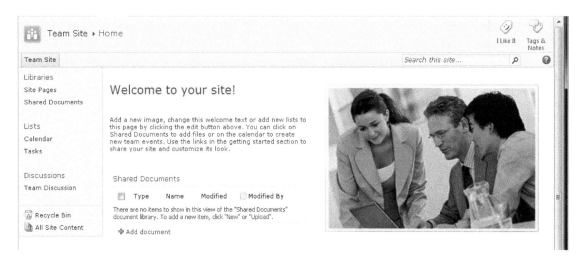

*Figure A-30. SharePoint 2010 page breadcrumb*

# Workspace

This ID is used to set the height and width to automatic and assign the overflow properties. Based on this ID, JavaScript is used to automatically set the height and width of the DIV based on the size of the browser window. Listing A-30 shows the standard CSS properties.

- **Style Sheet:** COREV4.CSS
- **ID:** s4-workspace

*Listing A-30. Workspace CSS*

```
body #s4-workspace{
overflow:visible !important;
width:auto !important;
height:auto !important;
}
body #s4-workspace{
overflow-y:scroll;
overflow-x:auto;
position:relative;
left:0px;
}
```

# Body Container

This ID includes a min-width for both the header and content elements. Listing A-31 shows the standard CSS properties.

- **Style Sheet:** COREV4.CSS
- **ID:** s4-bodyContainer

***Listing A-31.*** *Body Container CSS*

```
body #s4-bodyContainer{
min-width:760px;
}
```

# Title Row

This ID and CSS is a container for the logo, page breadcrumb, social tags, top navigation search, and the help icon. The `ms-titlerowborder` class adds a border to the right of these elements, as shown in Figure A-31. Listing A-32 shows the standard CSS properties.

***Figure A-31.*** *SharePoint 2010 title row*

- **Style Sheet:** COREV4.CSS
- **ID:** s4-titlerow
- **Class:** s4-pr s4-notdlg s4-titlerowhidetitle ms-titlerowborder ms-titlerowborder

***Listing A-32.*** *Title Row CSS*

```
body #s4-titlerow{
display:block !important;
}
.ms-titlerowborder{
border-right:1px solid #b8babd;
}
```

# Title Area

This CSS is used to add padding to the left of the site logo, set a minimum height, add a background image with color, and set the horizontal overflow to hidden, as shown in Figure A-32. Listing A-33 shows the standard CSS properties.

**Figure A-32.** *SharePoint 2010 title area*

- **Style Sheet:** COREV4.CSS
- **Class:** s4-title s4-lp

**Listing A-33.** *Title Area CSS*

```
.s4-title{
padding:0px 0px 0px 10px;
margin:0px;
min-height:64px;
background:url("/_layouts/images/bgximg.png") repeat-x -0px -1023px;
background-color:#f9f9f9;
word-wrap:break-word;
-ms-word-wrap:break-word;
overflow-x:hidden;
}
```

# Title Inner

This CSS is used to set a minimum height on the title area. Listing A-34 shows the standard CSS properties.

- **Style Sheet:** COREV4.CSS
- **Class:** s4-title-inner

**Listing A-34.** *Title Inner CSS*

```
.s4-title-inner{
min-height:64px;
}
```

# Title Table

This CSS is used to set the height, width, and font properties for the title table. Listing A-35 shows the standard CSS properties.

- **Style Sheet:** COREV4.CSS
- **Class:** s4-titletable

*Listing A-35. Title Table CSS*

```
.s4-titletable{
border:0px;
height:64px;
width:100%;
font-family:Verdana,Arial,sans-serif;
font-size:8pt;
}
```

Within this next section I will cover the elements that are contained within the site table. The first element is the site logo that gets displayed within the title area on the left.

# #6: Site Logo

The site logo shown in Figure A-30 includes the following CSS to add padding and alignment to the image, as shown in Figure A-33. Listing A-36 shows the standard CSS properties.

*Figure A-33. SharePoint 2010 site logo*

- **Style Sheet:** COREV4.CSS

- **Class:** s4-titlelogo

*Listing A-36. Site Logo CSS*

```
.s4-titlelogo{
padding:12px 10px 12px 0px;
text-align:center;
vertical-align:middle;
}
```

The second element within the site table is the page breadcrumb described below.

# #7: Page Breadcrumb

The page breadcrumb shown in Figure A-34 includes the following CSS elements. The page title and icon are visible only on publishing pages or wiki pages.

*Figure A-34. SharePoint 2010 page breadcrumb*

- Page Breadcrumb Container
- Page Breadcrumb Site Name
- Page Breadcrumb Arrow Icon
- Page Breadcrumb Page Name

# Page Breadcrumb Container

This class is used to set the TD width and vertical alignment. Listing A-37 shows the standard CSS properties.

- **Style Sheet:** COREV4.CSS
- **Class:** s4-titletext

*Listing A-37. Page Breadcrumb Container CSS*

```
.s4-titletext{
width:100%;
vertical-align:middle;
unicode-bidi:embed;
}
```

# Page Breadcrumb Site Name

This class is used to set the font size, font weight, padding, margin, and font color, as shown in Figure A-35. Listing A-38 shows the standard CSS properties.

Sub Site Level 1

*Figure A-35. SharePoint 2010 page breadcrumb site name*

- **Style Sheet:** COREV4.CSS
- **Class:** s4-title h1

*Listing A-38. Page Breadcrumb Site Name CSS*

```
.s4-title h1,.s4-title h2{
font-size:1.4em;
font-weight:normal;
display:inline;
padding:0px;
margin:0px;
}
.s4-title h1 a,.s4-title h2 a{
color:#003759;
display:inline-block;
}
```

# Page Breadcrumb Arrow Icon

This class is used to set the vertical alignment of the image, and the inline CSS on the image is used for positioning, as shown in Figure A-36. Listing A-39 shows the Standard CSS properties and the inline CSS.

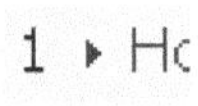

1 ▸ Hc

*Figure A-36. SharePoint 2010 page breadcrumb Arrow icon*

- **Style Sheet:** COREV4.CSS & Inline CSS
- **Container Class:** s4-nothome s4-bcsep s4-titlesep

*Listing A-39. Page Breadcrumb Arrow Icon CSS*

```
.s4-titlesep{
vertical-align:middle;
}
/* Inline CSS on IMG */
left: 0px !important;
top: -491px !important;
border: none;
position: absolute;
```

# Page Breadcrumb Page Name

This class is used to add margins, text color, and text decoration, as shown in Figure A-37. Listing A-40 shows the standard CSS properties.

Home

***Figure A-37.*** *SharePoint 2010 page breadcrumb page name*

- **Style Sheet:** COREV4.CSS
- **Class:** s4-title h2

***Listing A-40.*** *Page Breadcrumb Page Name CSS*

```
.s4-title h1,.s4-title h2{
font-size:1.4em;
font-weight:normal;
display:inline;
padding:0px;
margin:0px;
}
.s4-title h1 a,.s4-title h2 a{
color:#003759;
display:inline-block;
}
.s4-title h2{
color:#5d6878;
}
```

The third element within the site table is the social tags and notes element described below.

# #8: Social Tags & Notes

The social tags and notes shown in Figure A-38 include the following CSS elements.

***Figure A-38.*** *SharePoint 2010 social tags and notes*

- Social Tags Outer TD
- Social Tags Container
- Social Tags Group Separator
- Social Tag Item

- Social Tag Image
- Social Tag Label

## Social Tags Outer TD

This class is used to simply set the alignment of the containing information to the left. Listing A-41 shows the standard CSS properties.

- **Style Sheet:** COREV4.CSS
- **Class:** s4-socialdata-notif

**Listing A-41.** *Social Tags Outer TD CSS*

```
.s4-socialdata-notif{
text-align:left;
}
```

## Social Tags Container

This class is used to set the font properties, width, overflow, and padding for the social tags. Listing A-42 shows the standard CSS properties.

- **Style Sheet:** COREV4.CSS
- **Class:** ms-socialNotif-Container

**Listing A-42.** *Social Tags Outer TD CSS*

```
.ms-socialNotif-Container{
font-family:"Segoe UI",Tahoma,Verdana,sans-serif;
font-size:1em;
width:120px;
overflow-x:auto;
overflow-y:hidden;
padding:0px 3px;
text-align:right;
}
```

## Social Tags Group Separator

This class is used to set the height and position of the border to the left of the social icons, as shown in Figure A-39. Listing A-43 shows the standard CSS properties.

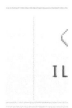

*Figure A-39. SharePoint 2010 social tags group separator*

- **Style Sheet:** COREV4.CSS
- **Class:** ms-socialNotif-groupSeparator

*Listing A-43. Social Tags Group Separator CSS*

```
.ms-socialNotif-groupSeparator{
display:inline-block;
height:60px;
position:relative;
top:4px;
margin:0px 3px;
border-right:1px solid;
border-right-color:#e7e7e8;
}
```

## Social Tag Item

This class is used to text align the icon and label text within the social item. It also sets the height, width, margin, and padding, as shown in Figure A-40. The hover state adds a border and background color. Listing A-44 shows the standard CSS properties that are used for both normal and hover state.

I Like It

*Figure A-40. SharePoint 2010 social tag item*

- **Style Sheet:** COREV4.CSS
- **ID:** AddQuickTag_ctl00_ctl37
- **Class:** ms-socialNotif
- **Hover Class:** ms-socialNotif:hover

**Listing A-44.** *Social Tag Item CSS*

```
.ms-socialNotif{
text-align:center;
vertical-align:top;
display:inline-block;
width:48px;
height:60px;
overflow:hidden;
margin:0px 1px;
padding:0px 2px;
border:1px solid transparent;
}
.ms-socialNotif:hover{
border:1px solid #f1c43f;
background-color:#fdeeb3;
}
```

## Social Tag Image

The inline CSS within the SPAN tag is used to add height, width, overflow, and positioning. The Inline CSS within the IMG sets the positioning of the "mossfgimg.png" image to display either the I Like It or the Tags & Notes icons shown in Figure A-41. Listing A-45 shows the inline CSS properties that are used within the SPAN and for each icon.

**Figure A-41.** *SharePoint 2010 social tag image*

- **Style Sheet:** Inline CSS

**Listing A-45.** *Social Tag Image Inline CSS*

```
/* Inline CSS on SPAN */
width: 32px;
height: 32px;
overflow: hidden;
display: inline-block;
position: relative;

/* Inline CSS on I Like It IMG */
left: 0px !important;
top: -132px !important;
border: none;
position: absolute;

/* Inline CSS on Tags & Notes IMG */
left: 0px !important;
```

```
top: -300px !important;
border: none;
position: absolute;
```

## Social Tag Label

This class is used to set the color and padding of the labels, as shown in Figure A-42. Listing A-46 shows the standard CSS properties.

**Figure A-42.** *SharePoint 2010 social tag label*

- **Style Sheet:** COREV4.CSS
- **Class:** ms-socialNotif-text

**Listing A-46.** *Social Tag Label CSS*

```
.ms-socialNotif-text{
color:#5d6878;
display:block;
padding-bottom:1px;
}
```

The next section that I will cover is the container for the top navigation, search, and help icon. These are all contained within a single DIV.

# #9: Top Header 2

This ID is used to set the height, background image, background color, and borders, as shown in Figure A-43. Listing A-47 shows the standard CSS properties.

**Figure A-43.** *SharePoint 2010 top header 2*

- **Style Sheet:** COREV4.CSS
- **ID:** s4-topheader2
- **Class:** s4-pr s4-notdlg

*Listing A-47. Top Header 2 CSS*

```
body #s4-topheader2{
background:url("/_layouts/images/selbg.png") repeat-x left top;
background-color:#f6f6f6;
vertical-align:middle;
min-height:25px;
border-top:1px solid #e0e0e0;
border-bottom:1px solid #b8babd;
}
```

This next section will cover the top navigation control that is included within the top header 2 container.

# #10: Top Navigation

The top navigation shown in Figure A-44 includes the following CSS elements.

*Figure A-44. SharePoint 2010 top navigation*

- Top Navigation Container
- Top Navigation
- Menu Horizontal
- Menu Item
- Menu Item Selected
- Menu Item Drop-Down Container
- Menu Item Drop-Down Container Item

## Top Navigation Container

This class is used to set padding of the top navigation container to 0px, as shown in Figure A-45. Listing A-48 shows the standard CSS properties.

*Figure A-45.* *SharePoint 2010 top navigation container*

- **Style Sheet:** COREV4.CSS
- **Class:** s4-lp s4-toplinks

*Listing A-48.* *Top Navigation Container CSS*

```
.s4-toplinks{
padding:0px;
}
```

# Top Navigation

This class is used to set the padding and margin of the top navigation to 0px, as shown in Figure A-46. Listing A-49 shows the standard CSS properties.

*Figure A-46.* *SharePoint 2010 top navigation*

- **Style Sheet:** COREV4.CSS
- **ID:** zz16_TopNavigationMenuV4
- **Class:** s4-tn

*Listing A-49.* *Top Navigation CSS*

```
.s4-tn{
padding:0px;
margin:0px;
}
```

# Menu Horizontal

This class is used to set the DIV to display as a table with a zoom of 1. Listing A-50 shows the standard CSS properties.

- **Style Sheet:** COREV4.CSS
- **Class:** menu horizontal menu-horizontal

***Listing A-50.*** *Top Navigation CSS*

```
.menu-horizontal{
display:table;
zoom:1;
}
```

# Menu Item

The following classes are used to stylize the individual top navigation item with padding, margins, text color, and height, and floating it to the left, as shown in Figure A-47. Listing A-51 shows the standard CSS properties.

```
Team Site
```

***Figure A-47.*** *SharePoint 2010 top navigation menu item*

- **Style Sheet:** COREV4.CSS

- **Item Container Class:** static

- **Item Link Class:** static menu-item

- **Item Link Additional Background Class:** additional-background

- **Item Link Text Class:** menu-item-text

***Listing A-51.*** *Top Navigation Menu Item CSS*

```
.menu ul,.menu li{
margin:0;
padding:0;
}
.menu-horizontal li.static,
.menu-horizontal a.static,
.menu-horizontal span.static{
float:left;
}
.s4-tn li.static > .menu-item{
color:#3b4f65;
white-space:nowrap;
border:1px solid transparent;
padding:4px 10px;
display:inline-block;
height:15px;
vertical-align:middle;
}
```

# Menu Item Selected

The following class is used to set the current navigation item to have padding, margins, borders, background image, background color, and a unique text color, as shown in Figure A-48. Listing A-52 shows the standard CSS properties.

Sub Site Level 1 ▼

*Figure A-48. SharePoint 2010 top navigation menu item selected*

- **Style Sheet:** COREV4.CSS
- **Item Link Class:** static selected menu-item

*Listing A-52. Top Navigation Menu Item Selected CSS*

```
.s4-toplinks .s4-tn a.selected{
border-color:#91cdf2;
border-bottom-color:#addbf7;
border-top-color:#c6e5f8;
background:url("/_layouts/images/selbg.png") repeat-x left top;
background-color:#ccebff;
color:#003759;
padding:4px 5px;
margin:0px 5px;
}
```

# Menu Item Drop-Down Container

The following class is used to set the drop-down background color, border, position, and minimum width, as shown in Figure A-49. Listing A-53 shows the standard CSS properties.

Sub Site Level 2
Sub Site Level 2a
Sub Site Level 2b
Sub Site Level 2c

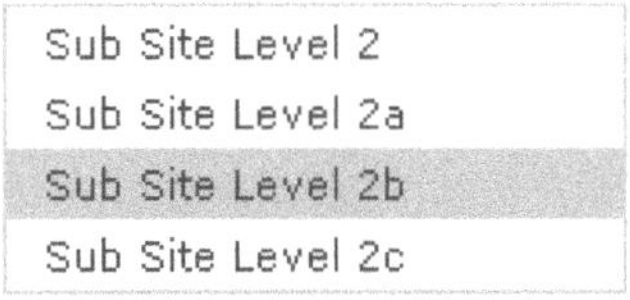

*Figure A-49. SharePoint 2010 top navigation menu item drop-down container*

- **Style Sheet:** COREV4.CSS
- **Class:** dynamic

*Listing A-53.* *Top Navigation Menu Item Drop-Down Container CSS*

```
.s4-tn ul.dynamic{
background-color:white;
border:1px solid #D9D9D9;
}
.menu ul.dynamic{
position:absolute;
left:-999em;
}
.menu span.dynamic, .menu a.dynamic{
min-width:150px;
}
```

## Menu Item Drop-Down Container Item

The following classes are used to stylize the individual menu item in the top navigation drop-down. These classes add padding, font weight, and also background color when your cursor hovers over it, as shown in Figure A-50. Listing A-54 shows the standard CSS properties.

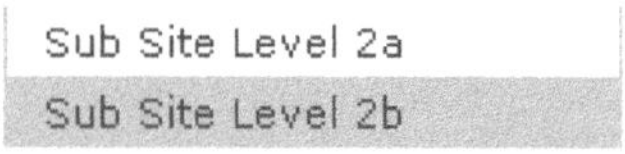

```
Sub Site Level 2a
Sub Site Level 2b
```

*Figure A-50.* *SharePoint 2010 top navigation menu item*

- **Style Sheet:** COREV4.CSS

- **Item Container Class:** dynamic

- **Item Link Class:** dynamic menu-item

- **Item Link Additional Background Class:** additional-background

- **Item Link Text Class:** menu-item-text

*Listing A-54.* *Top Navigation Menu Item CSS*

```
.menu ul,.menu li{
margin:0;
padding:0;
}
.s4-tn li.dynamic > .menu-item{
display:block;
padding:3px 10px;
white-space:nowrap;
font-weight:normal;
}
```

```
.s4-tn li.dynamic > a:hover{
font-weight:normal;
background-color:#D9D9D9;
}
```

This next section will cover the top navigation control that is included within the top header 2 container.

# #11: Search & Help

The top navigation shown in Figure A-51 includes the following CSS elements.

*Figure A-51. SharePoint 2010 search and help*

- Search Area
- Search Table
- Search Container
- Search Scope
- Search Box Cell
- Search Go
- Help Container
- Help Icon

## Search Area

The following classes are used to float the search area to the right of the top navigation; the padding is set to 0px per the s4-search class, as shown in Figure A-52. Listing A-55 shows the standard CSS properties.

*Figure A-52. SharePoint 2010 search area*

- **Style Sheet:** COREV4.CSS
- **ID:** s4-searcharea
- **Class:** s4-search s4-rp

*Listing A-55. Search Area CSS*

```
.s4-rp{
float:right;
padding:2px 10px 2px 5px;
}
.s4-search{
padding:0px !important;
}
```

# Search Table

The following class is specified in the search.css style sheet to give it a width and margin on the right to provide space between it and the help icon, as shown in Figure A-53. Listing A-56 shows the standard CSS properties.

*Figure A-53. SharePoint 2010 search table*

- **Style Sheet:** SEARCH.CSS
- **Table Class:** s4-wpTopTable

*Listing A-56. Search Table CSS*

```
.s4-search table{
width:212px;
float:left;
margin-right:17px;
}
```

# Search Box Container

The following classes are used to set the font styles and margins for the elements within the search container table. Listing A-57 shows the standard CSS properties.

- **Style Sheet:** SEARCH.CSS
- **Class:** ms-sbtable ms-sbtable-ex s4-search

*Listing A-57. Search Container CSS*

```
.ms-sbtable{
color:#000;
font-family:verdana,tahoma,sans-serif;
font-style:normal;
```

```
font-weight:normal;
}
.s4-search .ms-sbtable-ex{
float:right;
margin-right:2px;
margin-top:2px;
}
```

# Search Scope

The following classes are used to display the borders, text properties, width, height, margins, and padding for the search scope select box, as shown in Figure A-54. Listing A-58 shows the standard CSS properties.

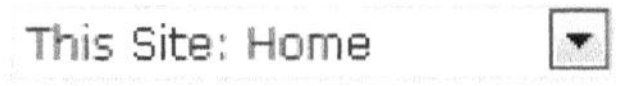

This Site: Home ▼

***Figure A-54.*** *SharePoint 2010 search box*

- **Style Sheet:** SEARCH.CSS

- **Select ID:** ctl00_PlaceHolderSearchArea_ctl01_SBScopesDDL

- **Container Class:** ms-sbscopes ms-sbcell

- **Input Class:** ms-sbscopes

***Listing A-58.*** *Search Box CSS*

```
td.ms-sbscopes{
border:none !important;
padding-right:10px;
}
select.ms-sbscopes{
font-family:verdana,tahoma,sans-serif;
font-size:1.3em;
width:170px;
border:thin solid #dbddde;
vertical-align:middle;
}
.s4-search select{
height:21px;
font-family:Verdana,Arial,sans-serif;
font-size:9pt;
padding:0 3px;
margin:3px 3px 0 0;
}
.s4-search select.ms-sbscopes,.s4-search input.ms-sbplain{
border:1px solid #e3e3e3 !important;
color:#476382;
```

```
margin-top:0;
}
.s4-search select.ms-sbscopes{
padding:0 0 2px;
}
```

# Search Box

The following classes are used to display the borders, text properties, width, background image, and background color for the search input box, as shown in Figure A-55. Listing A-59 shows the standard CSS properties.

*Figure A-55. SharePoint 2010 search box*

- **Style Sheet:** SEARCH.CSS

- **Input ID:** ctl00_PlaceHolderSearchArea_ctl01_S3031AEBB_InputKeywords

- **Class:** ms-sbplain s4-searchbox-QueryPrompt

*Listing A-59. Search Box CSS*

```
.s4-search select.ms-sbscopes,.s4-search input.ms-sbplain{
border:1px solid #e3e3e3 !important;
color:#476382;
margin-top:0;
}
.s4-search input.ms-sbplain{
font-size:1.1em;
border-right:0 !important;
width:191px !important;
background:url("/_layouts/images/bgximg.png") repeat-x -0px -511px;
border:1px solid #e3e3e3 !important;
background-color:#fff;
height:17px;
padding:2px 3px 0;
}
```

# Search Go

The following classes are used to set the vertical alignment, border, background image, and height of the IMG element, as shown in Figure A-56. Listing A-60 shows the standard CSS properties.

*Figure A-56.* *SharePoint 2010 search go*

- **Style Sheet:** SEARCH.CSS
- **Container Class:** ms-sbgo ms-sbcell
- **IMG Class:** srch-gosearchimg

*Listing A-60.* *Search Go CSS*

```
td.ms-sbgo img{
vertical-align:bottom;
border:1px solid #b6babf !important;
border-left:none !important;
}
.s4-search .srch-gosearchimg{
background:url("/_layouts/images/bgximg.png") repeat-x -0px -511px;
border:1px solid #e3e3e3 !important;
border-left:none !important;
background-color:#fff;
height:19px;
padding:0 !important;
}
```

# Help Container

The following class is used to add margins around the help icon, as shown in Figure A-57. Listing A-61 shows the standard CSS properties.

*Figure A-57.* *SharePoint 2010 help container*

- **Style Sheet:** COREV4.CSS
- **Class:** s4-help

*Listing A-61.* *Help Container CSS*

```
.s4-help{
display:inline-block;
margin:4px 4px 3px 21px;
}
```

# Help Icon

The following inline CSS used on the SPAN element defines the height, width, and overflow to display the help icon correctly. The inline CSS used on the IMG element defines the positioning of the "fgimg.png" sprite image. Listing A-62 shows the inline CSS properties that are used for both elements.

- **Style Sheet:** Inline CSS

*Listing A-62. Help Icon Inline CSS*

```
/* Inline CSS on SPAN */
width: 17px;
height: 17px;
overflow: hidden;
display: inline-block;
position: relative;

/* Inline CSS on IMG */
left: 0px !important;
top: -309px !important;
position: absolute;
```

This next section will cover the status bar control that is visible when a page is checked out or being edited.

# #12: Status Bar

The status bar shown in Figure A-58 includes the following CSS elements.

*Figure A-58. SharePoint 2010 status bar*

- Status Bar Container
- Status Bar Style 1 (Blue)
- Status Bar Style 2 (Green)
- Status Bar Style 3 (Yellow)
- Status Bar Style 4 (Red)

# Status Bar Container

The ID "s4-statusbarcontainer" is used for the containing DIV but does not have any styles applied to it, as shown in Figure A-59.

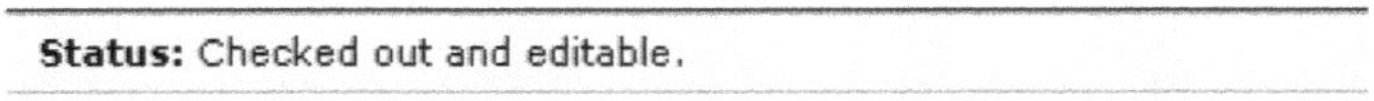

**Status:** Checked out and editable.

***Figure A-59.*** *SharePoint 2010 search area*

The next four classes are used based on the status type for the page.

# Status Bar Style 1 (Blue)

The following ID is used to set the padding, border width, and font for the status bar. The unique class is used to show the blue background image, font color, and border color within the status bar. Listing A-63 shows the standard CSS properties.

- **Style Sheet:** COREV4.CSS
- **Class:** pageStatusBar
- **Class:** s4-status-s1

***Listing A-63.*** *Status Bar Style 1 (Blue) CSS*

```
body #pageStatusBar{
display:none;
border-style:solid;
border-width:1px 0px;
padding:4px 5px 5px 10px;
font-family:verdana;
font-size:1em;
}
.s4-status-s1{
background:#c9d7e6 url("/_layouts/images/bgximg.png") repeat-x -0px -209px;
color:#3b4652;
border-color:#aaafbe;
}
```

# Status Bar Style 2 (Green)

The following ID is used to set the padding, border width, and font for the status bar. The unique class is used to show the green background image, font color, and border color within the status bar. Listing A-64 shows the standard CSS properties.

- **Style Sheet:** COREV4.CSS

- **Class:** pageStatusBar

- **Class:** s4-status-s2

*Listing A-64. Status Bar Style 2 (Green) CSS*

```
body #pageStatusBar{
display:none;
border-style:solid;
border-width:1px 0px;
padding:4px 5px 5px 10px;
font-family:verdana;
font-size:1em;
}
.s4-status-s2{
background:#71b84f url("/_layouts/images/bgximg.png") repeat-x -0px -83px;
color:#1a3807;
border-color:#3e8811;
}
```

# Status Bar Style 3 (Yellow)

The following ID is used to set the padding, border width, and font for the status bar. The unique class is used to show the yellow background image, font color, and border color within the status bar. Listing A-65 shows the standard CSS properties.

- **Style Sheet:** COREV4.CSS

- **Class:** pageStatusBar

- **Class:** s4-status-s3

*Listing A-65. Status Bar Style 3 (Yellow) CSS*

```
body #pageStatusBar{
display:none;
border-style:solid;
border-width:1px 0px;
padding:4px 5px 5px 10px;
font-family:verdana;
font-size:1em;
}
.s4-status-s3{
background:#fdf289 url("/_layouts/images/bgximg.png") repeat-x -0px -260px;
color:#4b3904;
border-color:#caac09;
}
```

## Status Bar Style 4 (Red)

The following ID is used to set the padding, border width, and font for the status bar. The unique class is used to show the red background image, font color, and border color within the status bar. Listing A-66 shows the standard CSS properties.

- **Style Sheet:** COREV4.CSS

- **Class:** pageStatusBar

- **Class:** s4-status-s4

*Listing A-66. Status Bar Style 4 (Red) CSS*

```
body #pageStatusBar{
display:none;
border-style:solid;
border-width:1px 0px;
padding:4px 5px 5px 10px;
font-family:verdana;
font-size:1em;
}
.s4-status-s4{
background:#df5a5b url("/_layouts/images/bgximg.png") repeat-x -0px -158px;
color:#1f0000;
border-color:#bc1213;
}
```

This next section will cover the Quick Launch, also referred to as the left-side navigation elements.

# #13: Quick Launch (Left Panel)

The Quick Launch (left panel) shown in Figure A-60 includes the following CSS elements.

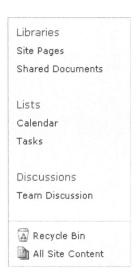

**Figure A-60.** *SharePoint 2010 Quick Launch (left panel)*

- Left Panel
- Left Panel Content
- Quick Launch Outer
- Quick Launch
- Quick Launch Menu
- Quick Launch Link Headers
- Quick Launch Link Items
- Special Navigation Links Container
- Recycle Bin
- All Site Content

# Left Panel

The following ID is used to float the Quick Launch panel to the left and provide it a set width. The class is used within the same DIV so that it does not get displayed within dialog windows. Listing A-67 shows the standard CSS properties.

- **Style Sheet:** COREV4.CSS
- **ID:** s4-leftpanel
- **Class:** s4-notdlg

***Listing A-67.*** *Left Panel CSS*

```
body #s4-leftpanel{
width:155px;
float:left;
}
```

## Left Panel Content

The following ID is used to set the padding, background color, and right and bottom border color. Listing A-68 shows the standard CSS properties.

- **Style Sheet:** COREV4.CSS

- **ID:** s4-leftpanel-content

***Listing A-68.*** *Left Panel Content CSS*

```
body #s4-leftpanel-content{
padding:0px 0px 5px;
background-color:#fcfcfc;
border:1px solid #dbddde;
border-top-width:0px;
border-right-width:1px;
border-bottom-width:1px;
border-left-width:0px;
}
```

## Quick Launch Outer

The following class is used to set the margin of this DIV to zero. Listing A-69 shows the standard CSS properties.

- **Style Sheet:** COREV4.CSS

- **Class:** ms-quicklaunchouter

***Listing A-69.*** *Quick Launch Outer CSS*

```
.ms-quicklaunchouter{
margin:0px;
}
```

## Quick Launch

The following class is used to apply 5px of padding to the top of the Quick Launch area Listing A-70 shows the standard CSS properties.

- **Style Sheet:** COREV4.CSS
- **Class:** ms-quickLaunch

*Listing A-70. Quick Launch CSS*

```
.ms-quickLaunch{
padding-top:5px;
}
```

# Quick Launch Menu

The following class is used to apply a bottom margin of 20px to the Quick Launch. Listing A-71 shows the standard CSS properties.

- **Style Sheet:** COREV4.CSS
- **ID:** zz18_V4QuickLaunchMenu
- **Class:** s4-ql

*Listing A-71. Quick Launch Menu CSS*

```
.s4-ql,.s4-specialNavLinkList{
list-style-type:none;
margin:0px 0px 20px 0px;
padding:0px;
}
```

# Quick Launch Link Headers

The following class is used to set the font size, font color, and padding for the Quick Launch header text, as shown in Figure A-61. Listing A-72 shows the standard CSS properties.

Libraries

Site Pages

*Figure A-61. SharePoint 2010 Quick Launch link headers*

- **Style Sheet:** COREV4.CSS
- **Class:** static menu-item

*Listing A-72. Quick Launch Link Headers CSS*

```
.s4-ql ul.root > li > .menu-item,.s4-qlheader,.s4-qlheader:visited{
font-size:1.2em;
color:#0072bc;
```

```
margin:0px;
padding:3px 4px 3px 10px;
border-width:1px 0px;
border-style:solid;
border-color:transparent;
word-wrap:break-word;
overflow-x:hidden;
}
```

# Quick Launch Link Items

The following class is used to set the padding, font color, and horizontal overflow for the Quick Launch link items shown in Figure A-62. Listing A-73 shows the standard CSS properties.

```
Libraries

Site Pages

Shared Documents
```

*Figure A-62.* SharePoint 2010 Quick Launch link items

- **Style Sheet:** COREV4.CSS
- **Class:** static menu-item

*Listing A-73.* Quick Launch Link Items CSS

```
.s4-ql ul.root ul > li > a{
padding:3px 4px 4px 10px;
border-width:1px 0px;
border-style:solid;
border-color:transparent;
color:#3b4f65;
overflow-x:hidden;
display:block;
zoom:1;
}
```

# Special Navigation Links Container

The following class is used to apply a 20px bottom margin, top border, and top padding, as shown in Figure A-63. Listing A-74 shows the standard CSS properties.

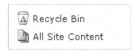

***Figure A-63.*** *SharePoint 2010 special navigation links container*

- **Style Sheet:** COREV4.CSS
- **Class:** s4-specialNavLinkList

***Listing A-74.*** *Special Navigation Links Container CSS*

```
.s4-ql,.s4-specialNavLinkList{
list-style-type:none;
margin:0px 0px 20px 0px;
padding:0px;
}
.s4-specialNavLinkList{
margin:0px;
border-top:1px solid #dbddde;
padding-top:5px;
}
```

# Recycle Bin

The following class is used to apply padding and font color for the recycle bin link as shown in Figure A-64. Listing A-75 shows the standard CSS for the text and inline CSS to position the IMG element.

***Figure A-64.*** *SharePoint 2010 Recycle Bin*

- **Style Sheet:** COREV4.CSS
- **Class:** s4-rcycl

***Listing A-75.*** *Recycle Bin CSS*

```
.s4-specialNavLinkList a{
display:block;
padding:3px 4px 3px 10px;
color:#3b4f65;
}
```

```
/* Inline CSS on fgimg.png IMG */
left: 0px !important;
top: -428px !important;
border: none;
position: absolute;
```

## All Site Content

The following inline CSS is used to show the All Site Content icon, as shown in Figure A-65. Listing A-76 shows the standard CSS for the text and inline CSS to position the IMG element.

 All Site Content

***Figure A-65.*** *SharePoint 2010 All Site Content icon*

- **Style Sheet:** Inline CSS

***Listing A-76.*** *All Site Content Inline CSS*

```
/* Inline CSS on fgimg.png IMG */
left: 0px !important;
top: 0px !important;
border: none;
position: absolute;
```

This next section will cover the main content areas within a site or a page.

# #14: Content Area

The content area includes the following CSS elements.

- Wide Content Area

- Content Area

- Body Area

- Body Area Cell

## Wide Content Area

The following class and ID are used to set the width and float the element to the left, as shown in Figure A-66. Listing A-77 shows the standard CSS properties.

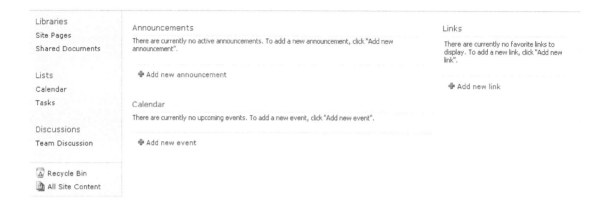

**Figure A-66.** *SharePoint 2010 wide content area*

- **Style Sheet:** COREV4.CSS
- **ID:** s4-mainarea
- **Class:** s4-pr s4-widecontentarea

**Listing A-77.** *Left Panel CSS*

```
.s4-widecontentarea{
width:100%;
}
body #s4-mainarea{
float:left;
clear:both;
}
```

## Content Area

The content area excludes the Quick Launch, and the class is used to set the background color and add a margin to the left so that it is pushed away from the Quick Launch. It also has a minimum height set, so when you do not have a lot of content on the page it will still have at least 324px in height, as shown in Figure A-67. Listing A-78 shows the standard CSS properties.

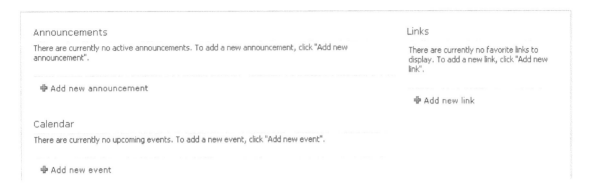

***Figure A-67.*** *SharePoint 2010 content area*

- **Style Sheet:** COREV4.CSS
- **ID:** MSO_ContentTable
- **Class:** s4-ca s4-ca-dlgNoRibbon

***Listing A-78.*** *Left Panel CSS*

```
.s4-ca{
background:#fff;
margin-left:155px;
margin-right:0px;
min-height:324px;
}
body #MSO_ContentTable{
position:relative;
}
```

# Body Area

The following class is used to add 5px of padding to the bottom of the body area. Listing A-79 shows the standard CSS properties.

- **Style Sheet:** COREV4.CSS
- **Class:** s4-ba

***Listing A-79.*** *Body Area CSS*

```
.s4-ba{
padding:0px 0px 5px 0px;
}
```

## Body Area Cell

The following class is used to set the vertical alignment of the content to the top. Listing A-80 shows the standard CSS properties.

- **Style Sheet:** COREV4.CSS
- **Class:** ms-bodyareacell

***Listing A-80.*** *Body Area Cell CSS*

```
.ms-bodyareacell{
vertical-align:top;
}
```

This next section will cover the main elements that make up a web part.

# #15: Web-Part Elements

The web-part elements shown in Figure A-68 include the following CSS elements.

Links

There are currently no favorite links to display. To add a new link, click "Add new link".

╬ Add new link

***Figure A-68.*** *SharePoint 2010 web-part elements*

- Web-Part Cell
- Web-Part Header
- Web-Part Header Space
- Web-Part Header TD
- Web-Part Title
- Web-Part Menu
- Web-Part Selection
- Web-Part Body
- Web-Part Border

- Web-Part Add New
- Web-Part Vertical Spacing

## Web-Part Cell

The list web-part class is applied around specific list and library web parts like announcements, events, and documents. You can use this class to stylize the outer part of these types of web parts. The basic web-part class shown below is used for web parts such as content editors and image viewer web parts.

- **List Web-Part Class:** s4-wpcell
- **Basic Web-Part Class:** s4-wpcell-plain

## Web-Part Header

The following class is used to add a white background, as shown in Figure A-69. Listing A-81 shows the standard CSS properties.

Links

*Figure A-69. SharePoint 2010 web-part header*

- **Style Sheet:** COREV4.CSS
- **Class:** ms-WPHeader

*Listing A-81. Web-Part Header CSS*

```
.ms-WPHeader{
background-color:#FFFFFF;
}
```

## Web-Part Header Space

The following class is used to add 5px of space before and after the web-part header. Listing A-82 shows the standard CSS properties.

- **Style Sheet:** COREV4.CSS
- **Class:** ms-wpTdSpace

*Listing A-82. Web-Part Header Space CSS*

```
.ms-WPHeader .ms-wpTdSpace{
width:5px;
border-bottom:1px solid transparent;
}
```

# Web-Part Header TD

The following class gives the web-part header element a border on the bottom. Listing A-83 shows the standard CSS properties.

- **Style Sheet:** COREV4.CSS
- **Class:** ms-WPHeaderTd

*Listing A-83. Web-Part Header TD CSS.*

```
.ms-WPHeader td,.ms-fakewptitle{
border-bottom:1px solid #EBEBEB;
border-collapse:collapse;
}
```

# Web-Part Title

The following classes are used to set the font properties and padding for the web-part title, as shown in Figure A-70. Listing A-84 shows the standard CSS properties.

Links

*Figure A-70. SharePoint 2010 web-part title*

- **Style Sheet:** COREV4.CSS
- **Class:** ms-standardheader ms-WPTitle

*Listing A-84. Web-Part Title CSS*

```
.ms-standardheader{
font-size:1em;
margin:0em;
text-align:left;
color:#525252;
}
.ms-WPTitle{
font-weight:normal;
font-family:Verdana,Tahoma,sans-serif;
padding-left:0px;
padding-right:4px;
padding-top:4px;
padding-bottom:5px;
font-size:10pt;
}
```

# Web-Part Menu

The following class is used to set the width, cursor, and border width for the web-part menu. As the user hovers over the arrow, the hover state adds a background image, background color, and border color, as shown in Figure A-71. Listing A-85 shows the standard CSS properties for normal state and hover state.

*Figure A-71. SharePoint 2010 web-part menu*

- **Style Sheet:** COREV4.CSS
- **Class:** ms-WPHeaderTdMenu
- **Hover Class:** ms-WPHeaderTdMenu:hover

*Listing A-85. Web-Part Menu CSS*

```
.ms-WPHeaderTdMenu{
width:21px;
cursor:pointer;
word-wrap:normal;
white-space:nowrap;
border:1px solid transparent;
}
.ms-WPHeaderTdMenu:hover{
border:1px solid #91CDF2;
background:url("/_layouts/images/selbg.png") repeat-x left top;
background-color:#CCEBFF;
}
```

# Web-Part Selection

The following class is used to set the width and text alignment for the input form, as shown in Figure A-72. Listing A-86 shows the standard CSS properties for normal state and hover state.

*Figure A-72. SharePoint 2010 web-part selection*

- **Style Sheet:** COREV4.CSS
- **Class:** ms-WPHeaderTdSelection

*Listing A-86. Web-Part Selection CSS*

```
.ms-WPHeaderTdSelection{
width:21px;
cursor:auto;
text-align:center;
}
```

# Web-Part Body

The following classes provide font properties and margins to the web-part body area. Listing A-87 shows the standard CSS properties.

- **Style Sheet:** COREV4.CSS

- **List Web-Part Class:** ms-wpContentDivSpace

- **Basic Web-Part Class:** ms-WPBody ms-wpContentDivSpace

*Listing A-87. Web-Part Body CSS*

```
.ms-WPBody{
font-size:8pt;
font-family:verdana,arial,helvetica,sans-serif;
}
.ms-wpContentDivSpace{
margin-left:5px;
margin-right:5px;
}
```

# Web-Part Border

If you have modified the web part to show a title and border or just a border with no title, the following class is used to add a 1px blue border around the web-part content, as shown in Figure A-73. Listing A-88 shows the standard CSS properties.

*Figure A-73. SharePoint 2010 web-part border*

- **Style Sheet:** COREV4.CSS

- **Class:** ms-WPBorder

***Listing A-88.*** *Web-Part Border CSS*

```
.ms-WPBorder,.ms-WPBorderBorderOnly{
border-color:#9ac6ff;
border-width:1px;
border-style:solid;
}
```

# Web-Part Line

The following class is used to add in a separator line between the web-part content and the summary toolbar link as shown in Figure A-74. Listing A-89 shows the standard CSS properties.

There are currently no upcoming events. To add a new event, click "Add new event".

✚ Add new event

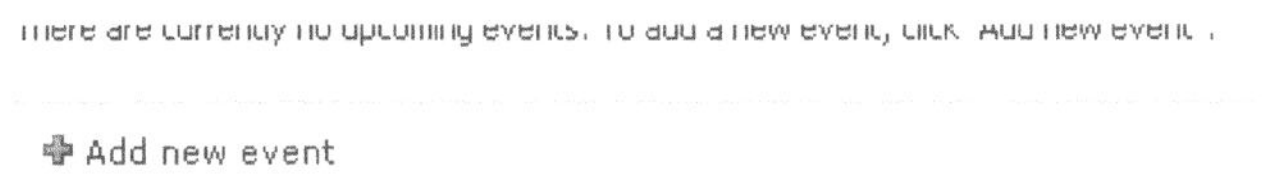

***Figure A-74.*** *SharePoint 2010 web-part line*

- **Style Sheet:** COREV4.CSS
- **Class:** ms-partline

***Listing A-89.*** *Web-Part Line CSS*

```
.ms-partline{
height:3px;
border-bottom:1px solid #EBEBEB;
}
```

# Web-Part Add New

The following class is used to add padding to the Add New element, as shown in Figure A-75. Listing A-90 shows the standard CSS properties.

✚ Add new event

***Figure A-75.*** *SharePoint 2010 web-part Add New*

- **Style Sheet:** COREV4.CSS
- **Class:** ms-addnew

*Listing A-90.* *Web-Part Add New CSS*

```
td.ms-addnew{
padding-left:10px;
padding-right:7px;
padding-top:9px;
}
```

## Web-Part Vertical Spacing

The following class is used to add spacing to the bottom of web parts. This adds in vertical space between two stacked web parts. Listing A-91 shows the standard CSS properties.

- **Style Sheet:** COREV4.CSS

- **Class:** ms-PartSpacingVertical

*Listing A-91.* *Web-Part Vertical Spacing CSS*

```
.ms-PartSpacingVertical{
font-size:1pt;
margin-top:12px;
}
```

This next section will cover the main elements that are used within dialog windows.

# #16: Dialog Windows

The Dialog Window shown in Figure A-76 includes the following CSS elements.

***Figure A-76.*** *SharePoint 2010 dialog window*

- Dialog Overlay (Gray Transparent Background)
- Dialog Content
- Dialog Border
- Dialog Title
- Dialog Title Text
- Dialog HTML Tag
- Dialog Title Buttons
- Dialog Frame Container

# Dialog Overlay (Gray Transparent Background)

The following class is used to add in a 70% transparent gray background color that draws the user's attention to the opened dialog window. Listing A-92 shows the standard CSS properties that are used.

- **Style Sheet:** COREV4.CSS
- **Class:** ms-dlgOverlay

*Listing A-92. Dialog Overlay CSS*

```
.ms-dlgOverlay{
position:absolute;
top:0px;
left:0px;
width:100%;
height:100%;
filter:alpha(opacity=70);
-ms-filter:"alpha(opacity=70)";
opacity:0.7;
background-color:#182738;
display:none;
}
```

# Dialog Content

The following class is used to set the positioning, background color, and border for the outer DIV container of the dialog window, as shown in Figure A-77. Listing A-93 shows the standard CSS properties.

*Figure A-77. SharePoint 2010 dialog content*

- **Style Sheet:** COREV4.CSS
- **Class:** ms-dlgContent

***Listing A-93.*** *Dialog Content CSS*

```
.ms-dlgContent{
position:absolute;
background-color:#ffffff;
display:none;
border:1px solid #161d25;
}
```

# Dialog Border

The following class is used to add an additional border around a dialog window. Listing A-94 shows the standard CSS properties.

- **Style Sheet:** COREV4.CSS
- **Class:** ms-dlgBorder

***Listing A-94.*** *Dialog Border CSS*

```
.ms-dlgBorder{
border:1px solid #0072bc;
}
```

# Dialog Title

The following class is used to set the background image, background color, and height, as shown in Figure A-78. Listing A-95 shows the standard CSS properties.

***Figure A-78.*** *SharePoint 2010 dialog title*

- **Style Sheet:** COREV4.CSS
- **Class:** ms-dlgTitle

***Listing A-95.*** *Dialog Title CSS*

```
.ms-dlgTitle{
background:url("/_layouts/images/bgximg.png") repeat-x -0px -51px;
background-color:#21374c;
height:32px;
white-space:nowrap;
```

```
cursor:default;
overflow:hidden;
}
```

# Dialog Title Text

The following class is used to set the font properties, padding, and overflow, as shown in Figure A-79. Listing A-96 shows the standard CSS properties.

Announcements - New Item

**Figure A-79.** *SharePoint 2010 dialog title text*

- **Style Sheet:** COREV4.CSS

- **Class:** ms-dlgTitleText

**Listing A-96.** *Dialog Title Text CSS*

```
.ms-dlgTitleText{
font-family:Verdana;
font-size:1.3em;
line-height:1.2;
font-weight:normal;
padding-left:10px;
padding-top:7px;
color:#ffffff;
float:left;
overflow:hidden;
text-overflow:ellipsis;
}
```

# Dialog Title Buttons

The following class is used to float the buttons to the right and add in padding, as shown in Figure A-80. Listing A-97 shows the standard CSS properties.

**Figure A-80.** *SharePoint 2010 dialog title buttons*

- **Style Sheet:** COREV4.CSS

- **Class:** ms-dlgTitleBtns

***Listing A-97.*** *Dialog Title Buttons CSS*

```
.ms-dlgTitleBtns{
float:right;
padding-top:2px;
padding-right:2px;
}
```

# Dialog Frame Container

The following container class is used to set the overflow to auto. The `iframe` class is used to set the width and height to 100% and no borders, as shown in Figure A-81. Listing A-98 shows the standard CSS properties.

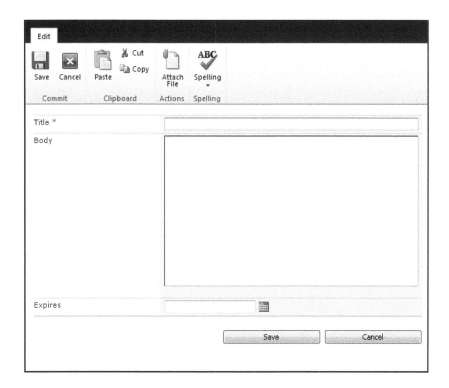

***Figure A-81.*** *SharePoint 2010 dialog frame container*

- **Style Sheet:** COREV4.CSS
- **Class:** ms-dlgFrameContainer
- **Iframe Class:** ms-dlgFrame

*Listing A-98. Dialog Frame Container CSS*

```
.ms-dlgFrameContainer{
overflow:auto;
}
.ms-dlgFrame{
width:100%;
height:100%;
border:none;
}
```

## Dialog HTML Tag

The "ms-dialog" class is used as a trigger to hide specific elements that are using the `s4-notdlg` class, as shown in Listing A-99. The `dlgframe.css` file is not located in the same place as the `corev4.css` file. The location of this file is at `/_layouts/styles/dlgframe.css`.

- **Style Sheet:** dlgframe.css
- **Class:** ms-dialog

*Listing A-99. Dialog HTML Tag CSS*

```
.ms-dialog .s4-notdlg{
display:none !important
}
```

This next section will cover some of the main elements within the blog site template.

# #17: Blog Posts

The blog post styles shown in Figure A-82 include the following CSS elements.

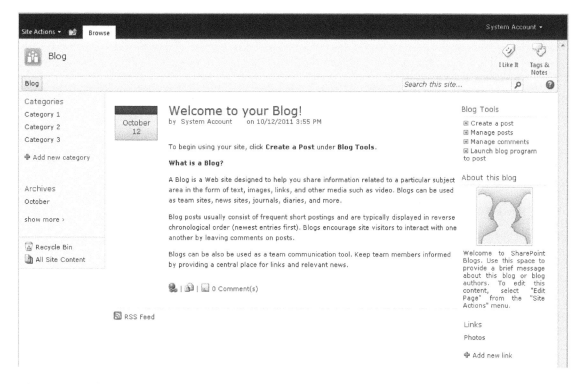

**Figure A-82.** *SharePoint 2010 Dialog Window*

- Left Blog Date
- Post Calendar Date Box Top
- Post Calendar Date Box Bottom
- Right Blog Post Container
- Post Title
- Post Footer
- Post Body
- Blog RSS
- Blog Right Zone

# Left Blog Date

The following class is used to set the width and padding for the blog date element, as shown in Figure A-83. Listing A-100 shows the standard CSS properties.

***Figure A-83.*** *SharePoint 2010 left blog date*

- **Style Sheet:** BLOG.CSS
- **Class:** ms-leftblogdate

***Listing A-100.*** *Left Blog Date CSS*

```
.ms-leftblogdate{
width:75px;
padding-right:10px;
}
```

# Post Calendar Date Box Top

The following class is used to set the margin, background color, background image, width, height, and margin, as shown in Figure A-84. Listing A-101 shows the standard CSS properties.

***Figure A-84.*** *SharePoint 2010 post calendar date box top*

- **Style Sheet:** BLOG.CSS
- **ID:** PostDateTopBox
- **Class:** ms-postcalendardateboxtop

***Listing A-101.*** *Post Calendar Date Box Top CSS*

```
.ms-postcalendardateboxtop{
margin-top:5px;
background:#0072bc url("/_layouts/images/calTopBkgd.png") repeat-x bottom left;
width:75px;
height:13px;
border:1px solid;
border-color:#00558d #004572 #003d66 #00558d;
margin-right:7px;
}
```

# Post Calendar Date Box Bottom

The following class is used to set height, width, padding, borders, font styles, background color, background image, and a few other properties, as shown in Figure A-85. Listing A-102 shows the standard CSS properties.

*Figure A-85. SharePoint 2010 post calendar date box bottom*

- **Style Sheet:** BLOG.CSS
- **ID:** PostDateBottomBox
- **Class:** ms-postcalendardateboxbottom

*Listing A-102. Post Calendar Date Box Bottom CSS*

```
.ms-postcalendardateboxbottom{
width:75px;
max-width:75px;
min-height:38px;
padding:4px 0px 2px 0px;
border:1px solid;
border-color:#c1c7cd #9ea3a8 #91959a #c1c7cd;
border-top-style:hidden;
font:1.1em verdana;
color:#65686b;
background:#f1f1f1 url("/_layouts/images/calMainBkgd.png") repeat-x bottom left;
margin-right:7px;
font:1.1em verdana;
word-wrap:break-word;
text-align:center;
color:#65686b;
word-spacing:10em;
line-height:1.3em;
display:table;
table-layout:fixed;
}
```

# Right Blog Post Container

The following class is used to set word wrap, horizontal overflow, and the width of the blog post content, as shown in Figure A-86. Listing A-103 shows the standard CSS properties.

## Welcome to your Blog!

by  System Account      on 10/12/2011 3:55 PM

To begin using your site, click **Create a Post** under **Blog Tools**.

**What is a Blog?**

A Blog is a Web site designed to help you share information related to a particular subject area in the form of text, images, links, and other media such as video. Blogs can be used as team sites, news sites, journals, diaries, and more.

Blog posts usually consist of frequent short postings and are typically displayed in reverse chronological order (newest entries first). Blogs encourage site visitors to interact with one another by leaving comments on posts.

Blogs can be also be used as a team communication tool. Keep team members informed by providing a central place for links and relevant news.

 | 📇 | 📧 0 Comment(s)

***Figure A-86.*** *SharePoint 2010 right blog post container*

- **Style Sheet:** BLOG.CSS
- **Class:** ms-rightblogpost

***Listing A-103.*** *Right Blog Post Container CSS*

```
.ms-rightblogpost{
word-wrap:break-word;
overflow-x:hidden;
width:680px;
}
```

# Post Title

The following class is used to set the width, font styles, and positioning of the post title, as shown in Figure A-87. Listing A-104 shows the standard CSS properties.

Welcome to your Blog!

***Figure A-87.*** *SharePoint 2010 post title*

- **Style Sheet:** BLOG.CSS
- **Class:** ms-PostTitle

*Listing A-104.* *Post Title CSS*

```
.ms-PostTitle{
font-size:16pt;
padding-top:0px;
width:600px;
word-wrap:break-word;
overflow-x:hidden;
}
.ms-PostTitle span{
position:relative;
left:-2px;
right:auto;
}
.ms-PostTitle a{
color:#4c4c4c;
text-decoration:none;
}
```

## Post Footer

The following classes are used to set the font size, font color, padding on the bottom, and hyperlink color to the elements below the title and below the post body, as shown in Figure A-88. Listing A-105 shows the standard CSS properties.

Welcome to your Blog!
by System Account      on 10/12/2011 3:55 PM

*Figure A-88.* *SharePoint 2010 post footer*

- **Style Sheet:** BLOG.CSS
- **Class:** ms-PostFooter

*Listing A-105.* *Post Footer CSS*

```
.ms-PostFooter,.ms-CommentFooter{
font-size:8pt;
color:#666666;
padding-bottom:22px;
}
.ms-PostFooter a,.ms-CommentFooter a{
:#6c90d8;
white-space:nowrap;
}
```

# Post Body

The following classes are used to set the font color, font size, line height, padding, hyperlink color, and paragraph margins spacing within the blog post body content, as shown in Figure A-89. Listing A-106 shows the standard CSS properties.

To begin using your site, click **Create a Post** under **Blog Tools**.

**What is a Blog?**

A Blog is a Web site designed to help you share information related to a particular subject area in the form of text, images, links, and other media such as video. Blogs can be used as team sites, news sites, journals, diaries, and more.

Blog posts usually consist of frequent short postings and are typically displayed in reverse chronological order (newest entries first). Blogs encourage site visitors to interact with one another by leaving comments on posts.

Blogs can be also be used as a team communication tool. Keep team members informed by providing a central place for links and relevant news.

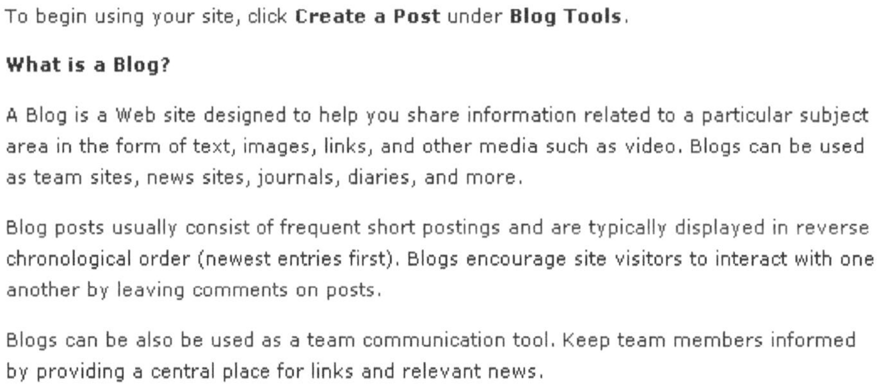

*Figure A-89. SharePoint 2010 post body*

- **Style Sheet:** BLOG.CSS
- **Class:** ms-PostBody

*Listing A-106. Post Body CSS*

```
.ms-PostBody{
color:#4c4c4c;
font-size:8pt;
line-height:1.7em;
padding-top:6px;
padding-bottom:12px;
}
.ms-PostBody a{
color:#0000CC;
}
.ms-PostBody p{
margin:0 0 1em 0;
}
```

# Blog RSS

The following classes are used to set the font color, width, top border, padding, hyperlink color, and icon style, as shown in Figure A-90. Listing A-107 shows the standard CSS properties.

RSS Feed

*Figure A-90. SharePoint 2010 blog RSS*

- **Style Sheet:** BLOG.CSS
- **ID:** BlogRSSMain
- **Class:** ms-blogrss

*Listing A-107. Blog RSS CSS*

```
.ms-blogrss{
color:#4c4c4c;
width:100%;
font-size:8pt;
border-top:solid 1px #e3efff;
padding-top:5px;
}
.ms-blogrss a{
color:#003399;
}
.ms-blogrss img{
vertical-align:middle;
border:none;
}
```

# Blog Right Zone

The following class and inline CSS is used to set the width, horizontal overflow, and word wrapping for the right blog panel, as shown in Figure A-91. Listing A-108 shows the standard CSS properties.

Blog Tools

▣ Create a post
▣ Manage posts
▣ Manage comments
▣ Launch blog program
to post

About this blog

**Figure A-91.** *SharePoint 2010 blog right zone*

- **Style Sheet:** BLOG.CSS & Inline CSS
- **Class:** ms-blogRightZone

**Listing A-108.** *Blog Right Zone CSS*

```
.ms-blogRightZone{
width:65px;
}
/* Inline CSS */
width: 165px;
overflow-x: hidden;
word-wrap: break-word;
```

This next section will cover some of the main elements on the Profile page within My Sites.

# #18: My Profile

The My Profile elements shown in Figure A-92 include the following CSS elements.

**Figure A-92.** *SharePoint 2010 My Profile*

- My Profile Content Area
- Profile As Seen By
- Profile Page Header
- Local Time
- Profile Picture
- Profile Name
- About Me Profile
- Status Bubble
- My Site Navigation Tabs

# My Profile Content Area

The following class is used to set the width of the profile information to 980px, as shown in Figure A-93. If you want the page to expand to the full width, set this class property to 100%. Listing A-109 shows the standard CSS properties.

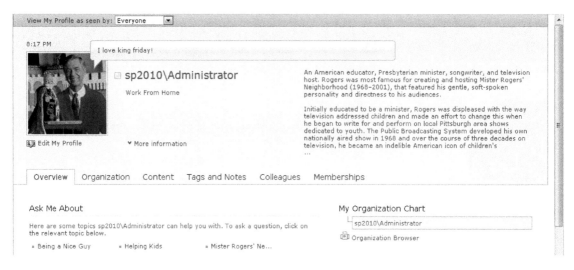

*Figure A-93. SharePoint 2010 My Profile content area*

- **Style Sheet:** mysitelayout.css
- **ID:** MSO_ContentTable
- **Class:** s4-ca s4-ca-dlgNoRibbon

*Listing A-109. My Profile Content Area CSS*

```
.s4-ca{
min-height: 0px;
float:left;
margin-left: 0px;
width:980px;
}
```

# Profile As Seen By

The following class is used to set the background image, border, font color, and padding, as shown in Figure A-94. Listing A-110 shows the standard CSS properties.

*Figure A-94. SharePoint 2010 Profile as seen by*

- **Style Sheet:** PORTAL.CSS
- **Class:** ms-profileasseenby

*Listing A-110. Profile As Seen By CSS*

```
.ms-profileasseenby{
background: url(/_layouts/images/asSeenBy_bg.png) repeat-x left bottom;
border: 1px solid #aaafbe;
border-top: none;
color: #3b4652;
vertical-align: middle;
padding-left: 24px;
line-height: 21px;
}
```

# Profile Page Header

The following class is used to set the background color and the border on the right, as shown in Figure A-95. Listing A-111 shows the standard CSS properties.

*Figure A-95. SharePoint 2010 profile page header*

- **Style Sheet:** mysitelayout.css
- **Class:** ms-profilepageheader

*Listing A-111. Profile Page Header CSS*

```
.ms-profilepageheader{
border-right: 1px solid #91cdf2;
background-color: #f8fcff;
}
```

# Local Time

The following class is a shared class used for other elements on the profile page to set the font family for the local time text, as shown in Figure A-96. Listing A-112 shows the standard CSS properties.

**Figure A-96.** *SharePoint 2010 local time*

- **Style Sheet:** mysitelayout.css
- **Class:** ms-contactcardtext3

**Listing A-112.** *Local Time CSS*

```
.ms-contactcardtext3{
font-family:verdana;
}
```

# Profile Picture

The following classes are used to set the alignment, height, border, background color, padding, and margins for the profile picture, as shown in Figure A-97. Listing A-113 shows the standard CSS properties.

**Figure A-97.** *SharePoint 2010 profile picture*

- **Style Sheet:** mysitelayout.css
- **Class:** ms-profilepicture ms-contactcardpicture ms-largethumbnailimage

**Listing A-113.** *Profile Picture CSS*

```
.ms-profilepicture{
text-align: center;
word-wrap: normal;
}
.ms-profilepicture img{
```

```
vertical-align: middle;
height: auto;
border: 1px solid #C5C7C9;
background-color: #ffffff;
padding: 2px;
}
.ms-largethumbnailimage{
width: 148px;
line-height: 148px;
}
.ms-largethumbnailimage img{
max-width: 148px;
}
.ms-contactcardpicture{
margin-right: 8px;
margin-top: 6px;
margin-bottom: 6px;
}
```

## Profile Name

The following class is used to set the font size for the user's profile name, as shown in Figure A-98. Listing A-114 shows the standard CSS properties.

sp2010\Administrator

*Figure A-98. SharePoint 2010 profile name*

- **Style Sheet:** mysitelayout.css
- **ID:** ProfileViewer_Name
- **Class:** ms-name ms-contactcardtext1

*Listing A-114. Profile Name CSS*

```
.ms-name{
font-size:1.8em;
}
```

## About Me Profile

The following class is used to set the font size for the user's profile name, as shown in Figure A-99. Listing A-115 shows the standard CSS properties.

An American educator, Presbyterian minister, songwriter, and television host. Rogers was most famous for creating and hosting Mister Rogers' Neighborhood (1968–2001), that featured his gentle, soft-spoken personality and directness to his audiences.

Initially educated to be a minister, Rogers was displeased with the way television addressed children and made an effort to change this when he began to write for and perform on local Pittsburgh area shows dedicated to youth. The Public Broadcasting System developed his own nationally aired show in 1968 and over the course of three decades on television, he became an indelible American icon of children's
...

*Figure A-99. SharePoint 2010 profile name*

- **Style Sheet:** Inline CSS
- **ID:** ProfileViewer_ValueAboutMe
- **Class:** ms-contactcardtext3

*Listing A-115. Profile Name Inline CSS*

```
/* Inline CSS */
height: 142px;
padding-top: 50px;
padding-right: 5px;
padding-bottom: 0px;
min-height: 142px;
```

# Status Bubble

The following classes are used to stylize the status bubble feature within the profile page, as shown in Figure A-100. Listing A-116 shows the standard CSS properties.

*Figure A-100. SharePoint 2010 status bubble*

- **Style Sheet:** PORTAL.CSS
- **Outer Container Class:** ms-contactcardtext2 ms-identitypiecenotediv
- **Inner Container Class:** ms-contactcardtext2
- **Left Side Bubble Class:** ms-edgebubble ms-identitypieceleftimagebig
- **Bubble Input Class:** ms-identitypiecenote ms-identitypiecenotebig

- **Right Side Bubble Class:** ms-edgebubble ms-identitypiecerightimagebig

- **Bottom Bubble Class:** ms-bottombubble ms-identitypiecebottomimagebig

***Listing A-116.*** *Status Bubble CSS*

```
.ms-identitypieceleftimagebig{
background: url("/_layouts/images/mossfgimg.png") no-repeat -0px -32px;
height:36px;
}
.ms-identitypiecenotebig{
background: url("/_layouts/images/mossbgximg.png") repeat-x -0px -0px;
height:20px;
padding:8px 0px;
width: 550px;
position: absolute;
left: 5px;
}
.ms-identitypiecerightimagebig{
background: url("/_layouts/images/mossfgimg.png") no-repeat -0px -212px;
left: 555px;
height:36px;
}
.ms-identitypiecebottomimagebig{
background: url("/_layouts/images/mossfgimg.png") no-repeat -0px -0px;
left: 7px;
top: 35px;
}
```

# My Site Navigation Tabs

The following classes are used to stylize the status bubble feature within the profile page, as shown in Figure A-101. Listing A-117 shows the standard CSS properties.

***Figure A-101.*** *SharePoint 2010 My Site navigation tabs*

- **Style Sheet:** mysitelayout.css

- **Outer Container ID:** zz17_MySiteSubNavigationMenu

- **Outer Container Class:** s4-sn

- **Inner Menu Class:** menu horizontal menu-horizontal

- **Link Item Class:** static

- **Selected Link Item Class:** static selected

*Listing A-117. My Site Navigation Tabs CSS*

```
.s4-sn{
padding: 0px 0px 5px 24px;
height: 22px;
border-bottom: 1px solid #91cdf2;
background-color: #f8fcff;
}
.s4-sn li.static > a {
padding: 5px 12px;
color: #3b4f65;
font-size: 1.3em;
min-height: 17px;
}
.s4-sn li.static > a.selected {
border: 1px solid #91cdf2;
border-bottom: white;
color: #003759;
background-color: white;
padding-bottom: 6px;
padding-top: 4px;
}
```

This next section will cover some of the main elements on the profile page within My Sites.

# #19: Search Results

The Enterprise Search Center Results page shown in Figure A-102 includes the following CSS elements.

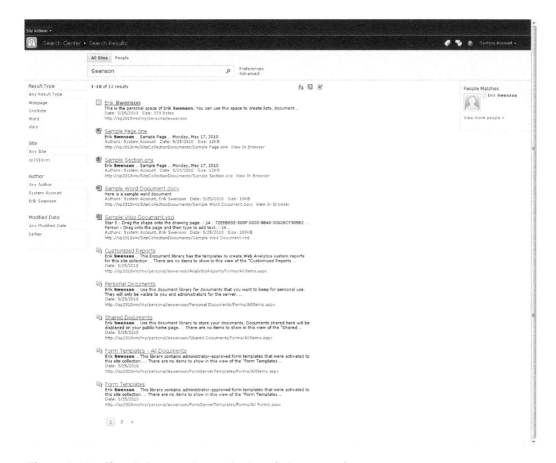

***Figure A-102.*** *SharePoint 2010 Enterprise Search Center results page*

- Search Box Results Container
- Search Center Tab Container
- Search Center Tabs
- Search Results Separator Line
- Search Left Cell
- Search Refine Area
- Search Refiners
- Search Refiner Category
- Search Refiner Item
- Search Main Top

- Search Statistics
- Search Results
- Search Result Icon
- Search Result Title
- Search Result Description
- Search Result Metadata
- Search Result URL
- Search Federation Area
- People Search Summary
- Search Pagination

## Search Box Results Container

The following class is used to set the background color, height, width, and padding for the top search box, as shown in Figure A-103. Listing A-118 shows the standard CSS properties.

*Figure A-103. SharePoint 2010 search box results container*

- **Style Sheet:** SEARCH.CSS
- **Class:** srch-sb-results

*Listing A-118. Search Box Results Container CSS*

```
.srch-sb-results{
background:#fcfcfc;
height:100%;
width:100%;
padding-top:7px;
padding-bottom:2px;
}
```

## Search Center Tab Container

The following class is used to add padding to the left side of the Search Center tabs. Listing A-119 shows the standard CSS properties.

- **Style Sheet:** SEARCH.CSS
- **Class:** srch-sb-results1

*Listing A-119. Search Center Tab Container CSS*

```
.srch-sb-results1{
padding-left:175px;
}
```

# Search Center Tabs

The following classes are used to stylize the tab item and the current tab item, as shown in Figure A-104. Listing A-120 shows the standard CSS properties.

*Figure A-104. SharePoint 2010 Search Center tabs*

- **Style Sheet:** SEARCH.CSS
- **Container Class:** ms-ptabarea
- **Tab Item Class:** ms-sctabcf
- **Current Tab Class:** ms-sctabcn

*Listing A-120. Search Center Tabs CSS*

```
.ms-sctabcf{
font-family:verdana,tahoma,sans-serif;
font-size:1em;
padding:0 10px;vertical-align:middle;
font-style:normal;
font-weight:normal;
}
.ms-sctabcn{
font-family:verdana,tahoma,sans-serif;
font-size:1em;
padding:0 10px;
font-style:normal;
font-weight:normal;
vertical-align:middle;
color:#003759;
background:url("/_layouts/images/selbg.png") repeat-x left top;
background-color:#ccebff;
border-top:solid 1px #c6e5f8;
border-right:solid 1px #91cdf2;
```

```
border-left:solid 1px #91cdf2;
border-bottom:solid 1px #91cdf2;
height:23px;
}
```

## Search Results Separator Line

The following class is used to add a border between the search box and the search results area, as shown in Figure A-105. Listing A-121 shows the standard CSS properties.

***Figure A-105.*** *SharePoint 2010 Search Results separator line*

- **Style Sheet:** SEARCH.CSS
- **Class:** srch-maincontent-separator

***Listing A-121.*** *Search Results Separator Line CSS*

```
.srch-maincontent-seperator{
border-color:#b6babf;
border-style:solid;
border-width:0 0 1px;
height:1px;
width:100%;
}
```

## Search Left Cell

The following class is used to set the width of the left side refining area, as shown in Figure A-106. Listing A-122 shows the standard CSS properties.

Result Type

Any Result Type

Webpage

OneNote

Word

Visio

Site

Any Site

**Figure A-106.** *SharePoint 2010 search left cell*

- **Style Sheet:** SEARCH.CSS
- **ID:** LeftCell
- **Class:** srchctr_leftcell

**Listing A-122.** *Search Left Cell CSS*

```
.srchctr_leftcell{
vertical-align:top;
width:175px;
}
```

# Search Refiners

The following class is used to set the width, height, font styles, padding, margins, background colors, background image, and borders for the refiners area. Listing A-123 shows the standard CSS properties.

- **Style Sheet:** SEARCH.CSS
- **ID:** SRCHREF
- **Class:** srch-WPBody ms-searchref-main

**Listing A-123.** *Search Refiners CSS*

```
.ms-searchref-main{
width:175px;
height:100%;
font-size:1em;
font-family:verdana,tahoma,sans-serif !important;
padding:7px 0 5px;
margin:0;
background-color:#fcfcfc;
```

```
border:1px solid #dbddde;
border-width:0 0 1px;
background-image:url("/_layouts/images/vertical_refinement_gradient.png");
background-repeat:repeat-y;
background-position:right;
}
```

# Search Refiner Category

The following class is used to set the padding, font color, font size, and height for the refiner category label, as shown in Figure A-107. Listing A-124 shows the standard CSS properties.

*Figure A-107.* *SharePoint 2010 search refiner category*

- **Style Sheet:** SEARCH.CSS
- **Class:** ms-searchref-categoryname

*Listing A-124.* *Search Refiner Category CSS*

```
.ms-searchref-categoryname{
padding:1px 3px 7px 11px;
COLOR:#3b4f65;
font-size:1.1em;
height:10px;
}
```

# Search Refiner Item

The following classes are used to set the padding, font color, and margins for the refiner item, and background and border around the selected refiner shown in Figure A-108. Listing A-125 shows the standard CSS properties for both of these types.

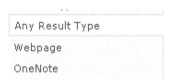

*Figure A-108.* *SharePoint 2010 search refiner item*

- **Style Sheet:** SEARCH.CSS

- **Refiner Item Class:** ms-searchref-filter ms-searchref-unselected

- **Selected Refiner Item Class:** ms-searchref-filter ms-searchref-selected

*Listing A-125. Search Refiner Item CSS*

```
li.ms-searchref-filter,li.ms-searchref-filtermsg{
padding:4px 20px 4px 5px;
color:#0072bc;
margin:1px 0 1px 6px;
}
li.ms-searchref-selected,li.ms-searchref-filtermsg{
background:#fff;
border-top:#dbddde 1px solid;
border-bottom:#dbddde 1px solid;
border-left:#dbddde 1px solid;
}
```

# Search Main Top

The following class is used to set the padding and max width for the statistics and icons, as shown in Figure A-109. Listing A-126 shows the standard CSS properties.

---

**1-10** of 13 results

*Figure A-109. SharePoint 2010 search main top*

- **Style Sheet:** SEARCH.CSS

- **Class:** srch-maintop

*Listing A-126. Search Main Top CSS*

```
.srch-maintop{
clear:both;
padding:8px 0 40px;
max-width:670px;
}
```

# Search Statistics

The following class is used to set the background color, font styles, and margin, as shown in Figure A-110. Listing A-127 shows the standard CSS properties.

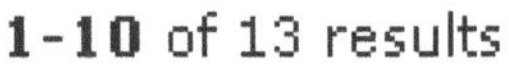

**1-10** of 13 results

***Figure A-110.*** *SharePoint 2010 search statistics*

- **Style Sheet:** SEARCH.CSS
- **Class:** srch-stats

***Listing A-127.*** *Search Statistics CSS*

```
.srch-stats{
background:#fff !important;
white-space:normal !important;
font-family:verdana,tahoma,sans-serif !important;
color:#3b4f65;
margin-left:10px;
}
```

# Search Results

The following class is used to add padding to the left of the results and also set a max width, as shown in Figure A-111. Listing A-128 shows the standard CSS properties.

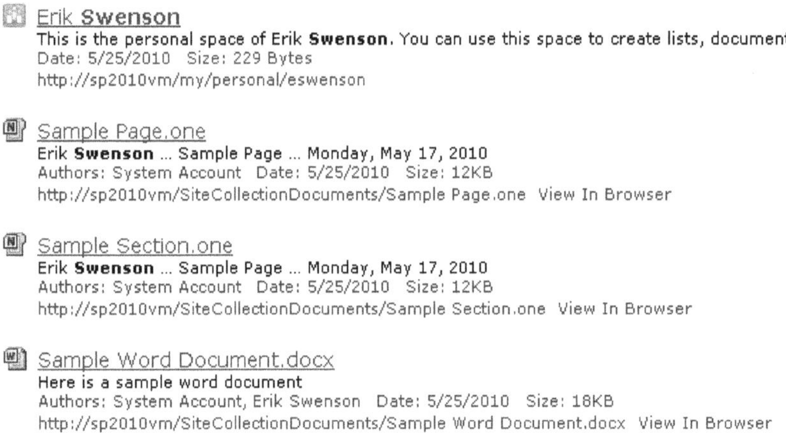

Erik **Swenson**
This is the personal space of Erik **Swenson**. You can use this space to create lists, document ...
Date: 5/25/2010   Size: 229 Bytes
http://sp2010vm/my/personal/eswenson

Sample Page.one
Erik **Swenson** ... Sample Page ... Monday, May 17, 2010
Authors: System Account  Date: 5/25/2010   Size: 12KB
http://sp2010vm/SiteCollectionDocuments/Sample Page.one  View In Browser

Sample Section.one
Erik **Swenson** ... Sample Page ... Monday, May 17, 2010
Authors: System Account  Date: 5/25/2010   Size: 12KB
http://sp2010vm/SiteCollectionDocuments/Sample Section.one  View In Browser

Sample Word Document.docx
Here is a sample word document
Authors: System Account, Erik Swenson  Date: 5/25/2010  Size: 18KB
http://sp2010vm/SiteCollectionDocuments/Sample Word Document.docx  View In Browser

***Figure A-111.*** *SharePoint 2010 Search Results*

- **Style Sheet:** SEARCH.CSS
- **Class:** srch-results

*Listing A-128. Search Results CSS*

```
.srch-results{
padding-left:24px;
max-width:630px;
}
```

# Search Result Icon

The following class is used to set the icons width, left float, and vertical alignment to the bottom, as shown in Figure A-112. Listing A-129 shows the standard CSS properties.

*Figure A-112. SharePoint 2010 Search Result icon*

- **Style Sheet:** SEARCH.CSS
- **Class:** srch-Icon

*Listing A-129. Search Result Icon CSS*

```
.srch-Icon img{
width:16px;
float:left;
vertical-align:bottom;
}
```

# Search Result Title

The following classes are used to add in padding to the left of the title and to set its font color and decoration, as shown in Figure A-113. Listing A-130 shows the standard CSS properties.

📄 Sample Word Document.docx

*Figure A-113. SharePoint 2010 search result title*

- **Style Sheet:** SEARCH.CSS
- **Container Class:** srch-Title2
- **Class:** srch-Title3

*Listing A-130. Search Result Title CSS*

```
.srch-Title3{
padding-left:24px;
}
.srch-Title2 a:link,.srch-Title2 a:visited,.srch-Title2 a:hover{
color:#0072bc !important;
font-size:1.3em;
text-decoration:underline !important;
}
```

## Search Result Description

The following class is used to set the font size, font color, left side margin, and max width, as shown in Figure A-114. Listing A-131 shows the standard CSS properties.

■ Sample Word Document.docx
Here is a sample word document

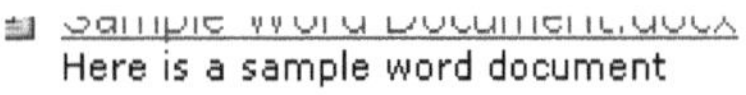

*Figure A-114. SharePoint 2010 search result description*

- **Style Sheet:** SEARCH.CSS
- **Class:** srch-Description2

*Listing A-131. Search Result Description CSS*

```
.srch-Description2{
font-size:1em;
color:#000;
margin-left:24px;
max-width:575px;
}
```

## Search Result Metadata

The following class is used to set the font color and left side margin, as shown in Figure A-115. Listing A-132 shows the standard CSS properties.

Here is a sample word document
Authors: System Account, Erik Swenson   Date: 5/25/2010   Size: 18KB

*Figure A-115. SharePoint 2010 Search Result Metadata*

- **Style Sheet:** SEARCH.CSS
- **Class:** srch-Metadata2

*Listing A-132. Search Result Metadata CSS*

```
.srch-Metadata2{
color:#666;
margin-left:24px;
}
```

# Search Result URL

The following class is used to set the font color max width and margin on the right, as shown in Figure A-116. Listing A-133 shows the standard CSS properties.

Authors: System Account, Erik Swenson   Date: 3/23/2010   Size: 16KB
http://sp2010vm/SiteCollectionDocuments/Sample Word Document.docx   View In Browser

*Figure A-116. SharePoint 2010 search result URL*

- **Style Sheet:** SEARCH.CSS
- **Class:** srch-URL2

*Listing A-133. Search Result URL CSS*

```
.srch-URL2{
color:#008000 !important;
max-width:575px;
word-wrap:break-word;
margin-right:8px;
}
```

# Search Federation Area

The following class is used to set the background color, borders, and float to the right, as shown in Figure A-117. Listing A-134 shows the standard CSS properties.

People Matches
☐ Erik **Swenson**

View more people »

*Figure A-117. SharePoint 2010 search federation area*

- **Style Sheet:** SEARCH.CSS
- **Class:** srch-federationarea

*Listing A-134. Search Federation Area CSS*

```
.srch-federationarea{
background:#fcfcfc;
border:solid #dbddde;
border-top-width:0;
border-right-width:0;
border-bottom-width:1px;
border-left-width:1px;
padding:0 0 5px;
float:right;
}
```

# People Search Summary

The following class is used to set the width, padding, and bottom margin for the people search summary, as shown in Figure A-118. Listing A-135 shows the standard CSS properties.

People Matches

☐ Erik **Swenson**

View more people »

*Figure A-118. SharePoint 2010 people search summary*

- **Style Sheet:** SEARCH.CSS
- **Class:** ms-searchsummarymain

*Listing A-135. People Search Summary CSS*

```
.ms-searchsummarymain{
width:190px;
padding:0 10px 0 0;
margin:0;
margin-bottom:25px;
}
```

# Search Pagination

The following classes are used to stylize the current search results pagination control that is visible below the results when there are more items, as shown in Figure A-119. Listing A-136 shows the standard CSS properties.

 1   2   ›

*Figure A-119. SharePoint 2010 search pagination*

- **Style Sheet:** SEARCH.CSS
- **Pagination Container Class:** srch-Page srch-Page-bg
- **Pagination Number Class:** srch-Page A
- **Current Pagination Number Class:** srch-Page STRONG
- **Pagination Next Icon Class:** srch-Page-img

*Listing A-136. Search Pagination CSS*

```
.srch-Page{
color:#666;
font-size:1em;
font-family:verdana,tahoma,sans-serif;
padding:0.7em 0 7em 48px;
clear:both;
}
.srch-Page A:link,.srch-Page A:visited{
border:1px solid transparent;
color:#1D71B6 !important;
font-size:1.1em;
font-weight:normal;
margin:0 3px;
padding:4px 7.5px;
text-decoration:none;
float:left;
display:block;
}
.srch-Page STRONG{
border-top:solid 1px #c6e5f8;
border-right:solid 1px #91cdf2;
border-left:solid 1px #91cdf2;
-bottom:solid 1px #91cdf2;
font-size:1.1em;
margin:0 3px;
padding:4px 7.5px;
background:url("/_layouts/images/selbg.png") repeat-x left top;
background-color:#ccebff;
```

```
text-decoration:none;
float:left;
display:block;
font-weight:normal;
}
.srch-Page-img a:link,.srch-Page-img a:visited{
border:none;
padding-left:4px;
padding-right:4px;
background:none;
border-top:1px solid transparent;
}
```

# Index

## B

## D

## T

## U

## V

## W, X, Y, Z